Eric Hobsbawm was a Fellow of the British Academy and the American Academy of Arts and Sciences. Before retirement he taught at Birkbeck College, University of London, and after retirement at the New School for Social Research in New York. His books include *The Age of Extremes*, *The Age of Revolution* and *The Age of Empire*. He died in 2012.

'A pioneering work opening up several little-explored themes. Its subject matter is of profound human interest . . . a very satisfying book. Written with a broad sociological slant, it continually thrusts ideas upon its readers, and it is inspired by a humanity and a deep sympathy for humble people' Christopher Hill, *History Today*

'Hobsbawm writes so fairly and with so much understanding and sympathy that many who disagree with him fundamentally will find their own views substantially altered by what he says' *Spectator*

'There is much more in this carefully considered book than a lively account of forgotten risings' *New Statesman*

'A book which is as fruitful as this one in posing problems as well as in providing answers deserves the careful attention of any reader. It is plausible, suggestive and intelligent' *Observer*

Also by Eric Hobsbawm

The Age of Revolution 1789–1848
The Age of Capital 1848–1875
The Age of Empire 1875–1914
The Age of Extremes 1914–1991

Labouring Men
Industry and Empire
Bandits
Revolutionaries
Worlds of Labour
Nations and Nationalism Since 1780
On History
Uncommon People
The New Century
Globalisation, Democracy and Terrorism
How to Change the World
Fractured Times
Viva La Revolución

Interesting Times

Primitive Rebels

Studies in Archaic Forms of Social Movement in the Nineteenth and Twentieth Centuries

ERIC HOBSBAWM

ABACUS

First published in Great Britain in 1959 by Manchester University Press
Reissued with a new preface in 1971
This paperback edition published in 2017 by Abacus

1 3 5 7 9 10 8 6 4 2

A CIP catalogue record for this book
is available from the British Library.

ISBN 978-0-349-14301-9

Typeset in Baskerville by M Rules
Printed and bound in Great Britain by
Clays Ltd, St Ives plc

Papers used by Abacus are from well-managed forests
and other responsible sources.

Abacus
An imprint of
Little, Brown Book Group
Carmelite House
50 Victoria Embankment
London EC4Y 0DZ

An Hachette UK Company
www.hachette.co.uk

www.littlebrown.co.uk

Contents

Introduction by Owen Jones   vii
Preface to the First Edition   xi
Preface to the Third Edition   xv

    I   Introduction   1
    II   The Social Bandit   17
    III   Mafia   40
    IV   Millenarianism I: Lazzaretti   75
    V   Millenarianism II: The Andalusian
        Anarchists   97
    VI   Millenarianism III: The Sisilian Fasci
        and Peasant Communism   123
    VII   The City Mob   143
    VIII   The Labour Sects   167
    IX   Ritual in Social Movements   199

Appendix: In Their Own Voices   233
    1.   *A letter from Pasquale Tanteddu, outlaw*
        and bandit (Sardinia 1954)
    2.   *The brigand Vardarelli helps the poor (Apulia 1817)*
    3.   *A Bourbon brigand examined (South Italy, early*
        1860s)

4. *Donato Manduzio confutes a false apostle (San Nicandro, early 1930s)*
5. *A peasant woman on the good society (Piana dei Greci, Sicily 1893)*
6. *A Commune unpoisoned by Cities (Ukraine 1918)*
7. *The peasants distrust governments (Ukraine 1917)*
8. *The Will of the Tsar (Poltava 1902; Chernigov 1905)*
9. *Conversation of Giovanni Lopez, cobbler (San Giovanni in Fiore 1955)*
10. *Two strike sermons (Loray, North Carolina 1929)*
11. *A Lincolnshire unionist: Joseph Chapman (Alford 1899)*
12. *The 'Men of Decision' recommend a brother (Lecce, Apulia 1817)*
13. *Some secret oaths (Britain 1830s, Naples 1815– 20, Paris 1834)*

Note on Further Reading	263
Geographical Index	267
Index of Names	273
Subject Index	279

Introduction to the 2017 Edition

A year and a half before his death in October 2012, I found myself pottering around the upstairs study of Eric Hobsbawm's Hampstead house. It was a surreal privilege: here was a historian who had had a profound impact on me, and I was now his employee, filing away and ordering his letters, notes, articles, you name it. Hobsbawm was by now very frail, but his mind was as sharp as ever; it was clear he was approaching the end of his life, and his reams of scattered writings needed to be archived. There I'd read correspondence with other intellectual luminaries, invites to conferences across the globe – alongside letters and articles he had penned as a young man in his twenties as the Nazis began their conquest of continental Europe.

At lunchtime, we would sit eating with his wonderful wife, Marlene. This was in the early days of Ed Miliband's leadership, after he defeated his brother, David. Hobsbawm knew their father, the iconic left-wing intellectual Ralph Miliband, and would recall two bright energetic teenagers shuffling around his house. We would talk about his profoundly influential lecture, *The Forward March of Labour Halted*, written in 1978 on the eve of Margaret Thatcher's destruction of Britain's post-war consensus. The transformation of the British working class, the divisions that had emerged within it, the stagnation in trade union membership and the long-term fall in Labour's vote all pointed to a halt in the 'forward march of labour'. This was not what the ascendant left felt at the time: among some, there was a sense of triumphalism, that the post-war consensus was disintegrating, industrial action was surging, and a radical departure – perhaps led by Tony Benn – could be possible. The calamity that was about to befall the left and the labour move-ment was not anticipated: Thatcher was held by some to be the last desperate gasp of a decaying British capitalist system. But Hobsbawm said he didn't write these things because he wanted to upset people, or even because he wanted them to be true: he was applying the Marxist method to examine the world as it was, not as he would like it to be.

It was his early life that would often fascinate me the most. Here was a man born in Egypt months before the Russian Revolution, orphaned by the age of fourteen, who was in Berlin when Adolf Hitler rose to power; he was on one of the last protests against Nazi rule, before fleeing for sanctuary in Britain as a sixteen-year-old Jewish leftist. Archiving work written in times of tumult in the quiet Hampstead house, the world in 2011 felt entirely divorced from the world Hobsbawm had grown up in. Thankfully we are not now reliving the rise of racist totalitarianism but, with the emergence of Trumpism and right-wing populism across the West since Hobsbawm's death, I've often wondered what he would make of it all. His *Age of Extremes* – defined as the short twentieth century, and beginning with the outbreak of the Great War in 1914 – ended with the collapse of the Soviet Union in 1991. Whether we were on the cusp of another 'age of extremes' will surely soon be decided.

Years before I worked in Hobsbawm's study, I would sit

in Oxford's Radcliffe Camera library poring over his texts. Hobsbawm, of course, cannot be separated from the other great British Marxist historians who were his contemporaries, like Christopher Hill, E. P. Thompson and Sheila Rowbotham. It is often said that the contribution of British intellectuals to Marxism was in the field of history, not least in refining often crude, 'vulgar Marxist' interpretations of class. Class, for many of the British Marxist historians, was not something static, but a process, a relationship, a dynamic lived experience. Hobsbawm was – more than any other historian – the reason I chose to study history in the first place and (like so many others inspired by him) why I nursed ambitions to follow his path into academia.

Hobsbawm and his contemporaries were inevitably defined in part by their relationship to the Soviet Union and its Eastern European satellite states. As Marxists, here was what was held to be 'real existing socialism'. For those who experienced the rise of Nazism and the barbarism it unleashed, who lived through the economic traumas of the capitalist West in the 1930s, who saw the undoubted critical role of Soviet forces in defeating Hitler at terrible human cost, who witnessed the supposed economic successes of the Soviet Union's planned economy (a mirage though they often proved to be) which were even admired by some anti-Communists at the time, and who lauded the rise of Soviet-backed anti-colonial liberation movements, breaking with Soviet tyranny was often a difficult and troubled path. History is often unkind to those who had sympathies for Stalinist totalitarianism. But it is notable that Hobsbawm was among those Communists who denounced Nikita Khrushchev's crushing of the Hungarian Revolution in 1956 and the Soviet invasion of Czechoslovakia in 1968. He was a Marxist, yes, and his Marxist method underpinned his work, but he was undogmatic, flexible, and independent of mind.

We live in an age of unrest: this reissue of *Primitive Rebels* – Hobsbawm's first major work – is undoubtedly timely. The best history paints back on to the canvas those who have been air-brushed from it. These are the complex stories of movements which generally emerged lacking clear political direction or a language to explain their grievances and place them into a broader context, let alone articulate an alternative vision of society. Liberation would inevitably happen, they often believed; it didn't need to be planned for. Here is a reminder of how struggle defines and shapes every age.

We live in frightening times. The chief beneficiary of our current crisis of capitalism has not been a renewed left, but the forces of nativism, xenophobia and racism. But it is worth noting that, while Hobsbawm's lifetime encompassed the failures of Stalinism, free-market capitalism and traditional social democracy, he never gave up. His belief in the a viable alternative to a system that places profit ahead of people's needs and aspirations endured, and remained to the very end. His optimism endured, and so should ours.

Owen Jones
London
April 2017

Preface to the First Edition

My interest in the subjects with which this book deals was first aroused some years ago by Professor Ambrogio Donini of Rome, who told me something about the Tuscan Lazzarettists and the sectarians of Southern Italy. Professor Max Gluckman arranged for me to be invited in 1956 to give three Simon Lectures on them at the University of Manchester, and I was fortunate enough on that occasion to be able to discuss the subject with him and with a group of anthropologists, historians, economists and political scientists, including such experts on millenarian movements as Dr Peter Worsley and Professor Norman Cohn. The present book is an expansion of these lectures, but contains additional chapters on some topics I had intended to include in the original lectures, but could not. I am grateful to the University of Manchester, and especially to Professor Gluckman without whose encouragement this book would certainly not have been written.

Those whose brains I have picked are too numerous to acknowledge individually. I have tried, where necessary, to do so in footnotes. These also show on which books I have drawn particularly heavily. I should like to thank also the library staffs of the British Museum, the Cambridge University Library, the British Library of Political Science, the London Library, the

Feltrinelli Library, Milan, the University Library of Granada, the International Institute for Social History, Amsterdam, the Giustino Fortunato Library, Rome, and the Municipal Libraries ☙f Cadiz, Spain, and Cosenza, Italy, for their kindness to a foreign student.

A subject such as this cannot be studied from documents alone. Some personal contact, however slight, with the people and even the places about which the historian writes, is essential if he is to understand problems which are exceedingly remote from the normal life of the British university teacher. Every reader of that classic study of primitive social rebellion, Euclides da Cunha's *Rebellion in the Backlands*, will be aware of how much that great work owes to the author's first-hand knowledge of, and 'feel' for, the Brazilian backwoodsmen and their world. Whether I have succeeded in understanding the places and people in this book I cannot tell. But if I have not, the fault is not in the numerous men and women who have tried, often unintentionally, to teach me. It would be silly to list them, even if I could. However, there are one or two whom I should like to thank especially, notably the Hon. Michele Sala, mayor and deputy of Piana degli Albanesi, Sicily; the mayor and Messrs. Luigi Spadaforo, peasant, and Giovanni Lopez, cobbler, of Abbot Joachim of Flora's town of San Giovanni in Fiore, Calabria; Mrs Rita Pisano, formerly peasant, now women's organizer for the Communist Party in the province of Cosenza, Calabria; Mr Francesco Sticozzi, cultivator, and Dr Rafaelle Mascolo, veterinary surgeon, of San Nicandro, Apulia; and some informants who had best remain anonymous, in prevailing circumstances, in Andalusia. None of them are responsible for the views expressed in this book, and it is perhaps comforting that some of them will not care one way or another, because they will never read it.

In conclusion I should like to observe that I am quite aware of the shortcomings of this essay as a piece of historical scholarship. None of the chapters are exhaustive or definitive. Though I have done a little work on primary sources and a little fieldwork, both are certainly inadequate, and any specialist will be as keenly aware as I am that no attempt has been made even to exhaust the secondary sources, and much more keenly than I am of my slips and errors. However, I should also like to observe that exhaustive scholarship is not the object of this book.

One chapter contains material published in the *Cambridge Journal* VII, 12, 1954. The substance of another was given as a broadcast talk in 1957. I am indebted to Mr P. Thirlby for the index.

E. J. H.
Birkbeck College
July 1958

Preface to the Third Edition

This book first appeared in 1959 and has been published and reprinted since then without substantial changes in Britain, the U.S.A., Federal Germany, France, Italy, Spain and Brazil. The present edition brings some of the references up to date and abandons or modifies a few statements which subsequent discussion or reconsideration have made untenable. However, for practical purposes the original text remains. To revise it substantially would have meant to rewrite the work; not because the author wishes to disclaim what he has written, but because, in the light of his own subsequent work in this field, and of the increasingly voluminous literature about it by historians and various kinds of social scientist, he would today have planned and written it rather differently. Since there are people who still find *Primitive Rebels* interesting, let it stand, until such time as it is possible to scrap the original book entirely, absorbing the material into a larger and more systematic treatment of the great theme of the 'archaic phase' of the history of social movements.

Nevertheless it may be convenient in the meantime to formulate a few 'second thoughts' on the specific topics treated in these essays.

My views on *social banditry* have been elaborated in a short book, *Bandits* (London, New York, 1969) in the light of material from a much wider area than that from which the chapter in *Primitive Rebels* is drawn, but with the minimum of duplication of evidence. This also contains a guide to the literature. Two modifications of substance in my view may be noted. I would now put more stress on the peculiar symbiosis between social banditry and primitive revolutionary (millenarian) movements, both of which tend to flourish in the same areas. The dialectical interplay between the primitive 'reformism' (by direct action) and primitive revolutionism, is evidently complex, though it is significant that where the two coexist, the bandits tend to regard themselves as subordinate to the wider movement or aspiration. As the ballad writes of the relations between the most famous bandit and the most famous Messiah of Northeastern Brazil

> Lampião from that day on
> Swore to be avenged
> saying 'An enemy,
> I'll kill him without questions.
> In this world I'll only respect
> Padre Cicero and no one else.'

The second modification concerns the stereotype of the 'social bandit'. It is clear that, though the 'noble bandit' or Robin Hood is the purest, and in a sense the most logical of such stereotypes, he is not the only one. One may also detect one or two others, such as the 'avenger' (whose role stresses his power and even cruelty, but not his redistributive function and moderation in the use of violence), and what may be called the *haiduk*, the organized military outlaw band which is always believed to have potentially political functions, e.g. of national liberation (as in the Balkans). For the further elaboration of the analysis of the present chapter, readers are referred to *Bandits*.

Since 1959 a great deal of new information has become available about the Sicilian *Mafia*, so that it is no longer true to say that the post-war history of this organization is poorly documented. Other analogous phenomena, though inadequately known, have also come to our knowledge, such as the so-called *cofradia de mayordomos* in the coffee-producing areas of Colombia, which also sees a potential rural middle class (of estate-administrators) establishing its wealth and power in a situation of violence, where the official state apparatus is absent or inoperative, at the expense both of the landowners and of the peasants, and by means of terror and blackmail.

Nevertheless, it would seem that the study of 'parallel systems' of the *Mafia* type can hardly be conducted adequately only on the basis of the few European or western examples of which we have record. As with so many examples of the popular politics of traditional societies, we may well find that they reached their most complete development in other continents, e.g. in this instance in Imperial China, where secret societies in some respects analogous to *Mafias*, played a very large role until the rise of the communist movement. They have recently attracted the attention of experts in East Asian studies.* I am not qualified to discuss them, and in any case they fall outside the geographical area to which *Primitive Rebels* confined itself. One point arising out of such studies may, however, be worth noting. As Chesneaux puts it, these secret societies

> never organized more than an active minority, anxious to defend its interests by all means, legal or illegal, but by and

* Cf. Jean Chesneaux, *Les Sociétés Secrètes en Chine* (Paris 1965).

large dissociated from the rest of the labouring population, and where occasion demanded, living at their expense ... To be a minority is almost a condition of existence of secret societies.

This may well explain the tendency of *Mafias*, whatever their origins, to turn into organizations for the emergence of a middle class or a criminal elite under the conditions of capitalism, and thus to grow more or less rapidly away from their popular roots.

Since 1959 there has been a vast amount of research of *millennial and messianic movements*, mainly in areas outside Europe. There has also been some work on the specific movements I discussed, though not very much, with the exception of the Andalusian rural anarchists, which have benefited from the revival of serious historic study of modern Spain. Some of these new discussions have specifically criticized the arguments of *Primitive Rebels* (though in general amicably enough), and it is, therefore, proper for me to draw attention to these criticisms.*

Essentially they concern the question how far millennial movements can be regarded as 'revolutionary' in the sense defined in this book, what the nature of their revolutionism is, what role they may be expected to play in the political life of the countries in which they occur and how far they are in fact likely to be absorbed into 'modern' political movements.

* The fullest critique occurs in the doctoral dissertation of Maria Isaura Pereira de Queiroz, *Movimentos Messianicos, Tentativa de Classificacão Sociologica* (Sao Paulo 1962); the published version of this work, *Réforme et révolution dans les sociétés traditionelles* (Paris 1968), implies rather than states these differences. Dr Pereira de Queiroz, the leading expert on Brazilian messianic movements, has summarized her views in English in 'Messiahs in Brazil' (*Past and Present* 31, July 1965).

They also raise the question under what social and historical circumstances such movements are likely to arise. Is it, as *Primitive Rebels* suggested, in periods of basic social transformation, such as the transition to a capitalist economy? Or do they rather occur in a more general situation of 'structural duality', which may be due to the coexistence and interaction of two completely different societies (e.g. western economic penetration or colonial conquest of primitive societies), to the tension between a developing new socioeconomic system and an old one (e.g. the penetration of capitalist relations into the countryside), or simply – and this, it is argued, is typical of the Brazilian hinterland – to a society so structured as to produce periodic breakdowns of the system of social relationships, which are then periodically reconstructed, among other methods through millennialist efforts? Criticism also points out that what all messianic movements have in common is not a specific historic situation, but a social structure based on *kinship*, and it is this which they attempt to reconstruct against internal and external challenge in one way or another (in Brazil, by reconstructing the pyramid of the extended family and its values from the apex of the messianic leader 'father' or 'godfather').

Messianic movements, it is argued, are thus in themselves neither revolutionary nor reformist, though they may be either or both, depending on the situation. In other words, the cases discussed in *Primitive Rebels* are special cases and of a more general one. This is not the place to discuss these matters at length, and the general point may well be valid. It is worth noting, however, both that the distinction between reform/restoration and revolution is necessarily unclear in certain historical situations, and that the bulk of the millennial movements with which recent work (including *Primitive Rebels*) has concerned itself, does in fact deal with breakdowns due to the

impact of new economic, social and political forces on traditional societies, and are, therefore, historically specific. This
is true even of the Northeast of Brazil, where the great age of
both bandits and messiahs occurs during a particular period
of transition, and comes to an end fairly suddenly around
1940. That they should reach their peak at a time when the
impact of the new forces is still comparatively marginal, is not
surprising. I would reserve judgment on the relations between
millennialism and kinship.

A more serious criticism is that which throws doubt on
the contention that millennial movements can be considered
as precursors of modern political movements. They may, of
course, and this is not questioned, 'predispose the minds of
individuals to accept (for instance) modern mass communism',
though this is also likely to be reinterpreted in the light of the
earlier movement's assumptions and practices. The discussion
on this point is lively among all students of millennial movements, and need not be pursued here. However, it leads me
to a substantial modification of *Primitive Rebels*, which, I now
believe, suffers from a failure to distinguish clearly enough
between millennial *movements* and millennial organizations
(typically, communities or sects).

The phenomena I wished to analyse is not so much the
formation and development of the messianic sect, as of millen-
narianism as a force which can and sometimes does mobilize
masses for revolutionary action; though a case such as that of
the Lazzarettists is much more characteristic of the sectarian
aspect. Sometimes this mass mobilization, which is almost by
definition temporary unless 'caught' by some organized mass
movement, crystallizes round a specific and organized millennial or messianic sect or group. This is clearly so in Brazil,
though perhaps we ought to distinguish here also between

the communities of the faithful, which finally settled down
in some Holy City under the wing of the messiah (or tried to
do so), and the mass of backwoodsmen for whom Antonio the
Counsellor or Padre Cicero are or were prophets and leaders of
self-assertion and liberation rather than 'fathers'. Sometimes,
as in Andalusian rural anarchism, there is virtually no 'sect'
in the narrow sense, unless we count the small and loose local
nuclei of *obreros conscientes* as such. There are only permanent
prophets and periodic mass mobilizations.

But what counts from the point of view of the masses is not
the – inevitably restricted – group or sect, but the 'common
myth of transcendental justice' which 'often can and does move
peasants into action, as other forms of organization cannot'.
Such a discovery of the possibility of freedom is – to continue
my quotation from the admirable work of Eric Wolf*—

> provides only a common vision, not an organizational frame-
> work for action. Such myths unite peasants, they do not
> organize them. If sometimes the peasant band sweeps across
> the countryside like an avalanche, like an avalanche, too, it
> spends itself against resistance and dissolves, if adequate lead-
> ership is not provided from without. Peasant movements . . .
> are unstable and shifting alignments of autonomous and
> antagonistic units, borne along only momentarily by a mil-
> lennial dream.

In defeat and retreat even such movements may shut themselves into a self-contained isolation like that of a sect: yet in
the best cases, it is the isolation not of a sect but of a small
mass. When the peasant of Piana in Sicily in the 1950s said

* Eric R. Wolf, *Peasants* (Prentice-Hall 1966), p. 108.

'we', he meant not the millenarian and communist minority, but *all* the people of the township (except the exploiters).* The distinction between movement and sect is fundamental, and readers of the book are asked to make it more clearly than the original text did.

In one respect both sectarian and unorganized millennialists are, however, even more revolutionary than I suggested. Subsequent work has shown that both are more persistently activist than I assumed, the phase of expectation being, generally, only a preliminary to a movement whose object is the active transformation of terrestrial existence. In any case it seems to me that subsequent work has confirmed that millennialism represents a rather ambitious form of primitive rebellion, a higher stage both ideologically and in its capacity to mobilize and to act, than local and individual phenomena of social rebellion such as banditry; and certainly one which represents a more ambitious vision of social change than these.

The study of urban *mobs* and riots, in both pre-industrial and modern cities, has also advanced considerably since 1959, and in recent years it has been stimulated by the revival of city riots in the western world. In general historians have followed lines similar to those suggested in this book. No major modification of my chapter seems called for, at least for the period and area covered. The same is broadly true of the chapter on *labour sects*.

* Cf. the statement of Franco P. of Piana recorded in Danilo Dolci, *Inchiesta a Palermo* (Turin 1956), 383 ff., which illustrates the combination of a primitive Christian revolutionism, incorporated in a modern movement of the Left, deliberately universal in scope. It reflects a certain isolation 'we are descended from exiled people' – but of the isolation of pioneers – 'sixty years of socialism have not passed in vain; compared to other villages, we are sixty years in advance'. This beautiful statement complements the documents from the same village quoted in the present book.

Not much work has been done on these, though the religious (generally millennial) aspects of early labour movements have attracted a growing amount of attention. For the time being I therefore refrain from comment on the original text. As for the chapter on *ritual in social movements*, several details might be modified in the light of the large literature on the secret political brotherhoods and the less flourishing research into *compagnonnages* and the ritual aspects of early trade societies. Still, the argument about the rise and decline of ritual brotherhoods still seems to me to be acceptable, and perhaps it had best be left to stand for the present.

Finally, a word of thanks to readers and critics. *Primitive Rebels*, fortunate in the time of publication, has been unusually well received both by non-expert readers and by historical, sociological and anthropological colleagues, who have evidently found its subjects interesting and its ideas worth pursuing. To this extent the purpose of the book, which was to start discussion, has been achieved, and the author, even when his views have not been accepted, cannot but be satisfied.

Birkbeck College
University of London
January 1971

Primitive
Rebels

Chapter I

Introduction

This essay consists of studies on the following subjects, all of which can be described as 'primitive' or 'archaic' forms of social agitation: banditry of the Robin Hood type, rural secret societies, various peasant revolutionary movements of the millenarian sort, pre-industrial urban 'mobs' and their riots, some labour religious sects and the use of ritual in early labour and revolutionary organizations. I have supplemented my accounts with 'case-papers' which illustrate the thoughts and assumptions of the people who took part in such movements as are here described, preferably in their own words. In the main, the field covered is Western and Southern Europe and especially Italy, since the French Revolution. The curious reader may simply read this book as a description of some social phenomena which are interesting, and surprisingly little known, having provoked only a rather sparse literature in English. However, the purpose of this book is analytical as well as descriptive – indeed, it contains no facts unfamiliar to the expert in these subjects – and it may therefore be as well to explain what it is trying to do.

The history of social movements is generally treated in two separate divisions. We know something about the ancient and medieval ones: slave revolts, social heresies and sects, peasant risings, and the like. To say that we possess a 'history' of them is perhaps misleading, for in the past they have been treated largely as a series of episodes, punctuating the general story of humanity, though historians have disagreed on their importance in the historical process and still debate their precise relationship to it. So far as modern times are concerned such agitations have been regarded by all, except anthropologists who are obliged to deal with pre-capitalist or imperfectly capitalist societies, simply as 'forerunners' or odd survivals. On the other hand 'modern' social movements, that is to say those of Western Europe from the later 18th century, and those of increasingly large sectors of the world in subsequent periods, have normally been treated according to a long-established and reasonably sound scheme. For obvious reasons the historians have concentrated on labour and socialist movements, and such other movements as have been fitted into the socialist framework. These are commonly regarded as having their 'primitive' stages – journeymen's societies and Luddism, Radicalism, Jacobinism and Utopian Socialisms – and eventually as developing towards a modern pattern which varies from one country to the next but has considerable general application. Thus labour movements develop certain forms of trade union and co-operative organization, certain types of political organization such as mass parties, and certain types of programme and ideology, such as secularist Socialism.

The subjects of this book fit into neither category. At first sight they belong to the first division. At any rate nobody would be surprised to encounter Vardarelli and bodies such as *Mafia*, or millenarian movements, in the European Middle Ages. But the point about them is that they do *not* occur in the Middle Ages, but in the 19th and 20th centuries, and indeed the past 150 years have produced them in abnormally large numbers, for reasons discussed in the text. Nor can they be simply written off as marginal or unimportant phenomena, though older historians have often tended to do so, partly out of rationalist and 'modernist' bias, partly because, as I hope to show, the political allegiance and character of such movements is often undetermined, ambiguous or even ostensibly 'conservative', partly because historians, being mainly educated and townsmen, have until recently simply not made sufficient effort to understand people who are unlike themselves. For, with the exception of the ritual brotherhoods of the Carbonaro type, all the phenomena studied in this book belong to the world of people who neither write nor read many books – often because they are illiterate –, who are rarely known by name to anybody except their friends, and then often only by nickname, who are normally inarticulate, and rarely understood even when they express themselves. Moreover, they are *pre-politcal* people who have not yet found, or only begun to find, a specific language in which to express their aspirations about the world. Though their movements are thus in many respects blind and groping, by the standards of modern ones, they are neither unimportant nor marginal. Men and women such as those with whom this book deals form the large majority in many, perhaps in most, countries even today, and their acquisition of political consciousness has made our century the most revolutionary in history. For this reason the study of their movements is not merely curious, or interesting, or moving for anyone who cares about the fate of men, but also of practical importance.

The men and women with whom this book is concerned differ from Englishmen in that they have not been born into the world of capitalism as a Tyneside engineer, with four generations of trade unionism at his back, has been born into it. They come into it as first-generation immigrants, or what is even more catastrophic, it comes to them from outside, insidiously by the operation of economic forces which they do not understand and over which they have no control, or brazenly by conquest, revolutions and fundamental changes of law whose consequences they may not understand, even when they have helped to bring them about. They do not as yet grow with or into modern society: they are broken into it, or more rarely – as in the case of the gangster middle class of Sicily – they break into it. Their problem is how to adapt themselves to its life and struggles, and the subject of this book is the process of adaptation (or failure to adapt) as expressed in their archaic social movements.

However, words like 'primitive' and 'archaic' should not mislead us. The movements discussed in this book all have considerable historical evolution behind them, for they belong to a world which has long known the State (i.e. soldiers and policemen, prisons, tax-collectors, perhaps civil servants), class differentiation and exploitation, by landlords, merchants and the like, and even cities. The bonds of kinship or tribal solidarity which – whether or not combined with territorial links* – are the key to what are normally thought of as 'primitive' societies, persist. But though they are still of considerable importance, they are no longer a man's primary defence against the vagaries of his social environment. The distinction between these two phases of 'primitive' social movements cannot be hard and fast, but should, I think, be made. The

---

* I do not propose to enter into the discussion revived in I. Schapera, *Government and Politics in Tribal Societies* (London 1956).

problems to which it gives rise are not discussed in this book, but may be illustrated fairly briefly, by examples taken from the history of social banditry.

This confronts us with two extreme types of the 'outlaw'. At one extreme we have the classical blood-vengeance outlaw of, say, Corsica, who was *not* a social brigand fighting the rich to help the poor, but a man who fought with and for his kin (including its rich) against another kin (including its poor). At the other extreme we have the classical Robin Hood who was and is essentially a peasant rebelling against landlords, usurers, and other representatives of what Thomas More called the 'conspiracy of the rich'. Between the two stretches a chain of historical evolution which it is not my purpose to uncover in detail. Thus all members of the kinship community, including the outlaws, may consider themselves as enemies of the exploiting foreigners who attempt to impose their rule on them. All may consider themselves as collectively 'the poor' as against, let us say, the wealthy inhabitants of the plains which they raid. Both these situations, which have in them the germs of social movements as we understand them, may be discerned in the past in the Sardinian highlands, which Dr Cagnetta has studied. The coming of the modern economy (whether or not it is combined with foreign conquest) may, and indeed probably will, disrupt the social balance of the kinship society, by turning some kins into 'rich' families and others into 'poor', or by disrupting the kin itself. The traditional system of blood-vengeance outlawry may – and indeed probably will – 'get out of hand' and produce a multiplicity of unusually murderous feuds and embittered outlaws, into which an element of class struggle begins to enter. This phase has also been documented and partly analysed for the Sardinian highlands, notably for the period between, say, the later 1880s and the end of the First World War. Other things remaining equal, this may eventually lead to a society in which the class conflicts are dominant, though the future Robin Hood may still – as often in Calabria – take to the hills for personal reasons which are similar to those which drove the classical Corsican into outlawry, notably blood-vengeance. The final result of this evolution may be the classical 'social bandit' who takes to outlawry through some brush with the State or the ruling class – e.g. a quarrel with a feudal retainer – and who is simply a rather primitive form of peasant rebel. This, broadly speaking, is the point at which the analysis of the present book begins, though it may cast an occasional glance backwards. The 'pre-history' of the movements here discussed, is left aside. However, readers should be warned of its existence, especially if they are inclined to apply the observations and conclusions of this book to primitive social agitations which still show its traces. It is not my intention to encourage careless generalization. Millenarian movements such as those of Andalusian peasants no doubt have something in common with, let us say, Melanesian cargo cults; the labour sects of North Rhodesian copper-miners have something in common with those of Durham coal-miners. But it must never be forgotten that the differences may also be great, and that the present essay provides no adequate guide to them.

The first set of social movements discussed in this book is overwhelmingly rural, at least in the Western and Southern Europe of the 19th and 20th centuries, though there is no *a priori* reason why they should be confined to peasants. (Indeed, *Mafia* had some of its strongest roots among the sulphur-miners in Sicily before they turned Socialist; but then, miners are a peculiarly archaic body of workers.) They are treated in order of increasing ambition. *Social banditry*, a universal and virtually unchanging phenomenon, is little more than endemic peasant protest against oppression and poverty: a cry for vengeance on the rich and the oppressors, a vague dream of some curb upon them, a righting of individual wrongs. Its ambitions are modest: a traditional world in which men are justly dealt with, not a new and perfect world. It becomes epidemic rather than endemic when a peasant society which knows of no better means of self-defence is in a condition of abnormal tension and disruption. Social banditry has next to no organization or ideology, and is totally inadaptable to modern social movements. Its most highly developed forms, which skirt national guerilla warfare, are rare and, by themselves, ineffective.

The *Mafia* and similar phenomena (Ch. II) are best regarded as a somewhat more complex development of social banditry. They are comparable to it, insofar as their organization and ideology are normally rudimentary, insofar as they are fundamentally 'reformist' rather than revolutionary – except, once again, when they take some of the forms of collective resistance to the invasion of the 'new' society – and insofar as they are also endemic, but sometimes epidemic. Like social banditry it is almost impossible for them to adapt to or to be absorbed by modern social movements. On the other hand *Mafias* are both more permanent and more powerful, since they are less a series of individual revolts and more of an institutionalized system of a law outside the official law. In extreme cases they may amount to a virtual parallel or subsidiary system of law and power to that of the official rulers.

Being extremely archaic, and indeed pre-political, banditry and *Mafia* are difficult to classify in modern political terms. They can be and are used by various classes, and indeed sometimes, as in the case of *Mafia*, become primarily the instruments of the men of power or of aspirations to power, and consequently cease to be in any sense movements of social protest.

The various *millenarian* movements with which I deal – the Lazzarettists in Tuscany (Chapter III), Andalusian and Sicilian peasant movements (Chapters IV and V) – differ from banditry and *Mafia* because they are revolutionary and not reformist, and because, for this reason, they are more easily modernized or absorbed into modern social movements. The interesting problem here is, how and how far this modernization takes place. I suggest that it does not take place, or takes place only very slowly and incompletely, if the matter is left to the peasants themselves. It takes place most completely and successfully, if the millenarian movement is fitted into a framework of organization, theory and programme which comes to the peasants from outside. This is illustrated by the contrast between the Andalusian village anarchists and the Sicilian village Socialists and Communists; the former converted to a theory which virtually told the peasants that their spontaneous and archaic form of social agitation was good and adequate, the latter converted to a theory which transformed it.

The second set of studies deals essentially with urban or industrial movements. It is naturally much less ambitious, for most of the main tradition of urban or working-class agitations has been deliberately left aside. There is, obviously, still a great deal to be said about the primitive and even the developed stages of labour and socialist agitations – for instance about the Utopian stages of socialism – but the object of this book is not so much to supplement or to revalue a story which is already reasonably well known in outline, but to attract attention to certain topics which have been very little studied and are still largely unknown. Hence we are here dealing with phenomena which may be much more correctly described as marginal.

The study of the '*mob*' (Chapter VI) deals with what is perhaps the urban equivalent to social banditry, the most primitive and pre-political of the movements of the urban poor, particularly in certain kinds of large pre-industrial cities. The mob is a particularly difficult phenomenon to analyse in lucid terms. Nearly the only certain thing about it is that its activity always was directed against the rich, even when also directed against someone else such as foreigners, and that it possessed no firm or lasting political or ideological allegiance except perhaps to its city or its symbols. Normally it may be regarded as reformist, insofar as it rarely if ever conceived of the construction of a new order of society, as distinct from the correction of abnormalities and injustices in a traditional old order. However, it was perfectly capable of mobilizing behind leaders who were revolutionaries, though perhaps not fully grasping the implications of their revolutionism, and, being urban and collective, was familiar with the concept of the 'seizure of power'. Consequently it is far from easy to answer the question of its adaptability to modern conditions. As it tended to disappear in the modern type of industrial city, the question very often answers itself, for an organized industrial working class operates on quite different lines. Where it did not disappear the question ought perhaps to be rephrased as follows: at what stage did the mob, when operating under ostensibly political slogans, cease to attach itself to traditional ones ('Church and King') and attach itself to modern ones, Jacobin, Socialist or the like? And how far was it capable of permanent absorption into the modern movements to which it attached itself? I am inclined to think that it was and is fundamentally rather inadaptable, as indeed one might expect.

The *Labour Sects* (Chapter VII) represent a more clearly transitional phenomenon between the old and new: proletarian organizations and aspirations of a sort expressed through traditional religious ideology. The phenomenon is exceptional in its developed form, and indeed largely confined to the British Isles, for elsewhere in Western and Southern Europe the industrial working class emerged from the beginning as a de-christianized group, except where it was Roman Catholic, a religion which lends itself much less well than Protestantism to this peculiar adaptation. Even in Britain it may be regarded as a phenomenon of archaic industrialism. Though there is no *a priori* reason why religious labour movements should not be revolutionary, and they have sometimes been so, there are some ideological and more sociological reasons why labour sects should have a bias towards reformism. Certainly labour sectarianism, though as a body fairly readily adaptable to moderate modern labour movements, has been somewhat resistant to adaptation to revolutionary ones, even when it continued to provide a breeding-ground for individual revolutionaries. However, this generalization is perhaps unduly based on British experience, that is to say on the history of a country in which revolutionary labour movements have been abnormally weak for the past century.

The last study, of *ritual in social movements* (Chapter VIII), is difficult to classify at all. It has been included chiefly because the peculiar ritualization of so many movements of this kind in the period between the late 18th and the middle of the 19th century is so patently primitive or archaic in the commonly accepted meaning of the word, that it could hardly be left out. But it belongs essentially to the history of the main stream of modern social movements which runs from Jacobinism to modern Socialism and Communism, and from the early craft journeymen's societies to modern trade unionism. The trade unionist side of it is fairly simple. I merely attempt to describe the character and function of the early rituals, which have since gradually faded away as the movement has become more 'modern'. The study of the revolutionary ritual brotherhood is more anomalous, for while all the other phenomena described in this book belong to the labouring poor, this is, at least in its initial stages, essentially a movement of people belonging to the middle and upper classes. It belongs to this story because modern forms of revolutionary organization among the poor may be traced by lineal descent to it, at least in part.

These observations naturally do not exhaust the problem of how primitive social movements 'adapt' to modern conditions, let alone the wider problem of which this one is a part. As I have already observed, certain types of primitive social protest have not been considered at all here. No attempt has been made to analyse the analogous or equivalent movements which have occurred and are occurring in the overwhelming bulk of the world which lies outside the narrow geographical area surveyed here – and the non-European world has produced primitive social movements in much greater profusion and variety than South-western Europe. Even within the chosen area, certain kinds of movement have been only glanced at. For instance, I have said little about the pre-history of what may be loosely called 'national' movements, at least insofar as they are mass movements, although elements of the phenomena discussed here may enter into them. *Mafia*, for instance, may at a certain stage of its evolution be regarded as a very young embryo of a subsequent national movement. On the whole I have confined myself to the pre-history of modern labour and peasant movements. All the subjects surveyed in this book occur, broadly speaking, in the period since the French Revolution, and deal fundamentally with the adaptation of popular agitations to a modern capitalist economy.

The temptation to point to analogies from earlier European history or from other types of movement, has been great, but I have attempted to resist it in the hope of avoiding irrelevant and possibly distracting arguments.

These limitations are not to be defended. A full comparative study and analysis of archaic social movements is badly needed, but I do not think that it can yet be undertaken, at least here. The state of our knowledge does not permit it yet. For our knowledge about even the best-documented of the movements in this book is capricious, and our ignorance of them vast. Very often what is remembered or observed about archaic movements of this kind is only that small corner of them which has, by some accident, been uncovered in the law-courts, or by journalists in search of sensation, or by some student with an eye for 'off-beat' matters. Our map of them, even in Western Europe, is as uncharted as that of the world in the period before proper cartography. Sometimes, as in social banditry, the phenomena are so standardized that this does not matter greatly for the purposes of a short survey. At other times the mere task of extracting a coherent, ordered and rational account from a mass of doubtful and mutually contradictory facts, is almost overwhelming. The chapters on *Mafia* and Ritual, for instance, can at best claim to be coherent. Whether the interpretations and explanations given are also true, is much harder to verify than in the case of, let us say, the social bandits. The student of *Mafias* has hardly more than a single reasonably attested phenomenon on which to base his views. Moreover, what material there is, is often contradictory, even when it has the air of common sense and does not consist of the sort of sensational gossip which this type of subject attracts, as pears attract wasps. Any historian who spoke with confidence, let alone finality, under such conditions, would be a fool.

This book is therefore tentative and incomplete, and pretends to be no more. It is open to criticism by all those on whose preserves it poaches, not only for poaching but in some cases for clumsy poaching. It is also open to the criticism of all who think a single and thorough monograph better than a set of necessarily cursory sketches. There is only one answer to such objections. It is high time that movements of the kind discussed in this book were seriously considered not simply as an unconnected series of individual curiosities, as footnotes to history, but as a phenomenon of general importance and considerable weight in modern history. What Antonio Gramsci said of the South Italian peasants in the 1920's applies to a great many groups and areas in the modern world. They are 'in perpetual ferment but, as a mass, incapable of providing a centralized expression for their aspirations and their needs'. That ferment, the inchoate strivings after an effective expression of these aspirations, and the possible ways in which both may evolve, are the subject of this book. I know of no other student in this country who has so far attempted to consider several of such movements together as a sort of 'pre-historic' stage of social agitation. Perhaps this attempt to do so is mistaken or premature. On the other hand, perhaps someone ought to make a start, even at the risk of making a false start.

NOTE This may be the place for a note clarifying some terms frequently used in this study. It would be pedantic to define all those which lend themselves to misinterpretation. My usage of such terms as 'feudal' may be open to criticism from medievalists, but since the argument of the text is not disturbed by the substitution of another term, or its omission, it is hardly necessary to explain or defend it. On the other hand the argument does in part rest on the acceptance of the distinction between 'revolutionary' and 'reformist' social movements. It is therefore desirable to say something about these terms.

The principle is quite clear. Reformists accept the general framework of an institution or social arrangement, but consider it capable of improvement or, where abuses have crept in, reform; revolutionaries insist that it must be fundamentally transformed, or replaced. Reformists seek to improve and alter the monarchy, or to reform the House of Lords; revolutionaries believe that nothing useful is to be done with either institution except to abolish them. Reformists wish to create a society in which policemen will not be arbitrary and judges at the mercy of landlords and merchants; revolutionaries, though also in sympathy with these aims, a society in which there will be no policemen and judges in the present sense, let alone landlords and merchants. For the sake of convenience the terms are used to describe movements which have views about the entire social order, rather than about particular institutions within it. The distinction is old. It was made, in effect, by Joachim of Fiore (1145–1202), the millenarian whom Norman Cohn has plausibly called the inventor of the most influential prophetic system known to Europe before the appearance of Marxism. He distinguished between the reign of *justice* or *law*, which is essentially the equitable regulation of social relations in an imperfect society, and the reign of *freedom*, which is the perfect society. It is important to remember that the two were in no sense the same, though one might be a necessary preliminary stage on the road to the other.

The point of this distinction is that reformist and revolutionary movements will naturally tend to behave differently, and to develop different organization, strategy, tactics, etc. It is therefore important, when studying a social movement, to know to which of the two groups it belongs.

This is by no means easy, except in extreme cases and for short periods of time, though this is no reason for abandoning the distinction. Nobody will deny the revolutionary aspirations of millenarian movements which reject the existing world to the point of refusing to sow, to reap, or even to procreate until it has ended, or the reformist character of, say, the Parliamentary Committee of the British T.U.C. in the later 19th century. But normally the situation is more complex, even when not obfuscated by the reluctance (which is universal in politics) of people to accept accurate descriptions whose implications they do not like; for instance, by the unwillingness of French Radical Socialists to forgo the electoral advantages of a name which conceals the fact that they are neither Radical nor Socialist.

In practice, every man who is not a Dr Pangloss and every social movement undergoes the pull of both reformism and revolutionism, and with varying strength at different times. Except at the rare moments just preceding or during profound crises and revolutions, the most extreme revolutionaries must also have a policy about the existing world in which they are obliged to live. If they want to make it more tolerable while preparing for revolution, or even if they want to prepare effectively, they must also be reformists, unless they abandon the world altogether by constructing some Communist Zion in the desert or on the prairie, or – like many religious bodies – transfer their hope entirely to the hereafter, merely seeking to traverse this vale of tears uncomplainingly until liberated by death. (In the latter case they cease to be either revolutionaries or reformists and become conservatives.) Conversely, the hope of a really good and perfect society is so powerful, that its ideal haunts even those who have resigned themselves to the impossibility of changing either the 'world' or 'human nature', and merely hope for lesser reforms and the correction of abuses. Inside the most militant reformist there is often a modest and overawed revolutionist hankering to be let out, though advancing age normally imprisons him more firmly. Given the total absence of the prospect of successful revolution, revolutionaries may turn into *de facto* reformists. In the intoxicating and ecstatic moments of revolution the great surge of human hope may sweep even reformists into the camp of the revolutionaries, though perhaps with some mental reservations. Between these two extremes a wide variety of positions may be occupied.

These complexities do not invalidate the distinction, whose existence can hardly be denied, since (whether they are right or not) there are plainly people and movements regarding themselves as revolutionary or reformist, and acting on revolutionary or reformist assumptions. It has, however, been attacked indirectly, chiefly by those who deny that any revolutionary transformation of society is possible, or to be envisaged by rational human beings, and therefore incapable of understanding what revolutionary movements are at. (Cf. the persistent tendency, first systematized by the positivist criminologists of the later 19th century, to regard them as psycho-pathological phenomena.) This is not the place to discuss these views. The reader of this book is not required to sympathize with revolutionaries, let alone primitive ones. He is merely advised to recognize that they exist, and that there have been at least some revolutions which have profoundly transformed society, though not necessarily in the way planned by revolutionaries, or as utterly and completely and finally as they may have wished. But the recognition that profound and fundamental changes take place in society does not depend on the belief that Utopia is realizable.

Chapter II

The Social Bandit

Bandits and highwaymen preoccupy the police, but they ought also to preoccupy the social historian. For in one sense banditry is a rather primitive form of organized social protest, perhaps the most primitive we know. At any rate in many societies it is regarded as such by the poor, who consequently protect the bandit, regard him as their champion, idealize him, and turn him into a myth: *Robin Hood* in England, *Janošík* in Poland and Slovakia, *Diego Corrientes* in Andalusia, who are probably all real figures thus transmuted. In return, the bandit himself tries to live up to his role even when he is not himself a conscious social rebel. Naturally Robin Hood, the archetype of the social rebel 'who took from the rich to give to the poor and never killed but in self-defence or just revenge', is not the only man of his kind. The tough man, who is unwilling to bear the traditional burdens of the common man in a class society, poverty and meekness, may escape from them by joining or serving the oppressors as well as by revolting against them. In any peasant society there are 'landlords' bandits' as well as 'peasant bandits' not to mention the State's bandits, though only the peasant bandits receive the

tribute of ballads and anecdotes. Retainers, policemen, merce-
nary soldiers are thus often recruited from the same material as
social bandits. Moreover, as the experience of Southern Spain
between 1850 and 1875 shows, one sort of bandit can easily turn
into another – the 'noble' robber and smuggler into the *bandolero*,
protected by the local rural boss or *cacique*. Individual rebelliousness is itself a socially neutral phenomenon, and consequently
mirrors the divisions and struggles within society. This problem
will be further considered in the chapter on *Mafia*.

However, something like an ideal type of social banditry
exists, and this is what I propose to discuss, even though few
bandits of recorded history, as distinct from legend, correspond
completely to it. Still, some – like Angelo Duca (Angiolillo) –
do even that.

To describe the 'ideal' bandit is by no means unrealistic.
For the most startling characteristic of social banditry is its
remarkable uniformity and standardization. The material
used in this chapter comes almost wholly from Europe in the
18th to 20th centuries, and indeed mainly from Southern
Italy.* But the cases one looks at are so similar, though drawn
from periods as widely separated as the mid-18th and the mid-
20th centuries and places as independent of one another as
Sicily and Carpatho-Ukraine, that one generalizes with very
great confidence. This uniformity applies both to the bandit
myths – that is, to the part for which the bandit is cast by the
people – and to his actual behaviour.

A few examples of such parallelism may illustrate the
point. The population hardly ever helps the authorities to

---

* For this area I have used not only the usual printed sources, but the invaluable information of Professor Ambrogio Donini, of Rome, who has had some
contact with ex-bandits, and some newspaper material.

catch the 'peasants' bandit', but on the contrary protects him. This is so in the Sicilian villages of the 1940s as in the Muscovite ones of the 17th century.* Thus his standard end – for if he makes too much of a nuisance of himself almost every individual bandit will be defeated, though banditry may remain endemic – is by betrayal. Oleksa Dovbush, the Carpathian bandit of the 18th century, was betrayed by his mistress; Nikola Shuhaj, who is supposed to have flourished *c.* 1918–20, by his friends.† Angelo Duca (Angiolillo), *c.* 1760–84, perhaps the purest example of social banditry, of whose career Benedetto Croce has given a masterly analysis,‡ suffered the same fate. So, in 1950, did Salvatore Giuliano of Montelepre, Sicily, the most notorious of recent bandits, whose career has lately been described in a moving book.§ So, if it comes to that, did Robin Hood himself. But the law, in order to hide its impotence, claims credit for the bandit's capture or death: the policemen shoot bullets into Nikola Shuhaj's dead body to claim the kill, as they did, if Gavin Maxwell is to be believed, into Giuliano's. The practice is so common that there is even a Corsican proverb to describe it: 'Killed after death, like a bandit by the police.'¶ And the peasants in turn add invulnerability to the bandit's many other legendary and heroic qualities. Angiolillo was supposed to possess a magic ring which turned away bullets. Shuhaj was

---

* J. L. H. Keep, Bandits and the Law in Muscovy, *Slavonic Review*, xxxv. 84, Dec. 1956, 201–23.

† Ivan Olbracht's novel *The robber Nikola Shuhaj* (*Nikola Šuhaj 'Loupežnilk*), German edn. Ruetten & Loening, (Berlin 1953), is not only, I am told, a modern Czech classic, but far and away the most moving and historically sound picture of social banditry I have come across.

‡ 'Angiolillo, capo di banditti', in *La Rivoluzione Napoletana del 1799* (Bari 1912).

§ Gavin Maxwell, *God preserve me from my friends* (1956).

¶ P. Bourde, *En Corse* (Paris 1887), 207.

invulnerable because – theories diverged – he had a green twig with which he waved aside bullets, or because a witch had made him drink a brew that made him resist them; that is why he had to be killed with an axe. Oleksa Dovbush, the legendary 18th-century Carpathian bandit-hero, could only be killed with a silver bullet that had been kept one year in a dish of spring wheat, blessed by a priest on the day of the twelve great saints and over which twelve priests had read twelve masses. I have no doubt that similar myths are part of the folklore of many other great bandits.* Obviously none of these practices or beliefs are derived from one another. They arise in different places and periods, because the societies and situations in which social banditry arises are very similar.

It may be convenient to sketch the standardized picture of the social bandit's career. A man becomes a bandit because he does something which is not regarded as criminal by his local conventions, but is so regarded by the State or the local rulers. Thus Angiolillo took to the hills after a quarrel over cattle-straying with a field-guard of the Duke of Martina. The best-known of the current bandits in the Aspromonte area of Calabria, Vicenzo Romeo of Bova (which is, incidentally, the last Italian village speaking ancient Greek), became an outlaw after abducting a girl he subsequently married, while Angelo Macri of Delianova killed a policeman who had shot his brother.† Both blood-feud (the *faida)* and marriage by abduction are common in this part of Calabria.‡ Indeed, of the

* For the actual belief in the efficacy of amulets (in this case a commission from the King), see Appendix 3: A Bourbon brigand examined.
† *Paese Sera* 6.9.1955.
‡ *La Voce di Calabria* 1–2.9.1955; R. Longnone in *Unità* 8.9.1955 observes that, even when the other functions of the local secret society have lapsed, the young men still 'rapiscono la donna que amano e che poi regolarmente sposano'.

160-odd outlaws reported at large in the province of Reggio Calabria in 1955, most of the forty who took to the hills for 'homicide' are locally regarded as 'honourable' homicides. The state mixes in 'legitimate' private quarrels and a man becomes a 'criminal' in its eyes. The State shows an interest in a peasant because of some minor infraction of the law, and the man takes to the hills because how does he know what a system which does not know or understand peasants, and which peasants do not understand, will do to him? Mariani Dionigi, a Sardinian bandit of the 1890s, went because he was about to be arrested for complicity in a 'just' homicide. Goddi Moni Giovanni, another, went for the same reason. Campesi (nicknamed Piscimpala) was admonished by the police in 1896, arrested a little later for 'contravention of the admonition' and sentenced to ten days and a year under surveillance; also to a fine of 12.50 lire for letting his sheep pasture on the grounds of a certain Salis Giovanni Antonio. He preferred to take to the hills, attempted to shoot the judge and killed his creditor.* Giuliano is supposed to have shot a policeman who wanted to beat him up for blackmarketing a couple of bags of wheat while letting off another smuggler who had enough money to bribe him; an act which would certainly be regarded as 'honourable'. In fact, what has been observed of Sardinia almost certainly applies more generally:

> The 'career' of a bandit almost always begins with some incident, which is not in itself grave, but drives him into outlawry: a police charge for some offence brought against the man rather than for the crime; false testimony; judicial error or

---

* Velio Spano, *Il banditismo sardo e i problemi della rinascita* (Rome, biblioteca di 'Riforma Agraria' n.d.), 22–4.

intrigue; an unjust sentence to forced residence (confino), or one felt to be unjust.*

It is important that the incipient social bandit should be regarded as 'honourable' or non-criminal by the population, for if he was regarded as a criminal against local convention, he could not enjoy the local protection on which he must rely completely. Admittedly almost anyone who joins issue with the oppressors and the State is likely to be regarded as a victim, a hero or both. Once a man is on the run, therefore, he is naturally protected by the peasants and by the weight of local conventions which stands for 'our' law – custom, blood-feud or whatever it might be – against 'theirs', and 'our' justice against that of the rich. In Sicily he will, unless very trouble-some, enjoy the goodwill of *Mafia*, in Southern Calabria of the so-called *Onorata Società*,† everywhere of public opinion. Indeed, he may – and perhaps mostly will – live near or in his village, whence he is supplied. Romeo, for instance, nor-mally lives in Bova with his wife and children and has built a house there. Giuliano did the same in his town of Montelepre. Indeed, the extent to which the ordinary bandit is tied to his territory – generally that of his birth and 'his' people – is very impressive. Giuliano lived and died in Montelepre territory, as his predecessors among Sicilian bandits, Valvo, Lo Cicero and Di Pasquale had lived and died in Montemaggiore or

* Il banditismo sardo e la rinascita dell'isola (*Rinascita*, X, 12, December 1953). For a full bibliography of Sardinian banditry, see F. Ferracuti, R. Lazzari, M. E. Wolfgang, *Violence in Sardinia* (Rome 1970), 147 ff.
† R. Longnone in *Unità* 8.9.1955: 'When, for instance, a man commits an offence of honour in some village, and takes to the hills, the local secret society feels the duty to help him to escape, to find a refuge and to sustain him and his family, even if he is not a member.'

Capraro in Sciacca.* The worst thing that can happen to a bandit is to be cut off from his local sources of supply, for then he is genuinely forced to rob and steal, that is to steal from his people, and may therefore become a criminal who may be denounced. The phrase of the Corsican official who regularly left wheat and wine for bandits in his country cottage, expresses one side of this situation: 'Better to feed them in this way than to oblige them to steal what they need.'† The behaviour of the brigands in the Basilicata illustrates the other side. In this area brigandage died out during the winter, some brigands even emigrating to work, because of the difficulty of getting food for outlaws. In spring, as food became available again, the brigandage season began.‡ These Lucanian cutthroats knew why they did not force the poor peasants to feed them, as they would certainly have done had they been an occupying force. The Spanish government in the 1950s ended Republican guerilla activity in the Andalusian mountains by moving against Republican sympathizers and suppliers in the villages, thus obliging the outlaws to steal food and alienate the non-political shepherds, who therefore became willing to inform against them.§

A few remarks may complete our sketch of the mechanics of the bandit's life. Normally he will be young and single or unattached, if only because it is much harder for a man to revolt against the apparatus of power once he has family responsibilities: two-thirds of the bandits in the Basilicata and Capitanata

---

* G. Alongi, *La Maffia* (Turin 1887), 109. In spite of its title this book is much more useful about brigandage than about *Mafia*.
† Bourde, *op cit.*, 218–19.
‡ G.Racioppi, *Storia dei Moti di Basilicata ... nel 1860* (Bari 1909), 304. An eyewitness account by a local liberal revolutionary and official.
§ J. Pitt-Rivers, *People of the Sierra* (1954), 181–3.

in the 1860s were under 25 years old.* The outlaw may of course remain alone – indeed, in cases where a man commits a traditional 'crime' which may, by custom, allow an eventual return to full legality (as in vendetta or abduction) this may be the usual case. Of the 160 or so existing South Calabrian outlaws most are said to be lone wolves of this sort; that is, individuals living on the margin of their villages, attached to them by threads of kin or support, kept from them by enmities and the police. If he joins or forms a band, and is thus economically committed to a certain amount of robbery, it will rarely be very large, partly for economic reasons, partly for organizational ones; for the band is held together only by the personal prestige of its leader. Some very small bands are known – e.g. the three men who were caught in the Maremma in 1897 (I need hardly say, by treachery).† Extremely large bands of up to sixty are reported among the Andalusian *bandoleros* of the 19th century, but they enjoyed the support of local lords (*caciques*) who used them as retainers; for this reason perhaps they do not belong in this chapter at all.‡ In periods of revolution, when bands become virtual guerilla units, even larger groups of some hundreds occurred, but in Southern Italy these also enjoyed financial and other support from the Bourbon authorities. The normal picture of even brigand-guerilla bands is one of a multiplicity of much smaller units, combining for operations.

* Quoted from Pani-Rossi, *La Basilicata* (1868), in C. Lombroso, *Uomo Delinquente* (1896), I, 612.

† E. Rontini: *I Briganti Celebri* (Florence 1898), 529. A sort of superior chap-book.

‡ See the constant complaints of the verbose Don Julián de Zugasti, governor of Cordoba province charged with bandit suppression, in his *El Bandolerismo* (Madrid 1876–80), ten volumes; e.g. Introduction, vol. I, 77–8, 181 and esp. 86 ff.

In the Capitanata under Joachim Murat there were something like seventy bands, in the Basilicata of the early sixties thirty-nine, in Apulia some thirty. Their average membership in the Basilicata is given as 'from twenty to thirty', but can be computed from the statistics as fifteen to sixteen. One may guess that a band of thirty, such as Giuseppe de Furia led for many years in Napoleonic and Restoration times, represents about the limit which can be dominated by an average leader without organization and discipline such as few brigand chieftains were capable of maintaining, larger units leading to secessions. (It may be observed that this is also something like the figure in tiny fissiparous protestant sects, such as the West Country Bible Christians, who averaged thirty-three members per chapel in the 1870s.*)

How long a band lasted we do not know exactly. It would depend, one imagines, on how much of a nuisance it made of itself, on how tense the social situation, or how complex the international situation was – in the period from 1799 to 1815 Bourbon and British help to local bandits might make it easy to survive for many years –, and how much protection it had. Giuliano (with heavy protection) lasted six years, but at a guess a Robin Hood of some ambition would be lucky to survive for more than two to four years: Janošik, the prototype bandit of the Carpathians in the early 18th century, and Shuhaj lasted for two years, Sergeant Romano in Apulia after 1860 for thirty months, and five years broke the back of the most tenacious Bourbon brigands in the South. However, an isolated small band without great pretensions, such as that of Domenico

* Lucarelli, *Il Brigantaggio Politico dell Mezzogiorno d'Italia, 1815–1818* (Bari 1942), 73; Lucarelli, *Il Brigantaggio Politico delle Puglie dopo il 1860* (Bari 1946), 102–3, 136–6; Racioppi, *op. cit., 299. Blunt's Dictionary of Sects and Heresies* (London 1874), Methodists, Bryanite.

Tiburzi on the confines of Latium, could carry on for twenty years (*c.* 1870–90). If the State let him, the bandit might well survive and retire into ordinary peasant life, for the ex-bandit was easily integrated into society, since it was only the State and the gentry who considered his activities criminal.*

It does not greatly matter whether a man began his career for quasi-political reasons like Giuliano, who had a grudge against the police and government, or whether he simply robs because it is a natural thing for an outlaw to do. He will almost certainly try to conform to the Robin Hood stereotype in some respects; that is, he will try to be 'a man who took from the rich to give to the poor and never killed but in self-defence or just revenge'. He is virtually obliged to, for there is more to take from the rich than from the poor, and if he takes from the poor or becomes an 'illegitimate' killer, he forfeits his most powerful asset, public aid and sympathy. If he is free-handed with his gains, it may only be because a man in his position in a society of pre-capitalist values shows his power and status by largesse. And if he himself does not regard his actions as a social protest, the public will, so that even a purely professional criminal may come to pander to its view. *Schinderhannes*, the most famous, though not the most remarkable of the gang-leaders who infested the Rhineland in the late 1790s,† was in no sense a social bandit. (As his name shows, he came from a low-caste trade traditionally associated with the underworld.) Yet he found it advantageous for his public relations to advertise the fact that he robbed only Jews, that is, dealers and money-lenders, and in return the anecdotes and chap-books which

* Pitt-Rivers, *op. cit.*, 183; Count Maffei, Brigand Life in Italy, 2 vols. (1865), I, 9–10.

† The main source is: B. Becker, *Actenmaessige Geschichte der Raeuberbanden an den beyden Ufern des Rheines* (Cologne 1804).

multiplied around him, gave him many of the attributes of the idealized Robin-Hood hero: the open-handedness, the righting of wrongs, the courtesy, sense of humour, cunning and valour, the ubiquity amounting to invisibility – all bandits in anecdotes go about the countryside in impenetrable disguises –, and so on. In his case the tributes are totally undeserved, and one's sympathies are entirely with Jeanbon St André, the old member of the Committee of Public Safety, who laid these gangsters low. Nevertheless, he may well have felt himself at least part of the time as a 'protector of the poor'. Criminals come from the poor and are sentimental about some things. So characteristic a professional crook as Mr Billy Hill, whose autobiography (1955) deserves more sociological study than it has received, lapses into the usual maudlin self-pity when he explains his continued career as a thief and gangster by the need to distribute money to 'his' people, that is to various families of Irish unskilled workers in Camden Town. Robin-Hoodism, whether they believe in it or not, is useful to bandits.

However, many do not need to have the role thrust upon them. They take to it spontaneously, as did Pasquale Tanteddu of Sardinia whose views (somewhat influenced by communism) are more fully set out in the Appendix. Again, I am told that a leading Calabrian bandit of pre-1914 vintage gave regular donations to the Socialist Party. Systematic Robin Hoods are known. Gaetano Vardarelli of Apulia, who was pardoned by the King and then betrayed and killed by him in 1818, was always distributing part of his booty to the poor, distributing salt free, ordering bailiffs to give bread to estate workers on pain of massacre, and commanding the local landed bourgeoisie to allow the poor to glean their fields. (For some of his activities, see the Appendix.) Angiolillo was exceptional in his systematic pursuit of a more general justice

than could be achieved by casual gifts and individual inter-
ventions. 'When he arrived in any village' it is reported 'he
had a tribunal set up, heard the litigants, pronounced sentence
and fulfilled all the offices of a magistrate'. He is even supposed to have prosecuted common-law offenders. He ordered
grain-prices to be lowered, confiscated the grain-stores held
by the rich and distributed them to the poor. In other words,
he acted as a parallel government in the peasants' interest. It
is hardly surprising that as late as 1884 his village wanted to
name the main street after him.

In their more primitive way the Southern brigands of the
1860s, like those of 1799–1815, saw themselves as the people's
champions against the gentry and the 'foreigners'. Perhaps
Southern Italy in these periods provides the nearest thing to
a mass revolution and war of liberation led by social bandits.
(Not for nothing has 'bandit' become a habitual term foreign
governments use to describe revolutionary guerillas.) Thanks
to a large scholarly literature the nature of these epochs of
brigandage is now well understood, and few students now share
the incomprehension of middle-class Liberals who saw in them
nothing but 'mass delinquency', and barbarism if not Southern
racial inferiority, an incomprehension which is still found
in Norman Douglas' *Old Calabria*.* And Carlo Levi, among
others, has reminded us in *Christ Stopped at Eboli* how profound
the memory of the bandit-heroes is among the Southern peasants, for whom the 'years of the brigands' are among the few
parts of history which are alive and real, because, unlike the
kings and wars, they belong to them. In their way the brigands,
dressed in torn peasant costume with Bourbon rosettes, or in

---

* F. Molfese, *Storia del brigantaggio dopo l'Unita* (Milan 1964) is the best general
treatment and contains a bibliography.

more gorgeous apparel, were avengers and champions of the people. If their way was a blind alley, let us not deny them the longing for liberty and justice which moved them.

Consequently also the characteristic victims of the bandit are the quintessential enemies of the poor. As recorded in tradition, they are always those groups which are particularly hated by them: lawyers (Robin Hood and Dick Turpin), prelates and idle monks (Robin Hood and Angiolillo), money-lenders and dealers (Angiolillo and Schinderhannes), foreigners and others who upset the traditional life of the peasant. In pre-industrial and pre-political societies they rarely if ever include the sovereign, who is remote and stands for justice. Indeed, the legend frequently shows the sovereign pursuing the bandit, failing to suppress him, and then asking him to court and making his peace with him, thus recognizing that in a profound sense his and the sovereign's interest, justice, is the same. Thus with Robin Hood and Oleksa Dovbush.*

The fact that the bandit, especially when he was not himself filled with a strong sense of mission, lived well and showed off his wealth did not normally put the public off. Giuliano's solitaire ring, the bunches of chains and decorations with which the anti-French bandits of the 1790s festooned themselves in Southern Italy, would be regarded by the peasants as symbols of triumph over the rich and powerful, as well as, perhaps,

---

* 'The Lord Emperor had heard that there was this man whom no power could subdue; so he ordered him to come to Vienna to make his peace with him. But this was a ruse. When Dovbush came near, he sent his whole army against him to kill him. He himself lay in his window to watch. But the bullets glanced off him and hit the riflemen and killed them. Then the Emperor ordered the fire to cease and made his peace with Dovbush. He gave him freedom to fight wherever he wished, only not against his soldiers. He gave him a letter and seal to prove this. And for three days and three nights Dovbush was the Emperor's guest at the Emperor's court.' Olbracht, *op. cit.*, 102.

evidences of the bandit's power to protect them. For one of the chief attractions of the bandit was, and is, that he is the poor boy who has made good, a surrogate for the failure of the mass to lift itself out of its own poverty, helplessness and meekness.* Paradoxically therefore the conspicuous expenditure of the bandit, like the gold-plated Cadillacs and diamond-inlaid teeth of the slum-boy who has become world boxing champion, serves to link him to his admirers and not to separate him from them; providing always that he does not step too far outside the heroic role into which the people have cast him.

The fundamental pattern of banditry, as I have tried to sketch it here, is almost universally found in certain conditions. It is rural, not urban. The peasant societies in which it occurs know rich and poor, powerful and weak, rulers and ruled, but remain profoundly and tenaciously traditional, and pre-capitalist in structure. An agricultural society such as that of 19th-century East Anglia or Normandy or Denmark is not the place to look for social banditry. (This is no doubt the reason why England, which has given the world Robin Hood, the archetype of the social bandit, has produced no notable example of the species since the 16th century. Such idealization of criminals as has become part of popular tradition, has seized upon urban figures like Dick Turpin and MacHeath, while the miserable village labourers have risen to little more than the modest admiration for exceptionally daring poachers.) Moreover, even in backward and traditional bandit societies, the social brigand appears only before the poor have reached

* 'This is how it was: he was a weakly shepherd, poor, a cripple and a fool. For as the preachers and the interpreters of scripture say, the Lord wished to prove by his example that all of us, everyone that is frightened, humble and poor, can do great deeds, if God will have it so.' Olbracht, *op. cit.*, 100. *N.B.* that the leaders of legendary bands are rarely the biggest and toughest members of them.

political consciousness or acquired more effective methods of social agitation. The bandit is a pre-political phenomenon, and his strength is in inverse proportion to that of organized agrarian revolutionism and Socialism or Communism. Brigandage in the Calabrian Sila went out before the First World War, when Socialism and peasant leagues came in. It survived in the Aspro-monte, the home of the great Musolino and numerous other popular heroes for whom the women prayed movingly.* But there peasant organization is less developed. Monteiepre, Giuliano's town, is one of the few places in Palermo province which lacked any peasant league of importance even during the national peasant rising of 1893† and where even today people vote much less than elsewhere for the developed political parties and much more for lunatic fringe groups like monarchists or Sicilian separatists.

In such societies banditry is endemic. But it seems that Robin-Hoodism is most likely to become a major phenomenon when their traditional equilibrium is upset: during and after periods of abnormal hardship, such as famines and wars, or at the moments when the jaws of the dynamic modern world seize the static communities in order to destroy and transform them. Since these moments occurred, in the history of most peasant societies, in the 19th or 20th centuries, our age is in some respects the classical age of the social bandit. We observe his upsurge – at least in the minds of the people – in Southern Italy and the Rhineland during the Revolutionary transformations and wars at the end of the 18th century; in Southern Italy after Unification, fanned by the introduction of capitalist

* See E. Morsello and S. De Sanctis, *Biografia di un bandito: Giuseppe Musolino difronte alia psichiatria ed alia sociologia* (Milan n.d.).
† See M. Ganci, 'Il movimento dei Fasci nella provincia di Palermo', in *Movimento Operaio*, N.S. VI, 6 (Nov.–Dec. 1954).

law and economic policy.* In Calabria and Sardinia the major
epoch of brigandage began in the 1890's, when the modern
economy (and agricultural depression and emigration) made
their impact. In the remote Carpathian mountains banditry
flared up in the aftermath of the First World War, for social
reasons which Olbracht has, as usual, described both accurately and sensibly.

But this very fact expressed the tragedy of the social bandit.
The peasant society creates him and calls upon him, when it
feels the need for a champion and protector – but precisely
then he is incapable of helping it. For social banditry, though
a protest, is a modest and unrevolutionary protest. It protests
not against the fact that peasants are poor and oppressed, but
against the fact that they are sometimes excessively poor and
oppressed. Bandit-heroes are not expected to make a world of
equality. They can only right wrongs and prove that sometimes oppression can be turned upside down. Still less can
they understand what is happening to Sardinian villages that
makes some men have plenty of cattle and others, who used
to have a few, have none at all; that drives Calabrian villagers
into American coal-mines, or fills the Carpathian mountains
with armies, guns and debt. The bandit's practical function is
at best to impose certain limits to traditional oppression in a
traditional society, on pain of lawlessness, murder and extortion. He does not even fulfil that very well, as a walk through
Montelepre will convince the observer. Beyond that, he is
merely a dream of how wonderful it would be if times were

* Article: 'Brigantaggio', in *Encicl. Italiana*. Even the Spanish *bandoleros* were
partly the victims of Free Trade. As one of their protectors says (Zugasti,
Introduction I, 94): 'Look sir, here we have many poor lads who used to go on
the highways to earn a peseta by smuggling; but now there's no more of that,
and the poor men don't know where their next meal is to come from.'

always good. 'For seven years he fought in our country,' the Carpathian peasants say about Dovbush, 'and while he lived things went well with the people.' It is a powerful dream, and that is why myths form about the great bandits which lend them superhuman power and the sort of immortality enjoyed by the great just kings of the past who have not really died, but are asleep and will return again. Just so Oleksa Dovbush sleeps while his buried axe moves every year nearer to the earth's surface by the breadth of a poppyseed, and when it emerges another hero will arise, a friend to the people, a terror to the lords, a fighter for justice, an avenger of injustice. Just so, even in the U.S.A. of yesterday in which small and independent men fought – if necessary by terror like the IWW – against the victory of big men and corporations, there were some who believed that the bandit Jesse James had not been killed but had gone to California. For what would happen to people if their champions were irrevocably dead?*

Thus the bandit is helpless before the forces of the new society which he cannot understand. At most he can fight it and seek to destroy it

> to avenge injustice, to hammer the lords, to take from them the wealth they have robbed and with fire and sword to destroy all that cannot serve the common good: for joy, for vengeance, as a warning for future ages – and perhaps for fear of them.†

---

* 'According to another version, truly strange and fantastic, it was not Romano who fell at Vallata, but another bandit, who looked like him; for the exalted imagination of the masses considered the Sergeant, as it were, invulnerable and "immortal" owing to the Papal benediction, and Gastaldi reports that he was supposed to have been seen for many years thereafter, roaming the countryside secretly and in solitude.' Lucarelli, *Brigantaggio ... dopo 1860*, 133 n.

† Olbracht, *op. cit.*, 98.

That is why the bandit is often destructive and savage beyond the range of his myth, which insists mainly on his justice and moderation in killing. Vengeance, which in revolutionary periods ceases to be a private matter and becomes a class matter, requires blood, and the sight of iniquity in ruins can make men drunk.* And destruction, as Olbracht has correctly seen, is not simply a nihilistic release, but a futile attempt to eliminate all that would prevent the construction of a simple, stable, peasant community: the products of luxury, the great enemy of justice and fair dealing. For destruction is never indiscriminate. What is useful for poor men is spared.† And thus the Southern brigands who conquered Lucanian towns in the 1860s, swept through them, opening jails, burning archives, sacking the houses of the rich and distributing what they did not want to the people: harsh, savage, heroic and helpless.

For banditry as a social movement in such situations was and is inefficient in every way. First, because it is incapable even of effective guerilla organization. Bandits certainly succeeded in launching a Bourbon rising against the Northern conquest – that is, genuine bandits, not simply political partisans so called by their opponents. But when a Spanish Bourbon soldier,

---

* There is a good description of the psychological effect of the burning of the business quarter in a Spanish city in Gamel Woolsey, *Death's Other Kingdom* (1939).

† 'Ils ont ravagé les vergers, les cultures scientifiques, coupé les arbres fruitiers. Ce n'est pas seulement par haine irraisonnée contre tout ce qui a appartenu au seigneur, c'est aussi par calcul. Il fallait égaliser le domaine, l'aplanir ... pour rendre le partage possible et equitable ... (Voilà) pourquoi ces hommes qui, s'ils ignorent la valeur d'un tableau, d'un meuble ou d'une serre, savent cependant la valeur d'une plantation d'arbres fruitiers ou d'une exploitation perfectionnée, brisent, brûlent et saccagent le tout indistinctement.' R. Labry, *Autour du Moujik* (Paris 1923), 76, on the sacking of country-houses in the Chernigov *gubernia* 1905. The source is the record of interrogations of peasants.

Borjes, attempted to form them into an effective guerilla movement, they resisted and threw him out:* the very structure of the
spontaneous band precluded more ambitious operations, and
though the thirty-nine Lucanian bands could continue to make
the country unsafe for some years to come, they were doomed.
Second, because their ideology debarred them from making
revolt effective. Not because bandits were generally tradition-
alists in politics – for their first loyalty was to the peasants – but
because the traditional force whose side they took were either
doomed, or because old and new oppression coalesced, leaving
them isolated and helpless. The Bourbons might promise to
distribute the land of the gentry to the peasants, but they never
did; at most they gave a few ex-bandits commissions in the
army. More likely than not they betrayed and killed them when
they had done with them. Giuliano became the plaything of
political forces he did not understand, when he allowed himself
to become the military leader of the (*Mafia*-dominated) Sicilian
Separatists. The one obvious fact about the men who used him
and threw him away is that their conception of an independent
Sicily was very different from his, which was certainly closer
to that of the organized peasants whose May Day meeting he
massacred at the Portella della Ginestra in 1947.

To be effective champions of their people, bandits had to
stop being bandits; that is the paradox of the modern Robin
Hoods. They could indeed assist peasant risings, for in these
mass movements it is generally the smallish band, rather
than the vast crowd, which prepares the ground for effective
action outside the actual village,† and what better nucleus for

* Racioppi, *op. cit.*, cap. XXI for all this.
† This emerges clearly from the study of the English Labourers' Rising of
1830, of which J. L. and B. Hammond, *The Village Labourer*, is still the only
real account in print.

such shock-troops than the existing bands of the brigands? Thus in 1905 the peasant activities of the Ukrainian village of Bykhvostova were largely initiated by the cossack Vassili Potapenko (the 'tsar' of his band), the peasant Pyotr Cheremok (his 'minister') and their band, two men who had been formerly expelled from the village community for crimes – we do not know whether voluntarily or under pressure – and later re-admitted. As in other villages, these bands who represented poor and landless peasants, and the sense of the community against the individualists and enclosers, were later killed by a village counter-revolution of the *kulaks*.* However, the band could not be a lasting form of organization for revolutionary peasants. It could at best be a temporary auxiliary for otherwise unorganized ones.

Thus the romantic poets who idealized the bandit, like Schiller in 'The Robbers', were mistaken in believing them to be the real 'rebels'. The Bakuninist anarchists, who idealized them more systematically because of their very destructiveness, and who believed that they could harness them to their cause, were wasting their and the peasants' time.† They might succeed from time to time. There is at least one case in which a primitive peasant movement in which anarchist doctrine

---

* Labry, *op. cit.*, reprints 'The Agrarian Troubles in the Gubernia of Chernigov in 1905' from *Istoricheski Vyestnik*, (July 1913), 202–26. Nine peasants and six cossacks were killed. Labry correctly notes that this area was on the borders of the zone in which the *mir* was powerful and resistant, and that in which its break-up, and the formation of individualist holdings, was advancing fast (p. 72 ff.).

† Cf. Bakunin: 'The bandit is always the hero, the defender, the avenger of the people, the irreconcilable enemy of every State, social or civil regime, the fighter in life and death against the civilization of State, aristocracy, bureau-cracy and clergy.' The problem is more fully discussed in F. della Peruta, 'La banda del Matese e il fallimento della teoria anarchica della moderna "Jacquerie" in Italia' (*Movimento Operaio*, N.S. 1954, 337–85).

was combined with 'a strong bandit streak' became a major if temporary regional revolutionary force. But who really believes that, with all its chief's genius for irregular warfare, the 'Makhnovshchina' of the Southern Ukraine 1918–21 would have faced anything but defeat, whoever won ultimate power in the Russian lands?*

The future lay with political organization. Bandits who do not take to the new ways of fighting for the peasants' cause, as many of them do as individuals, generally converted in jails or conscript armies, cease to be champions of the poor and become mere criminals or retainers of landlords' and merchants' parties. There is no future for them. Only the ideals for which they fought, and for which men and women made up songs about them, survive, and round the fireside these still maintain the vision of the just society, whose champions are brave and noble as eagles, fleet as stags, the sons of the mountains and the deep forests.

A note on pre-socialist left-wing bandits

Insofar as the social bandit had a political 'ideology' it was, as we have seen, a form of revolutionary traditionalism. The 'Church and King' brigand corresponds to the 'Church and King' city mob (see Chapter VII). Since the bandits'

* The quotation is taken from W. H. Chamberlin, *The Russian Revolution*, II, 232 ff.; for other uncommitted accounts, D. Footman, 'Nestor Makhno' (*St. Antony's Papers*, 6, 1959) and P. Avrich, *The Russian Anarchists* (Princeton 1967). The standard Maknovist account is P. Arshinov's (now available in French, Paris 1970). Makhno's own memoirs, from which extracts are printed in the Appendix, do not appear to go beyond 1918. He lived from 1884 to 1934, after 1921 in exile, and was converted to anarchism in his early twenties. The 'bandit streak' in this movement is strongly denied by anarchist and overemphasized by Bolshevik historians, but seems undeniable.

fundamental loyalty was to the peasants, with their permanent opposition to the actual authorities, even the most tradition-alist brigand had no difficulty in making common cause with other oppositionists and revolutionaries, especially if they were also persecuted. Carmine Donatello ('Crocco') could issue the following proclamation in 1863 (A. Lucarelli, *Il Brigantaggio Politico delle Puglie dopo il 1860*, 138):

> Out with the traitors, out with the beggars, long live the fair kingdom of Naples with its most religious sovereign, long live the vicar of Christ Pius IX, and long live our ardent republican brothers (i.e. the Garibaldians and Mazzinians, who were also in opposition).

Co-operation between Republicans and Bourbonists against moderate Liberals is frequently reported from all over the South – Garibaldi himself rejected offers of help from various brigands (G. Doria, 'Per la storia del brigantaggio,' in *Arch. Stor. Prov. Nap.*, N.S. 17, 1931, 390) – and a few ex-Garibaldian soldiers, presumably turned against Savoy by the bad treatment of their hero, became lesser brigand chiefs (Lucarelli, *op. cit.*, 82–3).

However, there are a few examples of pre-socialist Italian bandits with a distinctively left-wing ideology – Jacobin or Carbonarist, as well as of bandits idealized by urban Jacobins, e.g. Angiolillo. One would hazard the guess that these were socially somewhat exceptional figures. Thus both the Jacobin-Carbonaro bandits of 1815–18 described by Lucarelli are non-peasants, though the overwhelming majority of the normal brigands were peasants, herdsmen or – what comes to the same thing – ex-soldiers. Geatano Meomartino (Vardarelli), who was accepted into the Carbonari with his band in 1816 or 1817, was a *saddler*; Ciro Annicchiarico, who joined the sect of the *Decisi*, was a rural intellectual, i.e. a priest of peasant stock and Jacobin views, who had taken to the hills in the Napoleonic periods for purely non-political reasons, namely a quarrel over a woman. For his religio-illuminist millenarian visions, see Lucarelli, 1815–18, 129–31. Naturally it would be much easier for an intellectual or a village artisan – a class which did not normally furnish many bandits – to acquire a relatively modern political ideology than for illiterate goat-herds or poor peasants. However, in the absence of fuller data than are at present available, and in view of the confused and complex political atmosphere in which brigands often operated, one would not like to put forward any hypothesis at all firmly.

Chapter III

Mafia

There is no hard and fast line between the social banditry of the last chapter and the movements to be discussed in this, of which the Sicilian *Mafia* is the most interesting and persistent. Both are exceedingly primitive, not only in the ways originally denned, but also in so much as they tend to disappear as soon as more highly developed movements arise. They are collectively pretty inadaptable. Where they survive the rise of modern movements, such as peasant leagues, labourers' unions and left wing parties, they do so as something quite different from social movements.

Mafias – it is convenient to use the term for all phenomena of this kind – have a number of special characteristics. *First*, they are never pure social movements, with specific aims and programmes. They are, as it were, the meeting-places of all sorts of tendencies existing within their societies: the defence of the entire society against threats to its traditional way of life, the aspirations of the various classes within it, the personal ambitions and aspirations of individual energetic members. Hence they are to some extent, like national movements, of which perhaps they are a sort of embryo, fluid. Whether the tinge of social protest by the poor determines their general colour, as in Calabria, or that of the ambitions of the local middle classes, as in Sicily, or pure crime, as in the American *Mafia*, depends on circumstances. *Second*, they are to some extent unorganized. It is true that some *Mafias* are, at least on paper, centralized and with proper 'chains of command' and promotion, perhaps on the model of masonic orders. But the most interesting situation is that in which, as in the classical Sicilian *Mafia*, there is – or at one stage was – no proper organization above local level and only very primitive organization even there.

Under what conditions do *Mafias* arise? The question simply cannot be answered, because we do not know how many of them there are or have been. The Sicilian *Mafia* is the only body of its kind in modern Europe which has provoked description and analysis in any quantity. Apart from casual references to 'delinquent associations', 'secret associations of robbers' and protectors of robbers, and the like, we know hardly anything about the situation in other places, and what we know allows us at best to say that a situation out of which *Mafia could* have arisen, existed, not whether it actually did.* We cannot conclude that absence of information means that no such phenomenon existed. Thus, as we shall see, there is absolutely no doubt of the existence of a body of *mafia*-type in Southern Calabria. But apart from a passing reference to such secret societies in

---

* See Zugasti *op. cit.*, Introduction, vol. I for the *alcaldes'* reports on the state of crime in their areas of Cordoba province, *c.* 1870; e.g. a 'secret association of robbers' in Baena, a 'sociedad de ladrones' in Montilla, something that looks rather like *mafia* in the famous smugglers' pueblo of Benamejí, and the dumb opposition of Iznajar where 'according to the inveterate custom of this town, all these crimes have remained unpunished' (i.e. unsolved). I am inclined to accept Brenan's view that this was a *pioto-mafia* rather than a *Mafia* situation. Cf. also Chapter V on Andalusian anarchism, below.

Calabria and the Cilento (the region south of the gulf of Salerno)
it seems to have been wholly unrecorded in the past.* This is less
surprising than it might seem. Secret bodies composed largely
of illiterate countrymen work in obscurity. Middle-class townsmen are profoundly ignorant, and were normally profoundly
contemptuous, of the low life under their feet. The only thing
we can therefore do at present is to concentrate on one or two
examples of known *Mafias* and hope that these may eventually
throw light on the situation in hitherto uninvestigated areas.

The *Mafia* is less well known than one might suppose.
Though there is no dispute about the facts and much useful
descriptive and analytical literature,† public discussion has
been confused, partly by all manner of journalistic romancing,
partly by the simple failure to recognize that 'what appeared
to the Piedmontese or the Lombard as "Sicilian delinquency"
was in reality the law of a different society ... a semi-feudal
society'.‡ It may, therefore, be as well to summarize what we
know about it.

* G. Alongi, *La Camorra* (Turin 1890), 30. The note on La Camorra in
Calabria (*Archivio di Psichiatria*, IV, 1883, 295) appears to deal exclusively with
an organization of city crooks in Reggio Calabria, and appears to be quite
unaware of the rural body. It may be noted that nobody was more passionately
interested in this type of phenomenon than the Italian positivist (Lombroso)
school of criminology, whose organ the Archivio was.
† The main sources used in this article, besides some personal conversations
in Sicily, are N. Colajanni, *La Delinquenza in Sicilia* (1885), *La Sicilia dai Borboni
ai Sabaudi* (1900), A. Cutrera, *La Mafia ed i Mafiosi* (1900), G. Alongi, *La Maffia*
(1887), G. Montalbane, 'La Mafia' (*Nuovi Argomenti*, Nov.–Dec. 1953), various
official enquiries and standard works on Sicilian economic and social conditions, of which L. Franchetti, *Condizioni Politiche e Ammiistrative della Sicilia* (1877),
is a favourable specimen, and G. Mosca's articles in the *Giornale degli Economist*,
1900 and the *Encyclopedia of Social Sciences*. For more recent sources, see Notes
on Further Reading.
‡ E. Sereni, *Il Capitalismo mile Campagne, 1860–1900* (Turin 1948), 187.

The word *Mafia* stands here for several distinct things. First, it represents a general attitude towards the State and the State's law which is not necessarily any more criminal than the very similar attitude of, let us say, public schoolboys towards their masters. A *mafioso* did not invoke State or law in his private quarrels, but made himself respected and safe by winning a reputation for toughness and courage, and settled his differences by righting. He recognized no obligation except those of the code of honour or *omertà* (manliness), whose chief article forbade giving information to the public authorities. In other words *mafia* (which will be spelled with a small *m* when used in this sense) was the sort of code of behaviour which always tends to develop in societies without effective public order, or in societies in which citizens regard the authorities as wholly or partly hostile (for instance in jails or in the underworld outside them), or as unappreciative of the things which really matter (for instance in schools), or as a combination of both. One should resist the temptation to link this code with feudalism, aristocratic virtues or the like. Its most complete and binding rule was among the *souteneurs* and minor hoodlums of the Palermo slums, whose conditions approximated most closely to 'lawlessness', or rather to a Hobbesian state in which the relations between individuals or small groups are like those between sovereign powers. It has been rightly pointed out that in the really feudal parts of the island *omertà* tended to mean merely that only denunciation of the weak or defeated was permissible.* Where there is an established structure of power, 'honour' tends to belong to the mighty.

In lawless communities power is rarely scattered among an anarchy of competing units, but clusters round local strong-points. Its typical form is patronage, its typical holder the private

* Franchetti, 219–21.

magnate or boss with his body of retainers and dependants and the network of 'influence' which surrounds him and causes men to put themselves under his protection. *Mafia*, in the second sense of the word, is almost a synonym for this, though it tended to be applied to the retainers (the 'low *Mafia*') rather than to the patrons. Some of the forms of this system were certainly feudal, especially in the inland *latifundia*; and it is very probable that in Sicily (where legally feudal relations were not officially abolished until the 19th century, and their symbolism lives on even today in the painted battles between knights and Saracens on the sides of peasant carts) feudal forms of loyalty helped to shape it. However, this is a minor point, for retainership and patronage can come into existence without any feudal tradition. What characterized Sicily was the universal prevalence of such patronage and the virtual absence of any other form of constant power.

Mafia in the third, and most usual sense of the word, is not easy to distinguish from the second: it is the control of the community's life by a secret – or rather an officially unrecognized – system of gangs. So far as we know, this type of *Mafia* was never a single secret society, centrally organized, like the Neapolitan Camorra, though opinions about its degree of centralization have always differed.* The Palermo Procurator's report of 1931 probably expressed the situation best:

* *Mafia* by Ed. Reid, an American newspaper man (New York 1952), which holds the centralized view, is to be neglected, for the book – probably produced quickly to catch a market alerted by Sen. Kefauver's Crime Enquiry (which made vast accusations against *Mafia*) – shows a remarkable lack of appreciation of Sicilian problems. The strongest evidence for centralization comes from the U.S. *Mafia*, which can no longer be simply identified with its Sicilian parent. However, even here it is clear that interference by the 'national commission' in the relations between the leader of a 'family' and his 'soldiers' is regarded as illegitimate and passionately resented. Cf. H. A. Zeiger, *Sam the Plumber* (New York 1970), passim.

> The associations of the small localities normally exercise juris-
> diction within these and the neighbouring Communes. Those
> of the important centres are in relations with one another even
> to the most remote provinces, lending each other mutual aid
> and assistance.*

Indeed, being essentially a rural phenomenon to begin with,
it is difficult to see how *Mafia* could have been hierarchically
centralized, communications being what they were in the 19th
century. It was rather a network of local gangs (*cosche* – today
they seem to be called 'families') sometimes two or three
strong, sometimes much larger, each controlling a certain territory, normally a Commune or a *latifundium*, and linked with
one another in various ways. Each *cosca* milked its territory;
though sometimes, as during transhumance of cattle, the gangs
of the territories through which the beasts travelled would co-
operate. The migrations of harvest labourers, and especially
the links between *latifundia* and the urban lawyers and the mass
of cattle-markets and fairs all over the country, would provide
other contacts between local groups.†

Their members recognized one another less by accepted
secret signs and passwords than by bearing, dress, talk and
behaviour. Professional toughness and virility, professional
parasitism and outlawry, breed their specialized behaviour,
designed in a lawless society to impress the sheep – and perhaps also the lions – with the power of the wolves, as well as to
set them apart from the herd. The *bravi* in Manzoni's *Betrothed*
dress and behave very like the 'lads' (*picciotti*) in Sicily two
and a half centuries later. On the other hand each gang did

---

* Quoted in Montalbane, *loc. cit.*, 179.
† Alongi, *op. cit.*, 70 ff.

have strikingly standardized initiation rituals and passwords in the 1870s, though these seem to have been allowed to lapse subsequently.* Whether or not, as Cutrera holds, they had been evolved long since in Milazzo jail, and popularized through songs and such pieces of literature as the *Life and Brave Deeds of the Bandit Pasquale Bruno*, I do not know. But they were clearly the rituals of an old-fashioned Mediterranean blood-brotherhood. The crucial ritual – normally (except where this was impossible as in jails) carried out in front of a saint's image – was that of piercing the candidate's thumb and extracting blood, which was daubed on the saint's image, which was then burnt. This last act may have been designed to bind the novice to the brotherhood by the ceremonial breaking of a taboo: a ritual involving the firing of a pistol at a statue of Jesus Christ is also reported.† Once initiated the *Mafioso* was a *compadre*, co-godparenthood being in Sicily, as elsewhere in the Mediterranean, the form of artificial kinship which implied the greatest and most solemn obligations of mutual help on the contracting parties. The passwords also seem to have been standardized. However, this does not prove that the association was centralized, for the Camorra – a purely Neapolitan organization without Sicilian links – also had a blood-brotherhood initiation of a similar type.‡

So far as we can see, though standardized, each group seems

* Montalbane, *loc. cit.* The fullest description of these is for the *Stoppaglieri* of Monreale and the neighbourhood, and the *Fratellanza* of Favara (prov. Agrigento) and the neighbourhood. These are printed in various places, e.g. Montalbane. See also F. Lestingi, 'L'Associazione della Fratellanza', in *Archivio di Psicbiatria*, V (1884), 452 ff.

† Montalbane, 191. For the same ritual in the U.S., cf. P. Maas, *The Valachi Papers* (London 1968).

‡ Ed. Reid, *op. cit.*, for an initiation in New York 1917, 143–4; Alongi, 41.

to have regarded these rituals as its private bonds, rather as children adopt standardized forms of twisting words as strictly private languages. It may well be argued that *Mafia* evolved some sort of quasi-national co-ordination; its central direction, if this term is not too precise, settling in Palermo. However, as we shall see this reflected the economic and political structure and evolution of Sicily rather than any criminal master-plan.*

Beneath the rule of the Bourbon or Piedmontese state, though sometimes living in strange symbiosis with it, *Mafia* (in all the three senses of the word) provided a parallel machine of law and organized power; indeed, so far as the citizen in the areas under its influence was concerned, the only effective law and power. In a society such as Sicily, in which the official government could not or would not exercise effective sway, the appearance of such a system was as inevitable as the appearance of gang-rule, or its alternative, private posses and vigilantes in certain parts of *laissez faire* America. What distinguishes Sicily is the territorial extent and cohesion of this private and parallel system of power.

It was not, however, universal, for not all sections of Sicilian society were equally in need of it. Fishermen and sailors, for instance, never developed the code of *omertà* and – apart from the underworld – it was weakly developed in the towns, that is to say the real towns, not the great agglomerations in which Sicilian peasants lived in the midst of an empty, bandit-ridden or perhaps malarial countryside. Indeed, the urban artisans tended, especially during revolutions – as in Palermo in 1773 and 1820–1 – to organize their own 'train bands' or *ronde*, until

* It is also probable that *Mafia* among the immigrants in America was more centralized than at home, because these were transferred to the new world along relatively few lanes, and settled in a handful of big cities. However, this need not concern us.

the alliance of the ruling-classes, afraid of their revolutionary implications, imposed the socially more reliable National Guard and eventually the combination of policemen and *Mafiosi* on them after 1848.* On the other hand certain groups were in special need of private defences. Peasants on the large inland *latifundia*, and sulphur-miners, needed some means of mitigating their misery besides periodic jaqueries. For the owners of certain types of property – cattle, which was as easily rustled on the empty Sicilian ranges as in Arizona, and oranges and lemons, which invited thieves in the untended orchards of the coast – protection was vital. In fact, *Mafia* developed precisely in the three areas of this kind. It dominated the irrigated fruit-growing plain round Palermo, with its fertile, fragmented peasant tenancies, the sulphur-mining areas of the southern centre, and the open inland *latifundia*. Outside these areas it was weaker, and tended to disappear in the eastern half of the island.

It is a mistake to believe that institutions which look archaic are of great antiquity. They may, like public schools or the fancy dress part of English political life, have come into existence recently (though built of old or pseudo-ancient material) for modern purposes. *Mafia* is not a medieval, but a 19th- and 20th-century institution. Its period of greatest glory falls after 1890. No doubt Sicilian peasants have throughout history lived under the double regime of a remote and generally foreign central government and a local regime of slave or feudal lords; since theirs was *par excellence* the country of the *latifundium*. No doubt they were never, and could never be, in the habit of regarding the central government as a real State, but merely as a special form of brigand, whose soldiers, tax-gatherers, policemen and courts fell upon them from time to time. Their

* Montalbane, 194–7, for a valuable discussion of the problem.

illiterate and isolated life was lived between the lord with his strong-arm mien and parasites and their own defensive customs and institutions. In a sense, therefore, something like the 'parallel system' must always have existed, as it exists in all backward peasant societies.

Yet this was not *Mafia*, though it contained most of the raw material out of which the *Mafia* grew. In fact it hardly developed in its full sense until after 1860. The word itself, in its modern connotation, does not occur before the early 1860s,* and had in any case previously been confined to the argot of one district in Palermo. A local historian from western Sicily – a hotbed of *Mafia* – finds no trace of it in his town before 1860.† On the other hand by 1866 the word is already used as a matter of course by Maggiorani, and by the 1870s it is common currency in political discussion. It is fairly clear that in some regions – perhaps mainly in Palermo province – a developed *Mafia* must have existed earlier. Nothing could be more typically *mafioso* than the career of Salvatore Miceli, the boss of Monreale, who brought his armed *squadre* to fight the Bourbons in Palermo in 1848, was pardoned and made a captain of arms by them in the 1850s (a characteristic touch), took his men to Garibaldi in 1860 and was killed fighting the Piedmontese in the Palermitan rising of 1866.‡ And by 1872 the Monreale *Mafia* was developed to the point where the first of the subsequently endemic revolts of the 'young *Mafia*' against the 'old *Mafia*' took place, – aided by the police which sought to weaken the society – and produced the 'sect' of the Stoppaglieri.§ Nevertheless, something pretty fun-

---

* G. Pitré, *Usi e costume ... del popolo siciliano*, III, 287ff (1889); art. 'Mafia', in *Enc. Soc. Sciences*.
† S. Nicastro, *Dal Quarantotto a la Sessanta in Mazzara* (1913), 80–1.
‡ Cutrera, 170–4.
§ *Giornale di Sicilia* 21.8.1877, quoted by Montalbane, 167–74.

damental obviously happened to the 'parallel system' after the official abolition of feudalism in Sicily (1812–38), and especially after its conquest by the northern middle-class; and this is, after all, no more than we should expect. The question is what? To answer it, we must summarize what is known of the composition and structure of the developed *Mafia*. Its first, and by far its most important characteristic is, that *all* the heads of local *Mafias* were (and are) men of wealth, some ex-feudalists in the inland areas, but overwhelmingly men of the middle class, capitalist farmers and contractors, lawyers and the like. The evidence on this point seems conclusive.* Since *Mafia* was primarily a rural phenomenon, this in itself marks the beginnings of a revolution, for in mid-19th century Sicily bourgeois-owned land still amounted to only about 10 per cent of the cultivated area. The backbone of *Mafia* were the *gabellotti* – wealthy middle-class persons who paid the absentee feudal owners a lump rent for their whole estate and sublet at a profit to the peasantry, and who virtually replaced them as the real ruling class. Virtually all of them, in the *Mafia* areas, seem to have been *mafiosi*. The rise of *Mafia* thus marks a transfer of power in the 'parallel system' from feudal to rural middle class, an incident in the rise of rural capitalism. At the same time *Mafia* was one of the main engines of this transfer. For if the *gabellotto* used it to force terms on tenant and share-cropper, he also used it to force them on the absentee lord.

Because *Mafia* was in the hands of something like a local 'businessmen's' class, it also developed a range of influence which it could never have done had it merely been an affair of 'tough guys', whose horizon was bounded by the frontiers of their township. Most *gabellotti* were linked with Palermo, where

* Cutrera, 73, 88–9, 96. Franchetti, 170–2. The spectacle of gangsterism as a typically middle-class phenomenon amazed and troubled Franchetti.

the absentee barons and princes received their rents, as all Irish town-lands in the 18th century were linked with Dublin. In Palermo lived the lawyers who settled major property transfers (and were as like as not educated sons and nephews of the rural bourgeoisie); the officials and courts which had to be 'fixed'; the merchants who disposed of the ancient corn and cattle and the new cash crops of orange and lemon. Palermo was the capital in which Sicilian revolutions – i.e. the fundamental decisions about Sicilian politics – were traditionally made. Hence it is only natural that the local threads of the *Mafia* should converge there, though until after World War II the most eminent *mafiosi* (such as Vito Cascio Ferro, Calogero Vizzini and Genco Russo) represented inland latifundist areas.

The apparatus of coercion of the 'parallel system' was as shapeless and decentralized as its political and legal structure; but it fulfilled its purpose of securing internal quiet and external power – i.e. of controlling the local inhabitants and harassing a foreign government. It is not easy to give a lucid and brief account of its structure. In any society as miserably poor and oppressed as that of the Sicilians there is a vast potential reserve of strong-arm men, as there is of prostitutes. The 'bad man' is, in the expressive phrase of French criminal slang, *affranchi*; and there are no other individual methods of escaping the bondage of virtual serfdom but bullying and outlawry. In Sicily this great class consisted in the main of three groups: the retainers and private police-forces (such as the *guardiani* and *campieri* who guarded the orchards and ranges); the bandits and professional outlaws; and the strong and self-reliant among the legitimate labourers. We must bear in mind that the best chance the peasant or miner had of mitigating his oppression was to gain a reputation for being tough or a friend of toughs. The normal meeting-place of all these was in the entourage of the local great man, who provided employment for men of daring and swagger and protected the outlaws – if only because his prestige required him to demonstrate his power to do so. Thus a local network, which enmeshed estate guards, goatherds, bandits, bullies, and strong men, with the local property-owners, already existed.

Two things were almost certainly responsible for turning this into *Mafia*. First, there was the attempt of the feeble Bourbons to set up the 'Armed Companies'. Like most other attempts by feeble governments to hand over the maintenance of public security to private enterprise, spurred on by the fear of financial loss, this failed. The 'Armed Companies', which were set up independently in different areas, were responsible for making good what the thieves and robbers took. It follows, that under Sicilian conditions, each company had an overwhelming incentive to encourage its local bad men to rob elsewhere against the promise of local sanctuary, or to negotiate privately with them for the return of stolen goods. A small step separated this from the actual participation of the Armed Companies in crime, for they were naturally composed of the same kind of toughs as the brigands. Second, there was the increasing danger of urban and peasant discontent, especially after the abolition of feudalism. This, as usual, bore heavily on the peasants, and moreover involved them in the henceforth perennial tussle with the rural middle class about the ownership of the common and ecclesiastical lands, which the middle class tended to appropriate. At a period when revolutions occurred with terrifying frequency – four or five in 46 years – it was only natural that the rich tended to recruit retainers for the defence of their own interests – the so-called '*contro-squadre*' – as well as taking other measures to prevent the revolutions getting out of hand, and nothing lent itself to *mafioso* practices as well as such a combination of the (rural) rich and the toughs.

The relationship between the *Mafia*, the 'lads' or retainers and the brigands was therefore somewhat complex. As property-owners the *capi-mafia* had no interest in crime, though they had an interest in maintaining a body of armed followers for coercive purposes. The retainers, on the other hand, had to be allowed pickings, and a certain scope for private enterprise. The bandits, lastly, were an almost total nuisance, though they could occasionally be made use of to reinforce the power of the boss: the bandit Giuliano was called upon in 1947 to shoot up a May Day procession of peasants, the name of the influential Palermitan who arranged the transaction being known. However, in the absence of *central* state machinery, banditry itself could not be eliminated. Hence the peculiar compromise solution which is so typical of *Mafia*: a local monopoly of controlled extortion (often institutionalized so as to lose its character of naked force), and the elimination of interlopers. The orange-grower in the Palermo region would have to hire an orchard guard. If wealthy, he might from time to time have to contribute to the maintenance of the 'lads'; if he had property stolen, he would have it returned minus a percentage, unless he stood specially well with *Mafia*. The private thief was excluded.*

The military formations of *Mafia* show the same mixture of retainers' loyalty and dependence, and private profit-making by the fighting men. When war broke out, the local boss would raise his *squadre* – mainly, but perhaps not exclusively, composed of the members of the local *cosche*. The 'lads' would join the *squadra*, partly to follow their patron (the more influential

* One of the commonest misconceptions about *Mafia* – perpetuated in such works as the ineffable Prefect Mori's *Last Battle of the Mafia* and in the first edition of Guercio's *Sicily* – is the confusion between it and banditry. *Mafia* maintained public order by private means. Bandits were, broadly speaking, what it protected the public from.

the *capo-mafia*, the larger his troop), partly to raise their personal prestige by the only way open to them, acts of bravery and violence, but also because war meant profit. In the major revolutions the *capi-mafia* would arrange with the Palermo liberals for a daily stipend of four *tari* per man, as well as arms and munitions, and the promise of this wage (not to mention other pickings of war) swelled the numbers of the *squadre*.

2

Such, then, was the 'parallel system' of the *Mafia*. One cannot say that it was imposed on the Sicilians by anyone. In a sense, it grew out of the needs of all rural classes, and served the purpose of all in varying degrees. For the weak – the peasants and the miners – it provided at least some guarantee that obligations between them would be kept,* some guarantee that the usual degree of oppression would not be habitually exceeded; it was the terror which mitigated traditional tyrannies. And perhaps, also, it satisfied a desire for revenge by providing that the rich were sometimes fleeced, and that the poor, if only as outlaws, could sometimes fight back. It may even, on occasions, have provided the framework of revolutionary or defensive organization. (At any rate in the 1870s there seems to have been some tendency for Friendly Societies and quasi-*mafious* bodies like the *Fratellanza* of the sulphur-town of Favara, the *Fratuzzi* of Bagheria or the *Stoppaglieri* of Monreale to fuse.†)

---

* See N. Colajanni, *Gli Avvenimenti di Sicilia* (1894), cap 5, on the function of *mafia* as a code governing the relations between different classes of sulphur-miners, esp. pp. 47–8.

† I am not convinced that the rise of these bodies in the 1870s can be interpreted purely in terms of the revolt of young against old *Mafia* elements, as Montalbane suggests; though this may have been the case in Monreale.

For the feudal lords it was a means of safeguarding property and authority: for the rural middle class a means of gaining it. For all, it provided a means of defence against the foreign exploiter – the Bourbon or Piedmontese government – and a method of national or local self-assertion. So long as Sicily was no more than a static feudal society subject to outside rule, *Mafia's* character as a national conspiracy of non-co-operation gave it a genuinely popular basis. The *squadre* fought with the Palermo liberals (who included the anti-Bourbon Sicilian aristocracy) in 1820, 1848 and 1860. They headed the first great rising against the domination of northern capitalism in 1866. Its national, and to some extent popular character, increased the prestige of *Mafia*, and ensured it public sympathy and silence. Obviously it was a complex movement, including mutually contradictory elements. Nevertheless, however tiresome to the historian, he must resist the temptation to pigeon-hole *Mafia* more precisely at this stage of its development. Thus one cannot agree with Montalbane that the *picciotti* who then formed the revolutionary *squadre* were not really *Mafiosi* with a capital M but only *mafiosi* with a small m, while only the *contro-squadre*, already specialized strong-arm squads for the rich, were the 'real' *Mafia*. That is to read the *Mafia* of the 20th century into a period where it does not belong.*

Indeed, we may suspect that *Mafia* began its real rise to major power (and abuse) as a Sicilian regional movement of revolt against the disappointments of Italian unity in the 1860s, and as a more effective movement than the parallel and contemporary guerilla warfare of the brigands in continental southern Italy. Its political links as we have seen were with the extreme Left, for the Garibaldian Radicals were the

---

* Montalbane, 197.

main Italian opposition party. Yet three things caused *Mafia* to change its character.

First, there was the rise of capitalist relationships in island society. The emergence of modern forms of peasant and labour movement in place of the old alternation of silent conspiratorial hatred and occasional massacre faced the *Mafia* with an unprecedented change. 1866 was the last time it fought against the authorities with arms. The great peasant rising of 1894 – the *Fasci Siciliani* – saw it on the side of reaction, or at best neutral. Conversely, these risings were organized by new types of leaders – local socialists – connected with new types of organization, the *Fasci* or mutual defence societies, and independent of the 'lads'. The modern inverse proportion between the strength of *Mafia* and revolutionary activity began to appear. Even then it was observed that the rise of the Fasci had diminished the hold of *Mafia* on the peasants.* By 1900 *Piana dei Greci*, the socialist stronghold, though surrounded by *Mafia* strongholds, was markedly less riddled with it.† It

---

* E. C. Calon, *La Mafia* (Madrid 1906), 11.

† See the invaluable *Mafia* distribution map in Cutrera. Piana, though apparently slow to adopt peasant organization, became the great stronghold of the 1893 Fasci, and has remained a fortress of socialism (and later communism) ever since. That it was previously impregnated by *Mafia* is suggested by the history of *Mafia* in New Orleans, whose Sicilian colony which arrived in the 1880s had, to judge by the occurrence of the characteristic Albanian family names – Schirò, Loyacano, Matranga – a strong contingent of Pianesi. The Matrangas – members of the Stoppaglieri – controlled the dockside rackets, and were prominent in the *Mafia* incidents of 1889 in New Orleans. (Ed. Reid, *op. cit.*, 100 ff.) The family apparently continued its *Mafioso* activities, for in 1909 Lt. Petrosino of the New York police, later killed in Palermo – presumably by *Mafia* – was enquiring into the life of one of them (Reid, 122). I recall seeing the elaborate tomb of a Matranga in Piana in 1953, a man who had recently returned from emigration to the U.S.A. and had been found, in circumstances into which nobody was anxious to enquire, killed on a road a few years before.

is only in politically backward and powerless communities that brigands and *mafiosi* take the place of social movements. However, in spite of such local setbacks, there can be no doubt that *Mafia* as a whole was still expanding in the western part of Sicily throughout this period. At least a comparison of the Parliamentary Enquiries of 1884 and 1910 leaves one with a strong impression that it was.* Second, the new ruling class of rural Sicily, the *gabellotti* and their urban partners, discovered a *modus vivendi* with northern capitalism. They did not compete with it, for they were not interested in manufacture, and some of their most important products, such as oranges, were hardly produced in the north; hence the transformation of the south into an agrarian colony of the trading and manufacturing north did not greatly trouble them. On the other hand the evolution of northern politics provided them with an unprecedented and invaluable means of gaining power: the vote. The great days of *Mafia's* power, but days which portended its decline, begin with the triumph of 'Liberalism' in Italian politics and develop with the extension of the franchise.

From the point of view of the northern politicians, after the end of the conservative period which succeeded unification, the problem of the south was simple. It could provide safe majorities for whatever government gave sufficient bribes or concessions to the local bosses who could guarantee electoral victory. This was child's play for *Mafia*. Its candidates were always elected, in real strongholds almost unanimously. But the concessions and bribes which were small, from the point of view of northerners (for the south was poor) made all the difference to local power in a region as small as half Sicily.

* A. Damiani, *Inchiesta Agraria* (1884), Sicily, vol. III; G. Lorenzoni, *Inchiesta Parlamentare* (1910), Sicily, vol. VI, i–ii, esp. pp. 649–51.

Politics made the power of the local boss; politics increased it, and turned it into big business.

Mafia won its new power, not merely because it could promise and intimidate, but because, in spite of the new competitors, it was still regarded as part of the national or popular movement; just as big city bosses in the United States won their original power not simply by corruption and force, but by being 'our men' for thousands of immigrant voters: Irish men for the Irish, Catholics for the Catholic, Democrats (i.e. opponents of big business) in a predominantly Republican country. It is no accident that most American big city machines, however corrupt, belonged to the traditional party of minority opposition, as most Sicilians supported opposition to Rome, which, in the years after 1860, meant the Garibaldians. Thus the crucial turn in *Mafia's* fortunes could not come until the 'Left' (or men who sported its slogans) became the government party after 1876. The 'Left', as Colajanni put it, thus achieved 'a transformation in Sicily and the south which could not otherwise have been brought about: the complete subjection of the mass to the government'.* Sicilian political organization, i.e. *Mafia*, thus became part of the government system of patronage, and bargained all the more effectively because its illiterate and remote followers took time to realize that they were no longer voting for the cause of revolt. When they did (as for instance in the risings of the 1890s) it was too late. The tacit partnership between Rome with its troops and martial law and *Mafia* was too much for them. The true 'kingdom of *Mafia*' had been established. It was now a great power. Its members sat as deputies in Rome and their spoons reached into the thickest part of the gravy of government: large banks, national scandals. Its influence and patronage was now beyond the dream of old-

* *La Sicilia dai Borboni ai Sabaudi* (1951 ed.), 78.

fashioned local captains like Miceli of Monreale. It was not to be opposed; but it was no longer a Sicilian popular movement as in the days of the *squadre* of 1848, 1860 and 1866.

3

Hence its decline. Much has been published about this period since this book was written, but the main argument remains unaffected.* Some of the factors in the later history of *Mafia* may be briefly sketched.

First, there was the rise of the peasant leagues and the Socialists (later Communists), which provided the people with an alternative to *Mafia*, while at the same time alienating them from a body which became, with increasing openness and determination, a terrorist force directed against the Left.[†] The Fasci of 1893, the revival of agrarian agitation before the First World War, and in the disturbed years after 1918, were so many milestones on the roads which separated *Mafia* and the masses. The post-fascist period with its open warfare between *Mafia* and the Socialist-Communists – the massacres of Villalba (1944) and Portella della Ginestra (1947), the attempted assassination of the leading Sicilian Communist Girolamo Li Causi, and the killing of various union organizers – widened the gap.[‡] What mass basis *Mafia* had possessed among landless labourers, sulphur-miners, etc., has tended to diminish. There are still, according to Renda (a political

* See especially F. Renda, 'Funzione e basi sociali della Mafia', in *Il Movimento Contadino nella Società Siciliana* (Palermo 1956), and Montalbane, *loc. cit.* For recent literature see the Note on Further Reading.

† Prefect Mori, to do him justice, at least mentions this fact in passing.

‡ See M. Pantaleone, *Mafia e Politico* (Turin 1962) – the author comes from Villalba.

organizer as well as a good scholar), a few places which remain generally and 'spiritually' *mafiosi*, but 'the spirit and custom of mafia survive on the margins of the great popular sentiments'.

The rise of the Socialist-Communist vote has been marked in the most *Mafia*-riddled provinces, especially in the country-side. It is evident that the rise of the combined left wing vote in Palermo province from 11.8 per cent in 1946 to 22.8 per cent in 1953, or in Caltanissetta province from 29.1 per cent in 1946 to 37.1 per cent in 1953, marks a decline in the influence of the bitterly anti-left *Mafia*. The 29 per cent of Socialist-Communist votes in Palermo City (1958 election) continue the trend; for the Sicilian city was always, and still is, much less kind to the left wing parties than the village, and *Mafia* is proverbially strong in Palermo.* The Left has provided Sicilians with an alternative and more up-to-date organization, and with some direct and indirect protection against *Mafia*, especially since 1945, if only because the more extreme forms of its political terror now tend to cause major rows in Rome. In the second place, since *Mafia* can no longer control elections, it has lost much of the power that comes from patronage. Instead of being a 'parallel system' it is now only a very powerful pressure group, politically speaking.

Second, there were the internal divisions within *Mafia*. These took and take two forms: the rivalries between the 'ins' (generally the old generation) and the 'outs' (generally the 'young') in a country in which pickings are limited and unem-ployment high, and the tension between the old generation

* For election figures by provinces up to 1953, E. Caranti, *Sociologia e Statistica delle Elezioni Italiane* (Rome 1954). The 1958 figures are taken from the post-election Corriere della Sera, May 28th 1958. The total socialist-communist percentage for the four *Mafiose* provinces in 1958 was 33–9, against 43 for the Demochristians and most of the balance for the extreme right. (Palermo, Trapani, Agrigento, Caltanissetta electoral division.)

of illiterate and parochially-minded *gabellotti*, barely removed (except in wealth) from the peasants on whom they batten, and their sons and daughters, of higher social status. The lads who become white-collar workers and lawyers, the girls who marry into 'better' society – i.e. non-*Mafia* society – break up the family cohesion of *Mafia*, on which much of its strength depended. The first type of tension between 'old' and 'young' *Mafia* is old; as we have seen, it occurred in classic form in Monreale as early as 1872. The second is found in Palermo as early as 1875, but in the latifundist hinterland it has only developed in the last decades.* These ever-renewed rivalries between 'old' and 'young' *Mafia*, produce what Montalbane has called its 'strange dialectic': sooner or later the young toughs, who cannot solve the problem of life by working – for there is no work – must solve it in some other manner, e.g. crime. But the older generation of the *Mafiosi* have the lucrative rackets under control and are reluctant to make way for the young men, who therefore organize rival gangs, generally on the same lines as the old *Mafia*, often with the help of the police, which hopes thereby to weaken the old *Mafia*, and which the young *Mafiosi* wish to use for the same purpose. Sooner or later, if neither side has been able to suppress the other – most *Mafia* killings are the outcome of such internecine quarrels – old and young combine, after a redistribution of the spoils.

However, it is widely felt that *Mafia* has suffered from abnormally profound internal dissensions since the First World War, and this may be due to tensions of the second kind, intensified by genuine policy-differences which were bound to arise in an island whose economy, society and criminal horizons have changed with increasing rapidity. An example of such

* Renda, *loc. cit.*, 219.

policy-differences may be given from America. There *Mafia* originally refused to deal with any but Sicilian immigrants, and fought notable battles against the rival (Neapolitan) *Camorristi*, e.g. the famous Matranga-Provenzano feuds in New Orleans in the 1880s, and similar battles in New York in the 1910s. It has been plausibly suggested that a purge of the 'old' *Mafia* by the 'young' took place about 1930, the old organization being replaced by a more up-to-date version which was, unlike the old blood-brotherhood, prepared to co-operate with Neapolitan, or for that matter Jewish gangsters. The arguments about the survival or non-survival of *Mafia* among American gangsters are perhaps best explained in terms of such dissensions.* We shall consider the new 'business' horizons of the modern *Mafia* below.

Thirdly, there was Fascism. Mussolini, according to the plausible account of Renda, found himself obliged to fight *Mafia*, since the non-fascist Liberal Party relied heavily on its backing. (The Palermo election of 1924 had shown Liberal-*Mafia* capacity to resist the normal Fascist process of political conquest.) Admittedly the Fascist campaigns against *Mafia* revealed its growing weakness more than they contributed to it, and ended with very much the same tacit working agreement between the local men of wealth and power and the central government as before. But by abolishing elections Fascism certainly deprived *Mafia* of its main currency for purchasing concessions from Rome, and the Blackshirt movement provided discontented *Mafiosi* or would-be *Mafiosi* with a wonderful opportunity for using the state apparatus to supplant their established rivals, and thus intensified the internal tensions of *Mafia*. Its roots

* For the old feuds, cf. Ed. Reid, *The Mafia*, 100, 146. For the 1930 purge (unmentioned by Reid or Kefauver), Turkus & Feder, *Murder Inc.* (London 1953).

remained: after 1943 it re-emerged happily. However, the sub-stantial shocks and shifts that were forced upon it had far from negligible social effects. The big *Mafiosi* could come to terms with Rome easily enough. For most Sicilians all that happened was that the 'parallel system' and the official government merged into a single conspiracy to oppress; a step along the road opened in 1876 rather than a reversal of steps. The little *Mafiosi*, on the other hand, may well have suffered. It has even been argued that the Fascist campaigns 'brought to a stop the long process by which the middle strata of the *Mafia* increasingly inserted themselves into the system of large landed property as small and medium proprietors.'*

After 1943 the *Mafia* re-emerged under the wing of the Americans. It seems clear – according to Branca's report of 1946 – that it was closely linked with the Sicilian separatist movement with which the Allies flirted somewhat rashly after their occupation of the island, and perhaps also with the old party of property and the *status quo*, the Liberals. Subsequently the *Mafia* seems to have switched alliances, as the dramatic fall in the Liberal and Independentist vote (from half a million in 1947 to 220,000 in 1948) indicates. Though some old *mafiosi* may have turned for a time to the Monarchists and other parties, for obvious reasons the Christian Democrats, permanent party of govern-ment and patronage, in Italy, attracted most of their interest.†

* Renda, 213.

† In 1958, the parties of the pre-fascist régime – Liberals and Monarchists – still remained remarkably strong in certain areas, which may perhaps serve as a rough index of 'old *Mafia*' voting influence: in Trapani they ran ahead of both Demochristians and Socialist-Communists, in Partinico-Monreale – an old *Mafia* fief – ahead of the Socialist-Communists, though in such typically Mafia areas as Corleone-Bagheria they had dropped well behind the Left and far behind the Demochristians.

However, though the *Mafia* is deeply enmeshed in the complex and profitable business of Sicilian politics, it can no longer 'deliver the vote' as it could in its great days.

In return, however, *Mafia* has in the post-war period discovered two new sorts of profitable economic activity. On the simple criminal side the horizons of certain *Mafia* groups have certainly become international, partly due to the vast pickings to be made in black-marketing and wholesale smuggling in what historians will undoubtedly regard as the golden age in the world history of the organized criminals, partly because of the strong links between Sicily and the occupying American forces, strengthened by the expulsion to Italy of numerous well-known American gangsters. There seems little doubt that part of *Mafia* has taken to international drug-trafficking with enthusiasm. It is even possible – and a far cry from the old provincialism – that *Mafiosi* are prepared to subordinate themselves to criminal activities organized from elsewhere.*

Far more important is the method by which *Mafia* has been able to resist the destruction of its former mainstay, the latifundist economy. The estates have gone, and many barons have sacked their *campieri*. But the position of the *Mafiosi* as local men of influence has enabled them to cash in on the vast body of land-sales to peasants under the various reform laws. 'It may be affirmed', says Renda, 'that practically all purchases of small peasant property have been negotiated through the mediation of *Mafioso* elements'† to whose hands much of the land and other assets have therefore tended to cling. *Mafia* has thus once again played its part in the creation

---

* Cf. M. Pantaleone, *Mafia e Droga* (Turin 1966).
† Renda, 218.

of a Sicilian middle class, and will undoubtedly survive the fall of the old economy. The typical *Mafioso*, who used to be a *campiere*, has merely been replaced by the *Mafioso* landowner or businessman.

Finally, the great economic boom of the 1950s and 1960s provided the *Mafia* with vast new opportunities in the field of urban development, especially in Palermo, which the political autonomy of Sicily allowed them to exploit to the full; as witness the *Memoriale sulla Mafia* submitted by the Palermo Federation of the Communist Party to the Parliamentary Enquiry of 1963 (*Rinascità* 12 Oct. 1963, 11–21). Meanwhile the boom on the mainland and the mass migration of southerners to the North extended *Mafia* activities to the remainder of Italy. In the early 1960s the Italian government finally decided to take some action, but it can be said with some confidence that the *Mafia* has so far survived the attempt to stamp it out, though historians will benefit immeasurably from the information it has produced.

4

Mafia is the best-publicized but not the only phenomenon of its kind. How many comparable ones exist we simply do not know, because these things have only rarely attracted the attention of scholars, and that of journalists only intermittently. (Local journals are often reluctant to print news of matters which might reflect unfavourably on the 'good name' of the region, much as local journals in seaside resorts are disinclined to print too much news of cloudbursts.) Though the so-called *Honoured Society* (*'ndranghita, fibbia*) has long been known to one and all in Southern Calabria, and apparently came under the notice of the police in 1928–9, we owe most of our knowledge of it to a series of semi-fortuitous events in 1953–5.* In these years the number of homicides in the province of Reggio Calabria doubled. As the local activities of the *fibbia* had political implications nationally – the car of a government minister was held up by bandits at one stage, some said by mistake, and the various parties accused one another of utilizing local gangsters – the police drive of August–September 1955 was abnormally well reported in the national press. And, as it happened, an internal quarrel within the society into which the police were drawn, caused several of its secrets to be made public.† On such accidents does our knowledge of non-Sicilian *mafias* depend.

The *Onorata Società* appears to have developed about the same time as the Carbonari‡ and on the same model, for its structure and ritual is still reported to be masonic. However, unlike the Carbonari, who were a middle-class body specializing in opposition to the Bourbons, the Honoured Society 'developed rather as an association for mutual aid for persons who wished to defend themselves against feudal, state

* For more recent documentation on it, see G. G. Loschiavo, *100 Anni di Mafia* (Rome 1962), esp. pp. 393–421, which prints two police reports and a full version of the initiation ritual.

† C. Guarino, 'Dai Mafiosi ai Camorristi' (*Nord e Sud* 13, 1955, 76–107), claims that the gaff was blown by a member of the society, a certain Serafino Castagna, a rather unpopular man, who committed some extremely nasty private enterprise murders and then called on the society to help him escape. It refused and Castagna, desperate, made a bargain with the police. He was, however, sentenced, though testifying freely. Cf. also G. Cervigni, Antologia della "fibbia"' (*Nord e Sud* 18, 1956).

‡ My account is based on Guarino, Cervigni, *loc. cit.*, A. Fiumanò and R. Villari, 'Politica e malavita' (*Cronache Meridionali* II, 10, 1955, 653 ff.), but above all on newspaper accounts of Sept. 1955, especially the excellent articles by R. Longnone in *Unità. Leggenda e realtà della 'ndranghita* 8.9.1955 is particularly valuable.

or police power or against private assertions of power'. Like the *Mafia*, it underwent some historic evolution. On the other hand, unlike Sicilian *Mafia*, it seems to have maintained its character as a popular organization for self-defence and for the defence of the 'Calabrian way of life' to a much greater extent than *Mafia*. At least this is the testimony of the local communists who may be relied upon on this point, for their bias is very strongly hostile to organizations such as this. The Honoured Society has thus remained, at least in one of its aspects, 'a primitive, as it were pre-political, association joined by the peasant, the shepherd, the small artisan, the unskilled labourer who, living in a closed and backward environment such as that of certain Calabrian villages – especially in the mountains – strives for a consideration, a respect, a dignity not otherwise within reach of the propertyless and poor' (Longnone). Thus Nicola d'Agostino of Canolo, who later became Communist mayor of his village, is described as a man who, in his youth 'was, as they say in these parts, "a man who made himself respected"'. Naturally enough he was then a prominent member of the Society. (Like so many peasant communists he was 'converted' in jail.) As we have already seen, the Society regarded it as its duty to help not only its own members, but all who were in the eyes of local custom unjustly persecuted by the State, for instance blood-vengeance killers.

Naturally enough it also tended to function, like *Mafia*, as a parallel system of law, capable of returning stolen property or solving other problems (for a consideration) much more effectively than the foreign State apparatus. Naturally, again like *Mafia* and for analogous reasons, it tended to evolve into a system of local extortion rackets and local power-nuclei, which could be hired by anyone desirous of local 'influence' for their own purposes. Political opponents quote cases of local chiefs whose police sentences were suspended for the period of an election, so that they might exercise their influence in the right direction. *Mafia*-type lodges selling their influence to the highest bidders – i.e. mostly the local agrarian and business interests and government parties – are known. In the plain of Gioia Tauro an old landowners' fief (which the tourist traverses by train on his way to Sicily) it seems that local employers and authorities used *squadristi* – strong-arm squads drawn from the Society – extensively from 1949–50 on, which is not surprising for that year saw the peak of the Calabrian mass agitation for land reform. The Society there seems in consequence largely to have taken over the local mechanism for supplying employers with labour, a characteristically *Mafioso* development.* However, this is not necessarily typical, for in spite of its nominally hierarchical character the various village lodges of the Society appear to go very much their own ways, some of them tending even to make alliances with the Left.

The situation is further complicated by private rivalries within and between lodges, by blood-vengeance and other complexities of the Calabrian scene. When the Society is taken by emigrants to Liguria or Australia, it becomes even more obscure and sometimes bloody.† However, it seems clear

* Fiumanò and Villari, *loc. cit.*, 657–8.

† For a story combining two traditional Calabrian phenomena, the abduction of brides (see Chapter I) and the Society, see *La Nuova Stampa* 17.11.1956. The incident is reported from Bordighera. For the Society in Australia – a subject which Australian sociologists might profitably investigate – cf. the case of Rocco Calabro, local *fibbia* chief in Sinopoli, and three years an emigrant in Sydney, who was killed in 1955 in his home town, allegedly as the result of a Society quarrel in Sydney. (*Paese Sera* 7.9.1955, *Messagero* 6.9.1955.) Twenty per cent of Sinopolitans are in emigration in Australia.

that it has only partly evolved in the direction of the modern Sicilian *Mafia*.

Consequently also the Society has in many places gradually faded out as modern left wing movements have taken root. It has not invariably become a politically conservative force. In Gerace it is actually reported to have dissolved itself; in Canolo – thanks to the influence of the converted D'Agostino – it became bad form and slightly ridiculous to be a member; and even in those left wing villages in which it survives, it does so – or so it is reported – as a relatively somnolent local form of masonry. But – and this is the important point – it has nowhere, so far as we know, been *collectively* converted into a left wing organization, though it *has*, in some places, become a right wing pressure-group.

This is only natural. As we have seen, the chief tendency of *Mafia's* development is away from a social movement and towards at best a political pressure-group and at worst a complex of extortion rackets. There are very sound reasons why this should be so; why, in other words, no national or social movement of a modern type can be built on the foundations of a traditional *mafia*, unless it is profoundly transformed from within.

The first of these is, that it tends to reflect the unofficial distribution of power in the oppressed society: the nobles and the rich are its bosses simply because theirs was the effective power in the countryside. Hence, as soon as major cleavages between the men of power and the masses develop – e.g. with agrarian agitations – the new movements find it difficult to fit into the *Mafia* pattern. In turn, when socialist or communist peasant organization has a measure of local power, it no longer requires much help from bodies of the *Mafia* type.

The second reason is that the social aims of *Mafia*

movements, like those of banditry, are almost invariably limited, except perhaps insofar as they demand national independence. And even here they function best as tacit conspiracies to defend the 'old way of life' against the threat of foreign laws rather than as effective independent methods of throwing off the foreign yoke. The initiative in the Sicilian rebellions of the 19th century came from the urban liberals, not from the *Mafia*. The *mafiosi* merely joined them. Just because the *mafia* form of organization normally arises before the masses have crossed the threshold of political consciousness, just because its aims are limited and defensive, it will tend to become, in effect – to use an anachronistic term – reformist rather than revolutionary. It will be satisfied with a regulation of existing social relationships and will not demand their supersession. Hence, once again, the rise of revolutionary movements tends to weaken it.

Lastly, it will tend to social stability because, in the absence of conscious organization and ideology, it is normally unable to evolve an apparatus of physical force which is not at the same time an apparatus for crime and private enrichment. In other words, it inevitably tends to operate through gangsters, because it is incapable of producing professional revolutionaries. But gangsters have a vested interest in private property, as pirates have a vested interest in legitimate commerce, being parasitic upon it.

For all these reasons the *mafia* type of movement is least capable of being transformed into a modern social movement, except by the conversion of individual *mafiosi*. However, this does not mean that genuinely revolutionary movements operating under certain historic conditions may not develop a good many forms of behaviour and institutions reminiscent of *mafia*.

A note on the Camorra*

Since *Mafia* and the Camorra are often bracketed together as 'criminal associations' it may be as well to add a brief note. I do not think that the Camorra can be regarded as a 'social movement' in any sense of the word, even though, like all who are strong and break the laws of the oppressors, for whatever purposes, it enjoyed something of the admiration which the poor had for the brigand, and was invested with myth and commemorated in song 'as a sort of savage justice against the oppressors' (Alongi, 27).

Unless all authorities are mistaken, the Camorra was – and insofar as it may still exist, probably is – a criminal gild or fraternity, such as are sometimes recorded by the historian; perhaps like the underworld of Basel which had its own acknowledged court outside the town on the Kohlenberg[†] or the Cofradia del Monopodio of which Cervantes speaks in one of his Novelas Ejemplares. It represented no class or national interest or coalition of class interests, but the professional interest of an élite of criminals. Its ceremonies and rituals were those of a body designed to emphasize the separateness of the *milieu* from the mass of ordinary citizens; e.g. the obligation for candidates and novices to commit a certain number of common-law crimes, though the Camorra's normal activity was simple extortion. Its standard of 'honesty' – the concept is reminiscent of the criteria of admission to legitimate gilds – assumed that candidates belonged to the underworld: besides strength and courage, the candidate

---

* This note is primarily based on G. Alongi, *La Camorra* (Turin 1890); not a very good book, but one which embodies the previous literature.
† Avé-Lallemant, *Das deutsche Gaunerthum* I (1858), 48 n.

must not have sister or wife in prostitution and must not have been convicted of passive pederasty (presumably as a male prostitute), and must have no relations with the police (Alongi, 39). Its origin was almost certain in the jails, which normally, and in all countries, tend to produce camorras – though rarely institutionalized in so archaic a form – among the prisoners.

When it emerged from the jails is uncertain. Some time between 1790 and 1830 is the safest guess, perhaps as a result of the various revolutions and reactions in Naples. Once in the open, its power and influence grew rapidly, largely due to the goodwill of the Bourbons, who – after 1799 – regarded the *lumpenproletariat* of Naples and all that belonged to it as their safest allies against Liberalism. Since it came virtually to control every aspect of the life of the Neapolitan poor – though perhaps it made most of its money by various gambling rackets – it became increasingly indispensable to the local administration, and consequently increasingly powerful. Under Ferdinand II it functioned as the virtual secret police of the State against Liberals. Under Francis II it came to terms with the Liberals, though making a little money on the side by threatening to denounce such of their Liberal allies as suited them. The peak of its power was reached during the 1860 revolution when the Liberals actually handed over the maintenance of public order in Naples to the Camorra, a task it carried out with great efficiency and zeal, since it implied mainly the elimination of freelance crime as distinct from the Camorrist rake-off. In 1862 the new government undertook the first of a series of energetic campaigns against it. However, though it succeeded in suppressing the open operation of the society, it did not eliminate Camorra, which appears to have maintained itself – and perhaps strengthened itself – by the habitual process of 'going into politics', i.e. selling its support to the various political parties (Alongi, 32).

There is no evidence at all that it had any general political orientation, beyond looking after itself, though we must presume that, like all professional criminals, it had a bias towards private property as a system. Unlike *Mafias*, such organizations as Camorra live outside the entire 'legitimate' world, and consequently only impinge on its politics and movements incidentally.

Outside the jails it seems to have been confined exclusively to the city of Naples, though after 1860 it, or similar bodies, are said to have spread in other southern provinces such as Caserta, Salerno and Bari (Alongi, 111), perhaps as a result of better communications. Being confined to a single city, it was easier for it to be rather tightly, centrally and hierarchically organized. In this, as we have seen, it differed from the more decentralized *Mafias*.

Its recent history is obscure. Camorra as such appears to have disappeared, or at any rate the word is no longer used, except as a general description of any criminal secret society or fraternity or racketeering system. However, something like Camorra is once again in existence in the Neapolitan region, though its adepts seem to be known not as 'camorristi' but as 'i magliari'. It operates rackets mainly in tobacco, in petrol – specializing in fake permits for drawing petrol from the NATO stores –, in 'exemptions' of one kind or another, but especially in the trade with fruit and vegetables which appears to be largely under the control of racketeers. Gangs – whether of the ordinary or Camorra type is unknown – are also powerful elsewhere, e.g. in the Nola region, and in the lawless zone of the Salernitano, between Noca Inferiore, Angri and Scafati, which is said to be under the control of one Vittorio Nappi ('o studente').*

We may conclude that, while Camorra has much to interest the sociologist and anthropologist, it belongs into a discussion of social movements within the 'legitimate' as distinct from the 'crooked' world only insofar as the poor of Naples tend to idealize gangsters in a way vaguely reminiscent of social banditry. There is no evidence that the Camorristi or magliari have ever deserved any idealization whatsoever.

* Guarino, *loc. cit.*

Chapter IV

Millenarianism I: Lazzaretti

Of all the primitive social movements discussed in this book, millenarianism is the one least handicapped by its primitiveness. For the only thing really primitive about it is external. The essence of millenarianism, the hope of a complete and radical change in the world which will be reflected in the millennium, a world shorn of all its present deficiencies, is not confined to primitivism. It is present, almost by definition, in all revolutionary movements of whatever kind, and 'millenarian' elements may therefore be discovered by the student in any of them, insofar as they have ideals. This does not mean that therefore *all* revolutionary movements are millennial in the narrower sense of the word, let alone that they are primitive, an assumption which deprives Professor Norman Cohn's book of some of its value. Indeed, it is impossible to make much sense of modern revolutionary history unless one appreciates the differences between primitive and modern revolutionary movements, in spite of the ideal which they have in common, that of a totally new world.

The typical old-fashioned millenarian movement in Europe

has three main characteristics. First, a profound and total rejection of the present, evil world, and a passionate longing for another and better one; in a word, revolutionism. Second, a fairly standardized 'ideology' of the chiliastic type as analysed and described by Professor Cohn. The most important ideology of this sort before the rise of modern secular revolutionism is Judeo-Christian messianism, but the view suggested in the first edition of this book, that such movements are virtually confined to the countries affected by the Judeo-Christian-Moslem tradition does not seem tenable.* Religions such as Hinduism and Buddhism produce different rationalizations of millennial expectations, but plenty of movements which are recognizably like millenarian ones. Third, millenarian movements share a fundamental vagueness about the actual way in which the new society will be brought about.

It is difficult to put this last point more precisely, for such movements range from the purely passive at one extreme, to those which skirt modern revolutionary methods at the other – indeed, as we shall see, to those which merge naturally into modern revolutionary movements. However, it may perhaps be clarified as follows. Modern revolutionary movements have – implicitly or explicitly – certain fairly definite ideas on how the old society is to be replaced by the new, the most crucial of which concerns what we may call the 'transfer of power'. The old rulers must be toppled from their positions. The 'people' (or the revolutionary class or group) must 'take over' and then carry out certain measures – the redistribution of land, the nationalization of the means of production, or

* Yonina Talmon's 'Millenarism' (*Int. Encycl. Soc. Sciences* 1968) still maintains the old view, but cf. J. M. van der Kroef, 'Javanese Messianic Expectations: Their Origin and Cultural Context' (*Comp. Stud, in Society and History* I, 4, 1959, 299–323).

whatever it may be. In all this the organized effort of the revolutionaries is decisive, and doctrines of organization, strategy
and tactics, etc., sometimes very elaborate, are evolved to aid
them in their task. The sort of things revolutionaries do is,
let us say, to organize a mass demonstration, throw up barricades, march on the town hall, run up the tricolour, proclaim
the Republic one and indivisible, appoint a provisional government, and issue a call for a Constituent Assembly. (This,
roughly, is the 'drill' which so many of them learned from
the French Revolution. It is not, of course, the only possible
procedure.) But the 'pure' millenarian movement operates
quite differently, whether because of the inexperience of its
members or the narrowness of their horizons, or because of
the effect of millenarian ideologies and preconceptions. Its
followers are not makers of revolution. They expect it to make
itself, by divine revelation, by an announcement from on high,
by a miracle – they expect it to happen somehow. The part of
the people before the change is to gather together, to prepare
itself, to watch the signs of the coming doom, to listen to the
prophets who predict the coming of the great day, and perhaps
to undertake certain ritual measures against the moment of
decision and change, or to purify themselves, shedding the
dross of the bad world of the present so as to be able to enter
the new world in shining purity. Between the two extremes of
the 'pure' millenarian and the 'pure' political revolutionary all
manner of intermediate positions are possible. In fact, the millenarian movements discussed here occupy such intermediate
positions, the Lazzarettists nearest to one extreme, the Spanish
anarchists theoretically much nearer to the other.

When a millenarian movement turns into, or is absorbed
by, a modern revolutionary movement, it therefore retains the
first of its characteristics. It normally abandons the second at

least to some extent, substituting a modern, that is in general a secular, theory of history and revolution: nationalist, socialist, communist, anarchist or of some other type. Lastly it adds a superstructure of modern revolutionary politics to its basic revolutionary spirit: a programme, a doctrine concerning the transfer of power, and above all a system of organization. This is not always easy, but millenarian movements differ from some of the others discussed in this book in opposing no fundamental *structural* obstacles to modernization. At any rate, as we shall see, such movements have been successfully integrated into modern revolutionary ones; just possibly also into modern reformist ones. Their interest for the historian of the 19th and 20th centuries lies in the process by which they are so absorbed, or in the reasons why sometimes they are not. This will be sketched in this and the two subsequent chapters.

It is not always easy to recognize the rational political core within millenarian movements, for their very lack of sophistication and of an effective revolutionary strategy and tactics makes them push the logic of the revolutionary position to the point of absurdity or paradox. They are impractical and Utopian. Since they flourish best in periods of extraordinary social ferment and tend to speak the language of apocalyptic religion, the behaviour of their members is often rather odd by normal standards. They are therefore as easily misinterpreted as William Blake, who until quite recently was commonly regarded not as a revolutionary, but simply as an eccentric other-worldly mystic and visionary.* When they wish to express their fundamental critique of the existing world, they may, like

---

* The modern view was pioneered by J. Bronowski, *William Blake, A Man without a Mask* (London 1944 and Pelican Books).

the millenarian anarchist strikers in Spain, refuse to marry until the new world has been instituted; when they wish to express their rejection of mere palliatives and lesser reforms, they may (again like the Andalusian strikers of the early 20th century) refuse to formulate demands for higher wages or anything else, even when urged to do so by the authorities. When they wish to express their belief that the new world ought to be fundamentally different from the old, they may, like the Sicilian peasants, believe that somehow even the climate can be changed. Their behaviour may be ecstatic to the point where observers describe it in terms of mass hysteria. On the other hand their actual programme may be vague to the point where observers doubt whether they have one. Those who cannot understand what it is that moves them – and even some who do – may be tempted to interpret their behaviour as wholly irrational or pathological, or at best as an instinctive reaction to intolerable conditions.

Without wishing to make it appear more sensible and less extraordinary than it often is, it is advisable for the historian to appreciate the logic, and even the realism – if the word can be used in this context – which moves them, for revolutionary movements are difficult to understand otherwise. It is their peculiarity that those who cannot see what all the bother is about are disabled from saying anything of great value about them, whereas those who do (especially when among primitive social movements) cannot often speak in terms intelligible to the rest. It is especially difficult, but necessary, to understand that utopianism, or 'impossibilism' which the most primitive revolutionaries share with all but the most sophisticated, and which makes even very modern ones feel a sense of almost physical pain at the realization that the coming of Socialism will not eliminate *all* grief and sadness, unhappy love-affairs or mourning, and will not solve or make soluble *all* problems; a feeling reflected in the ample literature of revolutionary disillusionment.

First, utopianism is probably a necessary social device for generating the superhuman efforts without which no major revolution is achieved. From the historian's point of view the transformations brought about by the French and Russian Revolutions are astonishing enough, but would the Jacobins have undertaken their task simply to exchange the France of the Abbé Prévost for the France of Balzac, the Bolsheviks to exchange the Russia of Tchehov for that of Mr Khrushchev? Probably not. It was essential for them to believe that 'the ultimate in human prosperity and liberty will appear after their victories'.* Obviously they will not, though the result of the revolution may nevertheless be very worth while.

Second, utopianism can become such a social device *because revolutionary movements and revolutions appear to prove that almost no change is beyond their reach*. If the revolutionaries needed proof that 'human nature can be changed' – i.e. that no social problem is insoluble – the demonstration of its changes in such movements and at such moments would be quite sufficient:

> This other man had I dreamed
> A drunken vainglorious lout . . .
> Yet I number him in the song;
> He, too, has resigned his part
> In the casual comedy;

* M. Djilas, *The New Class* (1957), 32, discusses this point interestingly. This book by a disillusioned revolutionary is valuable for the light it throws on revolutionary psychology, including the author's own, and for very little else.

He, too, has been changed in his turn,
Transformed utterly:
A terrible beauty is born.

It is this consciousness of *utter* change, not as an aspiration but
as a fact – at least a temporary fact – which informs Yeats'
poem on the Easter Rising, and tolls, like a bell, at the end of
his stanzas: All changed, changed utterly. A terrible beauty is
born. Liberty, equality, and above all fraternity may become
real for the moment in those stages of the great social revolutions which revolutionaries who live through them describe
in the terms normally reserved for romantic love: 'bliss was it
in that dawn to be alive, but to be young was very Heaven'.
Revolutionaries not only set themselves a standard of morality
higher than that of any except saints, but at such moments
actually carry it into practice, even when it involves considerable technical difficulty, as in the relation between the sexes.*
Theirs is at such times a miniature version of the ideal society,
in which all men are brothers and sacrifice all for the common
good without abandoning their individuality. If this is possible
within their movement, why not everywhere?

As for the masses of those who do not belong to the revolutionary élite, the mere fact of becoming revolutionary and
of recognizing the 'power of the people' seems so miraculous
that anything else seems equally possible. An observer of the
Sicilian Fasci has correctly noted this logic: if a sudden vast

---

* Djilas, *op. cit.*, 153, 'Between men and women in the movement, a clean,
modest and warm relationship is fostered: a relationship in which comradely
care has become sexless passion', etc. Djilas, doubtless with the period of the
partisan war in mind, also stresses the historical moment ('on the eve of the
battle for power' when 'it is difficult to separate words from deeds'), but also
notes, perceptively, that 'these are the morals of a sect'.

mass movement could be stamped out of the ground, if thousands could be shaken out of the lethargy and defeatism of centuries by a single speech, how could men doubt that great and world-overturning events would soon come to pass? Men *had* been utterly changed and were being visibly transformed. Noble men who in their lives followed the dictates of the good society – poverty, brotherliness, saintliness, or whatever else they were – could be observed working among them even by the unregenerate, and provided further proof of the reality of the ideal. We shall see the political importance of these local revolutionary apostles among the Andalusian village anarchists, but every observer of modern revolutionary movements is aware of it in almost all of them, and of the pressure upon the revolutionary élite to live up to the role of moral exemplars: not to earn more or live better, to work harder, to be 'pure', to sacrifice their private happiness (as happiness is interpreted in the old society) in full public view. When normal modes of behaviour creep in again – for instance, after the triumph of a new revolutionary régime – men will not conclude that the changes for which they long are impracticable for long periods or outside exclusive groups of abnormally devoted men and women, but that there has been 'backsliding' or 'betrayal'. For the possibility, the reality, of the ideal relationship between human beings has been proved in practice, and what can be more conclusive than that?

The problems facing millenarian movements are or look simple in the intoxicating periods of their growth and advance. They are correspondingly difficult in those which follow revolutions or risings.

Since none of the movements discussed in this book have so far been on the winning side, the question what happens when they discover that their victory does not in fact solve *all* human problems does not greatly concern us. Their defeat does, for it faces them with the problem of maintaining revolutionism as a permanent force. The only millenarian movements which avoid this are the completely suicidal ones, for the death of all their members makes it academic.* Normally defeat soon produces a body of doctrine to explain why the millennium has not come and the old world can therefore expect to go on for a while. The signs of imminent doom were not read right or some other mistake has been made. (The Jehovah's Witnesses have quite a large exegetical literature to explain why the failure of the world to end on the date originally predicted does not invalidate the prediction.) To recognize that the old world will continue is to recognize that one must live in it. But how?

Some millenarians, like some revolutionaries, do indeed tacitly drop their revolutionism and turn into *de facto* acceptors of the *status quo*, which is all the easier if the *status quo* becomes more tolerable for the people. Some may even turn into reformist ones, or perhaps discover, now that the ecstasy of the revolutionary period is over, and they are no longer swept away by it, that what they wanted really does not require quite so fundamental a transformation as they had imagined. Or, what is more likely, they may withdraw into a passionate inner life of 'the movement', or 'the sect', leaving the rest of the world to its own devices except for some token assertions of millennial hopes, and perhaps of the millennial programme: for instance pacifism and the refusal to take oaths. Others, however, do not. They may merely retire to wait for the next revolutionary

* The best known, but not the only one, of this type was the movement of Antonio the Counsellor in the backwoods of Brazil in 1876–7, which provides the subject of a literary masterpiece, Euclides da Cunha's *Rebellion in the Backlands*. The rebel Zion of Canudos fought literally to the last man. When it was captured, no defender was left alive.

crisis (to use a non-millenarian term) which must surely bring with it the total destruction of the old world and the institution of the new. This is naturally easiest where the economic and social conditions of revolution are endemic, as in Southern Italy, where every political change in the 19th century, irrespective from what quarter it came, automatically produced its ceremonial marches of peasants with drums and banners to occupy the land,* or in Andalusia where, as we shall see, millenarian revolutionary waves occurred at roughly ten-year intervals for some sixty or seventy years. Others, as we shall see, retain enough of the old fire to attach themselves to, or to turn into, revolutionary movements of a non-millennial type even after long periods of apparent quiescence.

There, precisely, lies their adaptability. Primitive reformist movements are easily lost in a modern society, if only because the task of securing an equitable regulation of social relations within the existing framework, the creation of tolerable or comfortable conditions here and now, is technically specialized and complicated, and much better done by organizations and movements built to the specifications of modern societies: co-operative marketing organizations are better at the job of giving peasants a fair deal than Robin Hoods. But the fundamental object of social-revolutionary movements remains much more unchanged, though the concrete conditions of the fight for it vary, as may be seen by comparing the passages in which the great Utopian or revolutionary writers make their critique of existing societies with those in which they propose specific remedies or reforms. Millenarians can (as we shall see in the chapter on the Sicilian Fasci) readily exchange the

---

* Cf. A. La Cava, 'La rivolta calabrese del 1848', in *Arch. Stor. delle Prov. Napoletane*, N.S. XXXI, 1947–9, 445 ff., 540, 552.

primitive costume in which they dress their aspirations for the modern costume of Socialist and Communist politics. Conversely as we have seen even the least millenarian modern revolutionaries have in them a streak of 'impossibilism' which makes them cousins to the Taborites and Anabaptists, a kinship which they have never denied. The junction between the two is therefore readily made, and once made, the primitive movement can be transformed into a modern one.

I propose to discuss three movements of different degrees of millenarianism, and adaptation to modern politics, the Lazzarettists of Southern Tuscany (from *c.* 1875 onward), the Andalusian village anarchists (from the 1870s to 1936) and the Sicilian peasant movements (from *c.* 1893 onwards). In the 19th and 20th centuries such movements have been overwhelmingly agrarian, though there is no *a priori* reason why they should not be urban, and in the past they have sometimes been so. (But urban workers in our period have normally acquired more modern types of revolutionary ideology.) Of the three chosen here, the Lazzarettists are a laboratory specimen of a medieval millenarian heresy surviving in a backward corner of peasant Italy. The second and third are examples of the millenarian characteristics of social movements along an endemically revolutionary peasantry in very poor and backward areas. The anarchists are chiefly interesting in that they show millenarianism wholly divorced from traditional religious forms, and indeed in a militantly atheist and anti-Christian shape. On the other hand they also demonstrate the political weakness of millenarian movements which are transformed into imperfectly (i.e. ineffectively) revolutionary modern ones. The Sicilian Fasci, though in some senses much less 'modern' – for their members only abandoned their traditional ideology very incompletely – enable us to study the absorption of millenarianism into a modern revolutionary movement, the Communist Party, particularly clearly.

It only remains to note that the present account is sketchy and tentative, and that, in spite of considerable temptation, I have avoided all comparisons with the millenarian movements outside Europe which have lately received some very able scholarly attention.* My reasons for resisting the temptation are briefly outlined in the Introduction.

The Saviour on the Monte Amiata

The extraordinary impracticality of millenarian movements has often led observers to deny not only that they are revolutionary but also that they are social. This is very much so in the case of Davide Lazzaretti, the Messiah of the Monte Amiata.† It is argued, for instance, by Sig. Barzellotti, that the Lazzarettists were a purely religious movement. This is in any case an unwise statement to make. The kinds of community which produced millenarian heresies are not the ones in which clear distinctions between religious and secular things can be drawn. To argue about whether such a sect is religious *or* social is meaningless, for it will automatically and always be both in some manner. However, it is also clear that the Lazzarettists were passionately interested in politics. The slogan on their flag is variously described as 'The Republic and the kingdom of God' or 'The Republic is the kingdom of God', Italy being

* E.g. in Peter Worsley's *The Trumpet Shall Sound* (London 1957), a first-rate study of the Pacific 'cargo' cults.

† My attention was drawn to this movement by Prof. Ambrogio Donini, who has talked to the existing Lazzarettists and collected some of their unpublished scriptures. Besides information from him, I have drawn on the full contemporary monograph by a local scholar, Barzellotti, and on some other works.

at that time a monarchy. As they marched in procession they sang – probably echoing the songs of the Italian War of Liberation 1859–60:

> We go by faith
> To save our fatherland,
> Long live the Republic,
> God and Liberty*

And the Messiah himself addressed his people as follows and received the necessary responses:

> What do you want of me? I bring you peace and compassion.
> Is this what you want? (Response: Yes, peace and compassion.)
> Are you willing to pay no more taxes? (Response: Yes.)
> Are you for the Republic? (Response: Yes.)
> But don't think it will be the Republic of 1849. It will be the Republic of Christ. Therefore all cry with me: Long live the Republic of God.†

It is far from surprising that the authorities of the kingdom of Italy, as distinct from the Republic of God, regarded the Lazzarettians as a subversive movement.

The Monte Amiata lies in the extreme south-east of Tuscany, where it borders on Umbria and Latium. The Lazzarettist territory was and is composed partly of a very backward mountain area, pastoral and farming – there was also a very little mining – partly of an almost equally backward *maremma* or coastal plain, though the main Lazzarettist forces

---

* E. Lazzareschi, *David Lazzaretti* (Bergamo 1945), 248.
† Lazzareschi, *op. cit.*, 238.

seem to have come from the mountains. Both economically and culturally it was extremely backward. About two-thirds of the population of Arcidosso, the chief town in the region, were illiterate: to be precise 63 per cent of its 6491 inhabitants.[*] Most inhabitants were peasant proprietors or *mezzadri* (share-croppers). There was little absolute landlessness or industry. Whether the Amiatini were desperately poor or merely very poor is a matter for debate. What is not open to doubt is that the coming of Italian Unity began to involve this extremely backward zone in the economy of the liberal Italian state, and to create considerable social tension and unrest.

The irruption of modern capitalism into peasant society, generally in the form of liberal or Jacobin reforms (the intro-duction of a free land-market, the secularization of church estates, the equivalents of the enclosure movement and the reform of common land and forest laws, etc.) has always had cataclysmic effects on that society. When it comes suddenly, as the result of a revolution, a wholesale change of laws and policies, a foreign conquest or the like, having been relatively unprepared by the evolution of local social forces, its effect is all the more disturbing. On the Monte Amiata the most obvious way in which the new social system impinged on the old was by taxes; as indeed it was elsewhere. The construction of roads, begun in 1868, was paid for by local rates, and local towns and villages bore its brunt. In Castel del Piano, Cinigiano, Roccalbegna and Santa Fiora the amount of the provincial and communal extra taxes was more than double the amount of the central state tax while in Arcidosso it was three times as high.[†] These were primarily taxes on land and cottages. It

[*] Lazzareschi, *op. cit.*, 262.
[†] Barzellotti, *Monte Amiata e il Suo profeta* (Milan 1910), 77–8.

is not surprising that the collectors in Santa Fiora complained that some shopkeepers refused to pay them, because they had been promised by Lazzaretti that they would have to pay no more taxes.* Again, as usually happened, the introduction of Piedmontese law as the standard law of Italy, that is of an uncompromising code of economic liberalism, threw local society out of joint.† Thus the forest law, which virtually abrogated customary rights of common pasture, firewood collecting and the like, fell tragically on the marginal small proprietors, and incidentally exacerbated their relations with larger landowners.‡ It is thus equally natural to find Lazzaretti preaching a new order of things, in which property and land would be distributed differently, and leaseholders and share-croppers would enjoy a greater share of the crop.§ (The struggle for a larger share of the crop remains to this day the dominating economic issue in rural central Italy, and perhaps the major reason why that region is one of the most strongly Communist, in spite of the virtual absence of *latifundia* or industry. The province of Siena, in which the Monte Amiata lies in part, has the highest percentage of Communist votes in all Italy, 48.8 per cent in 1953.) Conditions were therefore favourable for a movement of social unrest. And in view of the abnormal remoteness of this corner of Tuscany, such a movement was bound to take a rather primitive form.

Let us now turn to Davide Lazzaretti himself. He was born in 1834 and became a carter, travelling up and down the

* Lazzareschi, *op. cit.*, 282–3.
† For the best discussion of this problem in general, E. Sereni, *Il capitalismo nelle campagne 1860–1900* (Turin 1949). The book mentions the Lazzarettians incidentally on pp. 114–15 n.
‡ Barzellotti, *op. cit.*, 79.
§ Barzellotti, *op. cit.*, 256.

region. Though he claimed to have had a vision at the age of fourteen – in the year of revolution, 1848 – he was known as a worldly-minded, not to say blasphemous man until his conversion in 1868. The year may be significant, for it was one of great popular unrest in Italy. The 1867 harvest had been bad, there was an industrial crisis, and above all, the milling tax which Parliament imposed in that year raised food-prices and created vast rural discontents.* In all but twelve provinces the imposition of this tax led to riots, and something like 257 people were killed, 1099 wounded, and 3788 arrested as a result.† Nothing would be more natural than for a peasant to pass through an intellectual and spiritual crisis in this year. Moreover, the impending Franco-Prussian conflict with its possible – and as it turned out actual – consequences for the Papacy greatly moved catholic minds. Lazzaretti was at this stage a papalist, though his preaching had certain left-wing and republican overtones, as was natural for a man who had fought as a volunteer in the national army in 1860. The papalists, being opposed to the godless government, were in any case at this time encouraging agrarian unrest – the riots were particularly marked in ex-papal provinces and Catholic slogans were heard – and it has also been argued that they protected the early Lazzaretti, whose preaching might form a counterweight to secular liberal influence. Certainly he had quasi-official Church support for a long time.

While Lazzaretti became locally known after 1868 as a holy man, he now began to elaborate his doctrines and prophesies. He believed himself to be the remote descendant

---

* N. Rosselli, *Mazzini e Bakunine (1860–1872)* (Turin 1927), for the best general account, pp. 213 ff.
† Sereni, *op. cit.*, 111.

of a French king (France being at the time the chief protector of the Papacy). By the end of 1870 in the *Rescritti Profetici*, also entitled *The Awakening of the Peoples*, he foresaw a prophet, a captain, a legislator and a reformer of laws, a new pastor from Sinai, who was to arise and liberate the peoples now groaning 'as slaves under the despotism of the monster of ambition, hypocrisy, heresy and pride'. A monarch, whose task was to reconcile the Church with the Italian people, was to 'descend from the mountain, followed by a thousand young men, all of Italian blood, and these are to be called the militia of the Holy Ghost', and these were to regenerate the moral and civil order.* He soon set about founding communist colonies on the Monte Amiata, where the faithful constructed a church and a tower for him. These things led to accusations of subversive activities, but Lazzaretti managed to escape sentence thanks to some influential local supporters.

Increasingly he now left the old orthodoxy behind him. In the course of various fasts and travels he gradually evolved the final version of his doctrine. He, Lazzaretti, was to be the king and Messiah. The Lord would construct seven sacred cities, one on the Monte Amiata, the rest in various suitable countries and places. Hitherto there had been the Kingdom of Grace (which he identified with the pontificate of Pius IX). It would be followed by the Kingdom of Justice and the Reform of the Holy Ghost, the third and last age of the world. Great calamities were to presage the final liberation of men by the hand of God.† But he, Lazzaretti, would die. Connoisseurs of medieval thought, and in particular of the Joachite doctrines,

---

* Barzellotti, *op. cit.,* 193–4.

† Barzellotti, *op. cit.,* 208, 235–6. One would normally expect the third age to be that of Freedom.

will recognize the striking parallelisms of this doctrine with those of traditional popular heresy.

The crucial moment came in 1878. Early in that year both Victor Emmanuel and Pius IX died and hence – according to Lazzaretti – the succession of pontiffs came to an end. Moreover, it is equally useful to recall that the agricultural depression was upon Italy. Wheat prices and wages fell from 1875, and though there is no special reason to single out 1878 – in fact, 1879 was the really catastrophic year, as in so many other parts of Europe – the preceding years of depression were quite enough to confirm the Tuscan peasants in the belief that the signs and portents of the end of the old world were at hand. Lazzaretti returned from France, where he had found some wealthy patrons, and declared himself to be the Messiah. When he informed the Vatican of this, he was very naturally excommunicated. But on the Monte Amiata his influence was very great. Men and women flocked to him, to the point where local churches were emptied.* He announced that he would descend from his mountain on the day before Assumption, August 14th. A crowd of 3000 gathered there, how many to watch, how many to support, we do not know. He had bought and made up for his followers a set of special costumes, which they wore as the 'Italian Legion' and the 'Militia of the Holy Ghost'. The flag of the Republic of God was run up. For various reasons the descent was postponed until August 18th. On that day the Lazzarettiani singing hymns descended from the mountain on Arcidosso, to be met by the *carabinieri*, who ordered them to turn back. Lazzaretti answered: 'If you want peace, I bring you peace, if you want compassion, you shall have compassion, if you want blood, here I am.' After a con-

---

* Barzellotti, *op. cit.*, 256–7.

fused exchange, the *carabinieri* fired, and Lazzaretti was among the killed. His leading apostles and Levites were tried and sentenced, the court attempting vainly to prove that they had hoped to sack the houses of the rich or to make a worldly revolution. But of course they had not. They were setting up the Republic of God, the third and final age of the world, which was a far vaster thing than sacking the houses of the Signori Pastorelli. Only, as it had turned out, the time was not ripe.

This looked like the end of the Lazzarettists, except for the close disciples who lingered on, the last of them dying in 1943. And indeed a book written in that year talked of 'the last of the Giurisdavidici'. However, there is an epilogue. When in 1948 an attempt was made to assassinate Togliatti, the Italian Communist leader, communists in various places believed that the great day had come, and promptly began to storm police-stations or to take power in other ways until calmed down by their leaders. Among the scattered places in which such risings took place was Arcidosso. Later a historically-minded Communist leader, who held a public meeting there, could not resist the temptation to refer to the prophet Lazzaretti and the massacre of 1878. After the meeting he was taken aside by various persons in the audience, who said how glad they were that he had spoken as he had done. They were Lazzarettiani, there were many of them in the area. They were naturally on the side of the Communists since they were against the police and the State. The prophet would certainly have taken the same line. But until that moment they had not known that the Communists themselves appreciated the noble work of Davide Lazzaretti. The original millenarian movement had thus continued underground – peasant movements are adept at existing below the level at which the townsmen take notice of them. It had been absorbed by a wider and more modern revolutionary movement. The Arcidosso rising of 1948 was a second, and somewhat rewritten, edition of the descent from the Monte Amiata.*

Who were or are the Lazzarettiani? As one might expect, few of them were rich. Few were landless. Their main strength seems to have lain among small peasants, share-croppers, artisans and the like in the smaller mountain villages. This is still so. The most recent information (1965) is that the nucleus of the faithful consists exclusively of small peasants, with the exception of the priest, a mason who is also a part-time peasant. Indeed, experience shows that the 'pure' heresies of the medieval type today tend to appeal perhaps less to absolutely landless men, who go straight to socialist and communist movements, than to small struggling peasants, agricultural craftsmen, village artisans and the like. Their situation pulls them both forward and backward: towards a new society and towards the dream of a pure past, the age of gold or the 'good old days'; and perhaps the sectarian form of millenarianism expresses this duality. At any rate the various heretical sects which have sprung up in Southern Italy, in an atmosphere which recalls the revolutionism of peasants in Luther's rather than Lenin's time, appear to show this tendency, though we cannot be certain until the much-needed study of southern rural heresies – older communities like the Valdensians or the 'Church of Christian Brothers', newer ones like the Pentecostal Church, the Adventists, Baptists, Jehovah's Witnesses, and

* 'Virtually the entire body of the Giurisdavidici voted for the Communist Party from the first (post-fascist) elections ... It is significant that all the most convinced Giurisdavidici maintain that support for the Communist Party is total, and that it could not be otherwise, since the C.P.s conception of social justice was analogous to their Church's.' Moscato-Pierini, *Rivolta Religiosa nelle campagne* (Rome 1965), 130.

Churches of Christ – has been seriously undertaken.* At all events Chironna the Evangelical, whose autobiography Rocco Scotellaro chooses as typical of this kind of peasant, is an agricultural craftsman and share-cropper 'born in a modest family of small direct cultivators'.† The famous Jews of San Nicandro seem to belong to analogous groups, their founder possessing at least a dwarf holding, and several leaders being artisans (shoemakers, etc.).‡ The Pentecostalists, according to Mrs Cassin, have a special attraction for artisans, and the trade union organizers for the General Italian Confederation of Labour (C.G.I.L.) in the province of Foggia, Apulia, consider the Protestants as a body chiefly composed of small peasants; 'a sect of gardeners', as I was told by one of them.§

Nor is the affinity of the Lazzarettists for socialism or communism unique. Religious ferment, among southern peasants, is merely one aspect of their endemic revolutionism, though – if the experience of the Monte Gargano is a guide – one which tends to be particularly prominent where it has not yet found, or has been denied, political expression. Thus protestantism made its first important advances after 1922, i.e. after the

---

* Meanwhile Elena Cassin, *San Nicandro* (Paris 1957) – a detailed study of the remarkable group of peasant converts to Judaism – contains invaluable material on the religious ferment in the Monte Gargano, the 'spur' of Italy, and also a distribution map of Pentecostal communities in Italy. A highly illuminating work. For the nature of the Pentecostal and other churches whose appeal has been greatest since the war, cf. the general description of the American cotton-mill sects in Chapter 8.

† Rocco Scotellaro, *Contadini del Sud* (Bari 1955), Vita di Chironna Evangelico.

‡ Elena Cassin, *op. cit.*, unfortunately only gives the social situation of five of the twenty-odd adult male members of the community.

§ I am grateful to Mr Lucio Conte and others of the Foggia provincial federation of the C.G.I.L. and to various members of the Communist Party in San Nicandro for information about the social composition and political allegiance of the sectarians in 1957.

defeat of the peasant leagues, the triumph of Fascism, and the closing of America to immigrants. Again, I am informed that in the province of Cosenza (Calabria) it has made most headway in the politically undeveloped zones of the North, and in Foggia there is a little evidence that sectarianism is rather stronger on either side of the Tavoliere plains, rather than in the plains with their strong and old socialist tradition. However, in conditions such as those of Southern Italy it is virtually impossible for a heretic in religion not to be also an ally of the secular anti-clerical movements, and very difficult not to be some sort of revolutionary sympathizer, and no sharp line between peasant socialist/communists and peasant sectarians can therefore be drawn. I am informed that the great majority of the San Nicandro convert Jews voted for the Communist Party (the township is a left-wing stronghold), while the local Communists – some of whom are related by blood to the local Protestants – describe them as 'mostly ours'. Several Protestants are even Communist militants, and cases of Jehovah's Witnesses being elected as secretaries of local *Camere del Lavoro*, or what is even more embarrassing to higher party organizations, of local Communist Party branches, are known. However, the tendency of heretic peasants also to join left-wing movements must not be identified with pure religio-political millenarianism such as that of the Lazzarettists. This appears to be a rather exceptional phenomenon, at least in Western and Southern Europe, though perhaps further research would yield other examples to set beside the Messiah of the Monte Amiata.

Chapter V

Millenarianism II:
The Andalusian Anarchists

The English reader possesses at least one book which is so excellent an introduction to Spain and to Spanish anarchism that it is hardly necessary to do more than refer him to it: Gerald Brenan's *The Spanish Labyrinth.** This chapter, even where it is not actually based on Brenan, is little more than slightly expanded and more detailed version of an account with which few students would wish to disagree.

---

* This chapter is largely based on Brenan and some of the works in his bibliography, especially J. Diaz del Moral, *Historia de las agitaciones campesinas andaluzas* (Madrid 1929), for which no praise is too high from the student of primitive social movements. It may also be worth mentioning Pitt-Rivers' *People of the Sierras* (1954), an anthropological monograph of the *pueblo* of Grazalema. Its observations on local anarchism are useful, but show too little appreciation of the fact that this little town was not just anarchist, but one of the classical centres of anarchism and known as such throughout Spain. No attempt is made to explain why Grazalema should have been so much more powerful a centre of the movement than other *pueblos*, or to explain the rise and rhythm of the movement, and this detracts from the value of the book, at least for the historian.

Andalusia, it has been observed, is the 'Sicily of Spain',*
and a great deal of the observations about that island
(e.g. in Chapters II and V) apply equally to it. It consists,
roughly, of the plain of the Guadalquivir and the mountains which enclose it like a shell. Taking it all in all, it
is overwhelmingly a country of concentrated settlements
(*pueblos*), an empty countryside into which the peasants
went for long periods to live in shelters or barracks, leaving
their wives in the town, of vast absentee-owned and inefficient estates, and a population of almost servile landless
braceros or day-labourers. It is classical latifundist country,
though this does not mean that all of it in the 19th century
was directly cultivated in vast estates and ranches; part was
let out in small farms on short leases. Only a very little –
politically conservative islands in a revolutionary sea – was
smallish or long-leased property. In Cadiz estates over 250
hectares occupied 58 per cent of the province in 1931: they
included three estates averaging over 10,000 hectares, 32
averaging almost 5000 and 271 averaging about 900. In
three of the administrative districts of the province *latifundia* occupied from 77 to 96 per cent of the total area. In
Seville large estates occupied 50 per cent of the total area:
they included 13 averaging almost 7000 hectares, and 104
averaging over 2000. The situation in Cordoba was similar, if slightly less extreme. It need hardly be said that the
large estates normally occupied the best land. The general
picture may be concisely summarized in the observation
that in the provinces of Huelva, Seville, Cadiz, Cordoba
and Jaen, 6000 large landowners owned at least 56 per cent
of the taxable income, 285,000 smaller owners shared the

* Angel Marvaud, *La Question Sociale en Espagne*, Paris 1910, 42.

98

rest, and something like 80 per cent of the rural population owned no land at all.* It may be observed in passing that Andalusia, like Southern Italy, was undergoing a process of de-industrialization in the 19th century – if not from the time of the Moors – being incapable of holding off its northern and foreign competitors. An exporter of farm-produce and of unskilled labourers, who began to migrate to the industrialized north, its countrymen depended almost exclusively on a particularly miserable and chancy agriculture.

A large literature unanimously paints their social and economic conditions in the most appalling colours. As in Sicily, the *braceros* worked when there was work for them and starved when there was none, as indeed they still do to some extent. An estimate of their food per month in the early 1900s makes them live virtually entirely on bad bread – 2½ to 3 lb. per day – a little oil, vinegar, dry vegetables and a flavour of salt and garlic. The death-rate in the *pueblos* of the Cordovese hills at the end of the 19th century ranged from 30 to 38 per thousand. In Baena, 20 per cent of all deaths in the quinquennium 1896–1900 were from lung diseases, almost 10 per cent from deficiency diseases. Male illiteracy in the early 1900s ranged from 65 to 50 per cent in the various Andalusian provinces; hardly any peasant women could read. It is hardly necessary to continue this misera-ble catalogue beyond observing that parts of this unhappy

* Brenan, 114 ff.; see also the maps, pp. 332–5; *La Reforma Agraria en España* (Valencia 1937); 'Spain: The distribution of property and land settlement', in *International Review of Agricultural Economics*, 1916, no. 5, which gives the per-centage of landlords per hundred of rural inhabitants doing agricultural work as under 17 in Western and under 20 in Eastern Andalusia, as compared with almost 60 in Old Castile (pp. 95 ff.).

region continue to be more poverty-stricken than any other part of Western Europe.*

It is not surprising that the area became solidly revolutionary as soon as political consciousness arose in Andalusia. Broadly speaking, the Guadalquivir basin and the mountain areas to the south-east of it were anarchist, that is, mainly the provinces of Seville, Cadiz, Cordoba and Malaga. The mining areas on the West and North (Rio Tinto, Pozoblanco, Almaden, etc.), working-class and socialist, sealed the anarchist zone off on one side; the province of Jaen, politically less developed and under the influence of both Castilian socialism and Andalusian anarchism, formed a frontier on another, Granada, in which conservatism was stronger – or at least the peasants more cowed – on the third. However, since Spanish election statistics give no reliable picture of the political complexion of this area, partly because the anarchists abstained from elections until 1936, and some may have abstained even then, partly because the influence of landlords and authorities vitiated them, the picture is bound to be impressionist rather than photographic.† Rural anarchism was by no means confined to the landless labourers. Indeed, it has been forcibly argued by Diaz del Moral and Brenan that smallholders as well as artisans played at least as important, and some would say a more tenacious, part in it, since they were economically

---

* Marvaud, *op. cit.*, 137, 456–7; F. Valverde y Perales, *Historia de la Villa de Baena* (Toledo 1903), 282 ff.

† Thus in the 1936 elections in Cadiz province there were Popular Front majorities everywhere except along part of the west coast and in the mountainous corner by Ronda, which, as it happened, contained some traditional and legendary strongholds of Anarchism, where the policy of abstention presumably operated. I have taken the figures of results published by the *Diario de Cadiz*, 17 Feb., 1936.

less vulnerable and socially not so cowed. Anyone who has seen a *pueblo* of *braceros*, in which, apart from the gentry, the ranch foremen and others 'born to rule', only the craftsmen and the smugglers walk with the indefinable mark of self-respect, will grasp the point.

Social revolution in Andalusia begins shortly after 1850. Earlier examples have been quoted – the famous village of *Fuenteovejuna* is Andalusian – but there is little evidence of specifically agrarian revolutionary movements before the second half of the 19th century. The affair of Fuenteovejuna (1476) was, after all, a special revolt against abnormal oppression by an individual lord, and, moreover, concerted with the townsmen of Cordoba, though the legend and drama do not stress this point. The hunger-riots of the 17th century, with their overtones of Andalusian separatism, appear also to have been urban rather than rural, and reflect the disintegration of the Spanish Empire at the time and the stronger contemporary revolts of Portugal and Catalonia rather than agrarian unrest as such. In any case there are few signs of any such movements specifically envisaging a peasant millennium, though no doubt research would reveal some. Andalusian peasants suffered and starved, as did peasants in all pre-industrial periods, and what revolutionism was in them found its outlet in an exceptionally passionate cult of social banditry and smuggling; of

> Diego Corrientes, the brigand of Andalusia
> Who robbed the rich and succoured the poor.*

---

* Pitt-Rivers, *op. cit.*, cap. xii, on the place of the bandit in the scheme of things of a modern Andalusian *pueblo*. But this discussion does not show a particularly good understanding of the phenomenon.

Perhaps also in a ferocious attachment to the Catholic Church Militant, whose Holy Inquisition smote the heretic, however rich and highly placed, whose (Spanish) theologians, like the Jesuit Mariana, defended the rising of Fuenteovejuna and attacked wealth and proposed radical social remedies, and whose monasticism sometimes embodied their primitive communist ideal. I have myself heard an old Aragonese peasant talk thus with approval of his son's order: 'They have communism there, you know. They put it all together and everyone draws out enough to live by.' While the Spanish Church retained that exceptional 'populism' which made its parish priests fight as guerilla leaders at the head of their flocks in the French wars, it certainly functioned as a very effective outlet for sentiments which might otherwise have become revolutionary in a more secular manner.

In the late 1850s there is news of roaming peasant bands, and even of villages 'taking power'.* The first indigenous revolutionary movement which attracted specific attention was the revolt in Loja and Iznajar in 1861, several years before the irruption of the Bakuninist apostles. (However, I understand there is some question of left-wing 'Carbonarist' Masonic influence in the Loja rising.†) The period of the International and the republican agitations of 1868–73 saw further movements: 'cantonalism', that is the demand for village independence, a characteristic of all Spanish peasant movements, in Iznajar and Fuenteovejuna, the demand for a division of lands in Pozoblanco and Benameji, 'this sadly famous pueblo, whose citizens in great number used formerly to practise contraband',

---

* 'The agrarian problem in Andalusia', in *Int. Rev. of Agric. Econ.* XI, 1920, 279.
† My friend Victor Kiernan, on whose profound knowledge of mid-19th-century Spanish affairs I have drawn, tells me that this is suggested – perhaps baselessly – in N. Diaz y Perez, *La Francmasoneria Española*.

where the bandits had often virtually besieged the rich and no crime was punished by the State, because nobody would inform.* As the 'sons of Benameji' (they still play their legendary role as individualist 'men who make themselves respected' in Garcia Lorca's Gipsy Romances) added social revolution to individualist revolt, a new age in Spanish politics began. Anarchism appeared on the scene, propagated by the emissaries of the Bakuninist wing of the International. As elsewhere in Europe, the early 1870s saw a rapid expansion of mass political movements. The main strength of the new revolutionism lay in the classical latifundist provinces, notably in Cadiz and southern Seville. The strongholds of Andalusian anarchism begin to appear: Medina Sidonia, Villamartin, Arcos de la Frontera, El Arahal, Bornos, Osuna, El Bosque, Grazalema, Benaocaz.

The movement collapsed in the later 1870s – not so badly in Cadiz province as elsewhere – revived again in the early 1880s, to collapse again. The earliest of the peasant general strikes occurred at this time in the Jerez area – then as later a fortress of extreme physical force anarchism. In 1892 there was another outburst, which culminated in the easily repressed march of several thousands of peasants on Jerez. In the early 1900s another revival occurred, this time under the banner of the General Strike, a tactic which had not hitherto been systematically seen as a means of achieving social revolutions. General peasant strikes took place in at least sixteen *pueblos*, mainly in Cadiz province, in the years 1901–3.† These strikes

---

* Julian de Zugasti, *El Bandolerismo*, Introduction, vol. I, 239–40. Iznajar, another of the pioneer centres of social revolution, also had an abnormally strong code of *omertà*, according to the same source.

† In *Cadiz*: Arcos, Alcala del Valle, Cadiz, Jerez, La Linea, Medina Sidonia, San Fernando, Villamartin. *Seville*: Carmona, Morón. *Cordoba*: Bujalance, Castro del Rio, Cordoba, Fernan-Nuñez. *Malaga*: Antequera. *Jaen:* Linares.

show marked millenarian characteristics. After another period of quiescence the greatest of the hitherto recorded mass movements was set off, it is said, by news of the Russian Revolution, which penetrated into this remote region. In this 'Bolshevik' period Cadiz for the first time lost its primacy among anarchist provinces to Cordoba. The Republic (1931–6) saw the last of the great revivals, and in 1936 itself the seizure of power in many anarchist *pueblos*. However, with the exception of Malaga and the Cordobese fringe, the anarchist zone fell under Franco's domination almost from the first days of the revolt, and even the Republican parts were soon conquered. 1936–7 therefore marks the end of at least this period of Andalusian anarchist history.

It is evident that, over a large area of Andalusia, peasant revolutionism was endemic from the late 1860s and epidemic at intervals of roughly ten years. It is equally clear that no movements of anything like comparable force and character existed in the first half of the 19th century. The reasons for this are not easy to discover. The rise of revolutionism was not simply a reflex of bad conditions, for conditions may have improved, though only to the point of eliminating the actual catastrophic famines, such as had occurred in 1812, 1817, 1834–5, 1863, 1868 and 1882. The last genuine famine (if we except some episodes since the Civil War) was that of 1905. Anyway, famine normally had its usual result of inhibiting rather than stimulating social movements when it came, though its approach sharpened unrest. When people are really hungry they are too busy seeking food to do much else; or else they die. Economic conditions naturally determined the timing and periodicity of the revolutionary outbreaks – for instance, social movements tended to reach peak intensity during the worst months of the year – January to March, when farm labourers have least work (the march on Jerez in 1892 and the rising of Casas Viejas in 1933 both occurred early in January), March–July, when the preceding harvest has been exhausted and times are leanest. But the rise of anarchism was not simply an index of growing economic distress. Again, it reflected outside political movements only indirectly. The relations between peasants and politics (which are a townsman's business) are peculiar in any case, and all we can say is that the vague news that some political cataclysm like a revolution or a 'new law', or some event in the international labour movement which seemed to herald the new world – the International, the discovery of the General Strike as a revolutionary weapon – struck a chord among the peasants, if the time was ripe.

The best explanation is, that the rise of social revolutionism was the consequence of the introduction of capitalist legal and social relationships into the Southern countryside in the first half of the 19th century. Feudal rights on land were abolished in 1813, and between then and the revolution of 1854 the battle for the introduction of free contract in agrarian matters continued. By 1855 it was won: the general liberation of civil and ecclesiastical property (state, church and waste lands, etc.) was reaffirmed, and directions for their sale on the open market given. Thereafter the sales continued without interruption. It is hardly necessary to analyse the inevitably cataclysmic consequences of so unprecedented an economic revolution on the peasantry. The rise of social revolutionism followed naturally. What is peculiar about Andalusia is the remarkably clear and early transformation of social disturbance and revolutionary unrest into a specific and politically conscious movement of agrarian social revolution under anarchist leaders. For, as Brenan points out,* Andalusia in 1860 had the makings of much the same primitive and undifferentiated ferment as Southern Italy. It might have produced the Italian combination of social and Bourbon-revolutionary brigandage and occasional jacqueries, or the Sicilian combination of both with *Mafia*, itself a complex amalgam of social banditry, 'landlords' banditry', and general self-defence against the outsiders. Clearly the preaching of the anarchist apostles, who welded the separate rebellions of Iznajar and Benameji, of Arcos de la Frontera and Osuna, together into a single movement, is partly responsible for this clarity of political outlines. On the other hand, anarchist apostles had also gone to Southern Italy, but without meeting anything like the same response.

It may be suggested that certain characteristics both of Church and State in Spain helped equally to produce the peculiar Andalusian pattern. The State was not a 'foreigners' State as in Sicily (the Bourbon's or Savoyards') or in Southern Italy (the Savoyards'); it was Spanish. To revolt against a legitimate ruler always requires considerably greater political consciousness than to reject a foreigner. Moreover, the Spanish State possessed a direct agency in every *pueblo*, omnipresent, efficient and the peasant's enemy: the *Guardia Civil*, formed in 1844 chiefly to suppress banditry, who watched over the villages from their fortified barracks, went about the countryside armed and in pairs, and were never 'sons of the *pueblo*'. As Brenan rightly observes, 'every Civil Guard became a recruiting officer for anarchism, and, as the anarchists increased their membership, the Civil Guard also grew'.† While the

* Brenan, 156.
† An illustration: before the rising at Casas Viejas (1933) there were four Civil Guards stationed in the village; today (1956) there are supposed to be twelve or sixteen.

State forced the peasants to define their rebellions in terms of hostility to it, the Church also abandoned them. This is not the place to analyse the evolution of Spanish Catholicism from the later 18th century.* We may merely note that, in the course of its losing struggle against the forces of economic and political liberalism, the Church became not simply a conservative-revolutionary force, as among the small proprietors of Navarre and Aragon (the backbone of the Carlist movement), but a conservative force *tout court*, in that it joined hands with the wealthy classes. To be the Church of the *status quo*, of the King and the past, does not disqualify an institution from also being the Church of the peasants. To be regarded as the Church of the rich does. As the social bandits became *bandoleros* protected by local rich *caciques* and the Church became the Church of the rich, the peasants' dream of a just and a free world had to find a new expression. This is what the anarchist apostles gave it.

The ideology of the new peasant movement was anarchist; or, to give it its more precise name, libertarian communist. Its economic programme aimed in theory at common ownership, in practice, in the early stages almost exclusively, at the *reparto*, the division of the land. Its political programme was republican and anti-authoritarian; that is, it envisaged a world in which the self-governing *pueblo* was the sovereign unit, and from which outside forces such as kings and aristocracies, policemen, tax-collectors and other agents of the supra-local State, being essentially agents of the exploitation of man by man, were eliminated. Under Andalusian conditions such a programme was less Utopian than it seems. Villages had run themselves, both economically and politically, in their primitive way with a minimum of actual organization

---

* Brenan's account is, as usual, both concise, lucid and perceptive.

for administration, government and coercion, and it seemed reasonable to assume that authority and the State were unnecessary intrusions. Why indeed should the disappearance of a Civil Guard post or of a nominated mayor and a flow of official forms produce chaos rather than justice in the *pueblo*? However, it is misleading to express the anarchists' aspirations in terms of a precise set of economic and political demands. They were for a new moral world.

This world was to come about by the light of science, progress and education, in which the anarchist peasants believed with passionate fervour, rejecting religion and the Church, as they rejected everything else about the evil world of oppression. It would not necessarily be a world of wealth and comfort, for if the Andalusian peasants could conceive of comfort at all, it was of hardly more than that all should have enough to eat always. The pre-industrial poor always conceive of the good society as a just sharing of austerity rather than a dream of riches for all. But it would be free and just. The ideal is not specifically anarchist. Indeed, if the programme which haunted the minds of the Sicilian peasants* or any other peasant revolutionaries were to have been carried out, the result would no doubt have resembled Castro del Rio in Cordoba province between the taking of power and its conquest by Franco's soldiers: the expropriation of land, the abolition of money, men and women working without property and without pay, drawing what they needed from the village store ('They put it all together and everyone draws out what he needs') and a great and terrible moral exaltation. The village bars were closed. Soon there would be no more coffee in the village store and the militants looked forward to the disappearance of yet

* See Appendix 5.

another drug. The village was alone, and perhaps poorer than before: but it was pure and free and those who were unfit for freedom were killed.* If this programme bore the Bakuninist label, it was because no political movement has reflected the spontaneous aspirations of backward peasants more sensitively and accurately in modern times than Bakuninism, which deliberately subordinated itself to them. Moreover, Spanish anarchism, more than any other political movement of our period, was almost exclusively elaborated and spread by peasants and small craftsmen. As Diaz del Moral points out, unlike Marxism it attracted practically no intellectuals, and produced no theorist of interest. Its adepts were hedge-preachers and village prophets; its literature journals and pamphlets which at best popularized the theories elaborated by foreign thinkers: Bakunin, Reclus, Malatesta. With one possible exception – and he a Galician – no important Iberian theorist of anarchism exists. It was overwhelmingly a poor men's movement and it is thus not surprising that it reflected the interests and aspirations of the Andalusian *pueblo* with uncanny closeness.

Perhaps it was closest of all to their simple revolutionism in its total and absolute rejection of this evil world of oppression, which found expression in the characteristic anarchist passion for burning churches, which has few parallels, and probably reflects the bitterness of the peasants' disappointment with the 'betrayal' of the cause of the poor by the Church. 'Malaga,' says the 1935 Guide Bleu to Spain with a poker face, 'is a city of advanced ideas. On the days of May 12th and 13th, 1931 forty-three churches and convents were burned there.' And an old anarchist, looking down on the same burning city some five years later, had the following conversation with Brenan:

* F. Borkenau, *The Spanish Cockpit* (1937), 166 ff.

'What do you think of that?' he asked.

I said: 'They are burning down Malaga.'

'Yes,' he said. 'They are burning it down. And I tell you – not one stone will be left on another stone – no, not a plant nor even a cabbage will grow there, so that there may be no more wickedness in the world.'*

And the conscientious anarchist did not merely wish to destroy the evil world – though he did not normally believe that this would in fact involve much burning or killing – but rejected it here and now. Everything that made the Andalusian of tradition was to be jettisoned. He would not pronounce the word God or have anything to do with religion, he opposed bull-fights, he refused to drink or even to smoke, – in the 'Bolshevik' period a vegetarian strain entered the movements also – he disapproved of sexual promiscuity though officially committed to free love. Indeed, at times of strike or revolution there is even evidence that he practised absolute chastity, though his was sometimes misinterpreted by outsiders.† He was a revolutionary in the most total sense conceivable to Andalusian peasants, condemning *everything* about the past. He was, in fact, a millenarian.

Fortunately, we possess at least one superb account of the millenarian aspects of village anarchism, as seen by a sympathetic and scholarly local lawyer: F. Diaz del Moral's massive *History of Agrarian Agitations in the Province of Cordoba* which takes the story up to the early 1920s. The sketch which follows is mainly based on Diaz del Moral, and a few other less ambitious

* Brenan, 189.
† Brenan, 175, Marvaud, 43, observes that during the Moron general strike of 1902 marriages were postponed to the day of the *reparto*, but merely puts this down to an excessively naïve optimism.

sources, supplemented by my own brief study of a single village revolution, that of Casas Viejas (Cadiz) in 1933.*

The village anarchist movement may be divided into three sections: the mass of the village population, who were only intermittently active, when the occasion seemed to demand it; the cadre of local preachers, leaders and apostles – the so-called 'conscious workers' (*obreros conscientes*), who are today retrospectively called 'those who used to have ideas' who were constantly active; and the outsider: national leaders, orators and journalists and similar external influences. In the Spanish anarchist movement the last section was abnormally unimportant. The movement rejected any organization, or at all events any rigidly disciplined organization, and refused to take part in politics; consequently it had few leaders of national standing. Its press consisted of a large number of modest sheets, much of it written by '*obreros conscientes*' from other villages and towns, and intended less to lay down a political line – for the movement, as we have seen, did not believe in politics – but to repeat and amplify the arguments for the Truth, to attack Injustice, to create that feeling of solidarity which made the village cobbler in a small Andalusian town conscious of having brothers fighting the same fight in Madrid and New York, in Barcelona and Leghorn, in Buenos Aires. The most active of outside forces were the wandering preachers and propagandists who, spurning all but hospitality, went about the country teaching the good word or starting local schools and the great shadowy names of the classics who wrote the standard pamphlets: Kropotkin, Malatesta. But if one or two men might

* My sources are the *Diario de Cadiz* and some survivors in the village. E. Malefakis, *Agrarian Reform and Peasant Revolution in Spain* (New Haven and London 1970), 241, 258–61 is the best brief account.

get a national reputation through their oratorical tours, they were not distinct from the village. It was just as likely that a local villager might get such a reputation, for *every* conscious worker regarded incessant propaganda, wherever he went, as his duty. What influenced men was not, they believed, other men, but the truth, and the entire movement was geared to the propagation of the truth by every person who had acquired it. For, having acquired the tremendous revelation that men need no longer be poor and superstitious, how could they do anything but pass it on?

The *oberos conscientes* were therefore educators, propagandists, agitators rather than organizers. Diaz del Moral has given a splendid description of their type – small village craftsmen and smallholders perhaps more often than landless labourers, but we cannot be sure. They read and educated themselves with passionate enthusiasm. (Even today, when one asks the inhabitants of Casas Viejas about their impressions of the former militants, now often dead or dispersed, one is most likely to hear some such phrase as 'He was always reading something; always arguing'.) They lived in argument. Their greatest pleasure was to write letters to and articles for the anarchist press, often full of high-flown phrases and long words, glorying in the wonders of modern scientific understanding which they had acquired and were passing on. If specially gifted, they clearly developed the sort of popular eloquence which multiplied pamphlets and tracts in 17th-century England. José Sanchez Rosa of Grazalema (born 1864) wrote pamphlets and dialogues between the worker and the capitalist, novelettes and orations on the model of the old 'dramatic pieces' encouraged by the Spanish friars (but naturally, with a rather different content) which were performed – and indeed partly improvised – in the ranch-houses and labourers' quarters of the large *latifundia* where the men, working away from their villages, spent the week.

Their influence in the village rested on no social position, but primarily on their virtue as apostles. Those who had first brought the good news to their fellows, perhaps by reading out newspapers to their illiterate company, might come to enjoy the almost blind trust of the village, especially if the puritan devotion of their lives testified to their worth. After all, not everyone was strong enough to abandon smoking, drinking and wenching or to resist the pressure of the church for baptism, church marriage and church burial. Men like M. Vallejo Chinchilla of Bujalance, or Justo Heller of Castro del Rio, says Diaz del Moral 'had the same sort of ascendancy over the masses as the great Conquistadors had over their men'; and in Casas Viejas old Curro Cruz ('Six Fingers') who issued the call for revolution and was killed after a twelve hours' gunfight with the troops, seems to have exercised a similar function. In the nature of things the small band of the elect drew together. The case of Casas Viejas, where personal and family relationships linked the leading anarchist cadre, is probably typical: Curro Cruz's granddaughter Maria ('La Libertaria') was engaged to José Cabanas Silva ('The Little Chicken'), the chief of the younger militants, another Silva was secretary to the labourers' union, and the Cruz and Silva families were decimated in the subsequent repression. The *obreros conscientes* provided leadership and continuity.

Normally the village would merely accept them as its most influential citizens, whose word would be taken for anything, from the advisability of attending the visiting circus (travelling showmen soon learned to get a recommendation from the local leader) to making a revolution. But of course revolutions would only be made if in fact the village itself wanted them: for the *obreros conscientes* did not regard it as their function to *plan* political agitation, but merely to make propaganda, so that action in fact occurred only when the peculiar groundswell of village opinion, of which they themselves formed part, made it not only advisable, but virtually inescapable. (The development of anarcho-syndicalism, with rather more organization and trade union policies, began to undermine this reliance on complete spontaneity; but we are not at the moment concerned with the decline and fall of village anarchism, but with its golden age.) In fact we know this happened at about ten-year intervals. So far as the village was concerned, however, it normally happened either when something in the local situation made action imperative, or when some impetus from outside fanned the glow of latent revolutionism into a flame. Some piece of news, some portent or comet proving that the time had come, would penetrate into the village. It might be the original arrival of the Bakuninist apostles in the early 1870s; the garbled news of the Russian Revolution; the news that a Republic had been proclaimed, or that an Agrarian Reform Law was under discussion.

> At the beginning of last autumn (1918, EJH) . . . the conviction seized the minds of the men of the Andalusian countryside, that something they called 'the new law' had been instituted. They did not know who had decreed it, or when, or where, but everyone talked of it.*

Before the rising at Casas Viejas all sorts of rumours had gone round: the time had come, two hundred *pueblos* had already

---

* C. Bernaldo de Quiros, *El Espartaquismo Agrario Andaluz* (Madrid 1919), 39.

declared for communism, the land was about to be divided, and so on. (This last rumour may have been due to the news that a large neighbouring *latifundium* was in fact due for land-reform under a recently passed law.)

At such moments endemic anarchism would become epidemic. Diaz del Moral has described it admirably:

We who lived through that time in 1918–19 will never forget that amazing sight. In the fields, in the shelters and courts, wherever peasants met to talk, for whatever purpose, there was only one topic of conversation, always discussed seriously and fervently: the social question. When men rested from work, during the smoking-breaks in the day and after the evening meal at night, whoever was the most educated would read leaflets and journals out aloud while the others listened with great attention. Then came the perorations, corroborating what had just been read and an unending succession of speeches praising it. They did not understand everything. Some words they did not know. Some interpretations were childish, others malicious, depending on the personality of the man; but at bottom all were agreed. How else? Was not all they had heard the *pure truth* which they had *felt* all their lives, even though they had never been able to express it? Everyone read at all times. There was no limit to the men's curiosity and to their thirst for learning. Even the riders read on their animals, leaving reins and halters trailing. When they packed their lunch, they always put some piece of literature into the wallet . . . Admittedly 70 or 80 per cent were illiterate, but this was not an insuperable obstacle. The enthusiastic illiterate bought his paper and gave it to a comrade to read. He then made him mark the article he liked best. Then he would ask another comrade to read him the marked article and after a few readings he had it by heart and would repeat it to those who had not yet read it. There is only one word to describe it: frenzy, (pp. 190.)

Under such conditions the good word would spread from one to the other spontaneously.

In a few weeks the original nucleus of 10 or 12 adepts would be converted into one of 200s; in a few months practically the entire working population, seized by ardent proselytism, propagated the flaming ideal frenziedly. The few who held out, whether because they were peaceable or timid, or afraid of losing public respect, would be set on by groups of the *convinced* on the mountainside, as they ploughed the furrow, in the cottage, the tavern, in the streets and squares. They would be bombarded with reasons, with imprecations, with contempt, with irony, until they agreed. Resistance was impossible. Once the village was *converted*, the agitation spread . . . Everyone was an agitator. Thus the fire spread rapidly to all the *combustible* villages. In any case the propagandist's job was easy. He had only to read an article from *Tierra y Libertad* or *El Productor* for the hearers to feel themselves to be suddenly illuminated by the new faith.

But how would the great change come about? Nobody knew. At bottom the peasants felt that it must somehow come about if only all men declared themselves for it at the same time. They did so in 1873, and it did not come. They formed the union in 1882 and the girls sang

All the pretty girls
Have it written down in their houses

In letters of gold it says:
I shall die for a Union man.*

But the union collapsed. In 1892 they marched on the town of Jerez, took over the town and killed a few people. They were easily scattered. Then around 1900 the news of the international debates on the General Strike which was then convulsing the Socialist movements reached Andalusia, and the general strike seemed the answer. (In fact the discovery of this new patent method of achieving the millennium probably roused the villages out of their apathy.) Such strikes were completely spontaneous and solid; even the servant girls and nurses of the gentry left work. The taverns were empty. Nobody formulated any petitions or demands, nobody attempted to negotiate, though sometimes the authorities succeeded in getting the peasants to say that they wanted higher wages and to make some sort of agreement. Such efforts were irrelevant. The village struck for more important things than higher wages. After two weeks or so, when it was clear that the social revolution had not broken out in Andalusia, the strike would end suddenly, as solid on the last day as on the first, and everybody would return to work and wait. In fact, as Diaz del Moral notes acutely, the attempts by anarchist and other leaders to use such strikes for the strengthening of organization or the achievement of limited ends met with opposition or lack of enthusiasm: the peasants wanted 'messianic strikes' (p. 358).

It is not easy to analyse these strikes and the rather similar risings which sometimes took place. They were of course revolutionary: the achievement of a fundamental, overwhelming

* Todas las niñas bonitas/ tienen en casa un letrero/ con letras de oro que dicen/ Por un *asociado* muero. Bernaldo de Quiros, *op. cit.*, 10.

change was their sole object. They were millenarian in the sense of this discussion, insofar as they were not themselves makers of the revolution: the men and women of Lebrija or Villamartin or Bornos downed tools not so much to over-throw capitalism as to demonstrate that they were ready for its overthrow which must, somehow, occur now that they had demonstrated their readiness. On the other hand what looks like millenarianism may sometimes have been only the reflec-tion of the village anarchists' lack of organization, isolation and relative weakness. They knew enough to be aware that communism could not be introduced in a single village, though they had little doubt that, if it were so introduced, it would work. Casas Viejas tried it in 1933. The men cut the telephone lines, dug ditches across the roads, isolated the police-barracks and then, secure from the outside world, put up the red-and-black flag of anarchy and set about dividing the land. They made no attempt to spread the movement or kill anyone. But when the troops came from outside they knew they had lost, and their leader told them to take to the hills, while he and his immediate companions fought it out in one cottage, and were killed, as they obviously expected to be. Unless the rest of the world acted as the village did, the revolution was doomed; and they were powerless to affect the rest of the world except perhaps by their example. Under the circumstances what looked like a millenarian demonstration might only be the least hopeless among available revolutionary techniques. There is no sign that a village refrained from making a classical revo-lution – taking power from the local officials, policemen and landlords, when it saw the chance of doing so profitably; for instance in July 1936. And yet, even if we find a functional rather than an historical explanation for the apparently mil-lenarian behaviour of Spanish village anarchism, they would hardly have behaved in quite that way unless their picture of the 'great change' had been Utopian, millenarian, apocalyptic, as all witnesses agree it to have been. They did not see the revolutionary movement as one engaged in a long war against its enemies, a series of campaigns and battles culminating in the seizure of national power, followed by the construction of a new order. They saw a bad world which must soon end; to be followed by the Day of Change which would initiate the good world, where those who had been at the bottom would be at the top, and the goods of this earth would be shared among all. 'Señorito,' said a young labourer to a gentleman, 'when is the great day coming?' 'What great day?' 'The day when we shall all be equal and the land will be shared among all.' Just because the change would be so complete and apocalyptic, they talked – and once again the witnesses are agreed – so freely about it 'publicly, with complete ingenuousness, even in front of the gentry, with a tranquil joy'.* For the force of the millennium was such that, if it was really coming, even the gentry could not stand out against it. Its achievement would be the result, not so much of a class struggle – for the class struggle belonged, after all, to the old world – as of something inexpressibly bigger and more general.

Spanish agrarian anarchism is perhaps the most impressive example of a modern mass millenarian or quasi-millenarian movement. For this reason its political advantages and disadvantages are also very easily analysed. Its advantages were that it expressed the actual mood of the peasantry perhaps more faithfully and sensitively than any other modern social movement; and consequently, that it could at times secure an effortless, apparently spontaneous unanimity of action

* Bernaldo de Quiros, 39, Diaz del Moral, 207.

which cannot but impress the observer profoundly. But its disadvantages were fatal. Just because modern social agitation reached the Andalusian peasants in a form which utterly failed to teach them the necessity of organization, strategy, tactics and patience, it wasted their revolutionary energies almost completely. Unrest such as theirs, maintained for some seventy years, spontaneously exploding over large areas of the kingdom every ten years or so, would have sufficed to overthrow regimes several times as strong as the rickety Spanish governments of the time; yet in fact Spanish anarchism, as Brenan has pointed out, never presented more than a routine police problem to the authorities. It could do no more: for spontaneous peasant revolt is in its nature localized, or at best regionalized. If it is to become general, it must encounter conditions in which every village takes action simultaneously on its own initiative, and for specific purposes. The only time when Spanish anarchism came near to doing this was in July 1936, when the Republican government called for resistance against the Fascists; but so far as anarchism was concerned, the call came from a body which the movement had always refused, on principle, to recognize, and had thus never prepared to utilize. Admittedly, the disadvantages of pure spontaneity and messianism had slowly come to be recognized. The substitution of anarcho-syndicalism, which allowed for a shadowy trade union direction and trade union policy, for pure anarchism, had already meant a halting step towards organization, strategy and tactics, but that was not sufficient to instil discipline, and the readiness to act under direction into a movement constructed on the fundamental assumption that both were undesirable and unnecessary.

Similarly, in defeat anarchism was and is helpless. Nothing is easier than illegal organization in a unanimous village.

Piana degli Albanesi in Sicily, as we shall see, illustrates the point. But when the millenarian frenzy of the anarchist village subsided, nothing remained but the small group of the *obreros conscientes*, the true believers, and a dispirited mass waiting for the next great moment. And if that small group should be dispersed – by death, or emigration, or the systematic attentions of the police, nothing at all remains except a bitter consciousness of defeat. It may be true, as Pitt-Rivers observes, that since the Civil War Andalusian anarchism has ceased to play any active part, what little illegal activity there is being that of the previously unimportant communists.* If so, it is only what we would expect, for a peasants' movement of the anarchist type is incapable of resisting in an organized fashion the sort of genuinely efficient repression and constant control which Spanish governments before Franco never troubled about, preferring to let the occasional outbreaks flare up and die down in isolation.

Classical anarchism is thus a form of peasant movement almost incapable of effective adaptation to modern conditions, though it is their outcome. Had a different ideology penetrated the Andalusian countryside in the 1870s, it might have transformed the spontaneous and unstable rebelliousness of the peasants into something far more formidable, because more disciplined, as communism has sometimes succeeded in doing. This did not happen. And thus the history of anarchism, almost alone among modern social movements, is one

---

* *Op. cit.*, 223. For the revival of guerilla action after the Civil War – characteristically in anarchist Andalusia it recalls the 'noble bandit' pattern – see Tomas Cossias, *La lucha contra el 'Maquis' en España* (Madrid 1956), 73–6; Andres Sorel, *Guerilla española del siglo XX* (Paris 1970). For the views of Andalusian labourers in the 1960s, J. Martinez Alier, *La Estabilidad del Latifundio* (Paris 1968), esp. caps. 1–7.

of unrelieved failure; and unless some unforeseen historical changes occur, it is likely to go down in the books with the Anabaptists and the rest of the prophets who, though not unarmed, did not know what to do with their arms, and were defeated for ever.

Chapter VI

Millenarianism III: The Sicilian Fasci and Peasant Communism

This account of the Sicilian Fasci and some of their political consequences is intended to illustrate the complete process by which a primitive social movement is absorbed into a wholly modern one, for Sicilian (like other South Italian) peasants have not become stuck at the half-way stage of rural anarchism, but have in general come to join the highly organized Socialist and Communist movements, if they have advanced beyond primitivism at all. Hence the content of peasant millenarianism, which in Andalusia has determined the simple forms of village anarchist organization has, in Italy, been fitted into a considerably more elaborate political framework. This does not mean that the individual Sicilian or Lucanian peasant communist or socialist – both are revolutionary Marxists in that country – differs greatly in his personal approach to politics from his Andalusian brother. It does mean that the political history of his village and movement is different, because the 'cause' which he has joined commits him to different and more complex activities; for instance, to voting and running agricultural co-operatives as well as to the forcible occupation of the land or general strikes.

Why the revolutionary Italian peasant movement should have – almost alone among peasant movements in Western Europe – come under primarily Marxist domination, is not easy to say. At any rate it is clear that the Bakuninist apostles made no less strenuous efforts to evangelize the Italian South than they did in Spain. They met with indifferent success, except among the young intellectuals of the South, whom that region then as now produced in excessive numbers and considerable brilliance. It is no accident that the great names of Italian anarchism are intellectuals, often men of the 'revolutionary gentry' like Errico Malatesta and Carlo Cafiero, whereas the great names of Spanish anarchism are men of the people and the opposite of theorists. So far as we can tell there have been no serious anarchist risings in the endemically revolutionary Italian South. The best-known attempt of the anarchists to start one, the Benevento rising of 1877, failed to come alive, because it was not geared to the rhythm of peasant discontent. Had it been, the peasants of Letino and Gallo would not have met the noble Malatesta's invitation to expropriate the land with the sensible and un-Spanish observation that 'our parish can't defend itself against the whole of Italy. This is not a general rising. Tomorrow the soldiers will come and everybody will be shot.' Southern peasants have, in their own time, marched to expropriate the land on many occasions.

Perhaps the most useful provisional explanation is the following. In Southern Spain, as we have seen, there was little sign of active agrarian revolutionism before the middle of the 19th century, and the anarchist apostles, as we have seen, got in on the ground floor. The Andalusian agrarian movement was thus from the beginning influenced by their ideology. In the kingdom of the Two Sicilies, on the other hand, agrarian revolutionism of a primitive sort had been endemic, even before the arrival of any modern ideology. Any political impetus from outside, whether Liberal as in 1820–1, 1848–9 or 1859–60, or Bourbonist, as in 1799 produced its crop of *jacqueries*. The anarchists arrived before the peasants had learned that the various earlier ideologies – brigandism or *mafia*, Bourbonism, touches of Garibaldianism – were inadequate, and at a time when they were therefore not in urgent need of a new faith. By the time they were the anarchist tide had receded and revolutionary state Socialism, with strong Marxist undertones, was the prevailing 'new' ideology, and they therefore came to adopt that.* There are other differences, which only a very profound knowledge of the history and sociology of Spain and the Kingdom of the Two Sicilies would allow us to analyse with any conviction. In any case it is not my purpose to suggest explanations of the differences, but merely to note them.

Sicily is too large and complex a country for its agrarian and social problems to be summarized here, however cursorily. For our purposes we need note no more than a marked generic similarity with Andalusia, and one or two other points. *First*, that it lagged, economically and socially, behind other parts of Italy. It remained officially feudal until 1812, and even the legal abolition of feudalism was not

---

* I am speaking of most of Southern Italy. The case of areas like the Romagna, where anarchism was influential, is somewhat different, but neither economically, socially or politically comparable to the South or to Andalusia.

substantially complete until 1838, or even 1862. Thanks to the British occupation, the radical reforms the French introduced on the continent were here postponed and modified. Large parts of the country remained, and continued to remain after the official legal changes, under the control of latifundist barons with their apparatus of armed retainers and agents, cultivated by landless labourers or dependent tenants, mostly producing cattle and grain, at least in the inland areas. The new rural bourgeoisie, as we have seen in the chapter on *Mafia*, utilized the legal and illegal apparatus of the feudal landowner at least as much as the more modern apparatus of the business-minded capitalist farmer or landlord. The lord, his armed *campiere*, the *gabellotto* ruled; the peasant suffered and obeyed.* *Second*, that Sicilian peasants were miserable, poverty-stricken, ignorant and exploited, and relatively undifferentiated in their misery even by contemporary standards. Thus among the several thousand inhabitants of *Piana dei Greci* in the 1870s only four families were reckoned to belong to the 'gentlemen' (*galantuomini* or *boiardi*), and only six to the 'burghers' (*borghesi*); that is, to take part in the grain trade, to have leased ex-feudal estates etc.† *Third*, that Sicily was then, and to some extent still is, in a state which combined latent agrarian revolutionism, barely suppressed class war and an impressive absence of public law and order, especially in the inland areas which

---

* E. Sereni, *Il Capitalismo nelle Campagne 1860–1900*, 175–188, gives an excellent brief picture, which may be supplemented by any contemporary account and enquiry, e.g. that of Sonnino and Franchetti in 1876. These two blameless Tuscan liberals were bitterly attacked as inciters of class war by outraged local property-owners' newspapers in consequence. See G. Procacci, *Le elezioni del 1874 e l'opposizione meridionale* (Milan 1956), 78–9.

† P. Villari, *Le lettere meridionali* (Turin 1885 edn.), 27.

no government had ever been able to bring under anything like effective administration.*

The traditional forms of peasant discontent had been, as we have observed, extremely primitive and virtually devoid of any explicit ideology, organization or programme. At all times the peasants hated the lords, their retainers, and the middle classes: the 'caps' – Sicilian peasants wore the traditional Mediterranean stocking cap or Phrygian bonnet – hated the 'hats'. In sub-revolutionary times they would idealize brigands or *mafiosi*, at any rate insofar as they represented peasant vengeance and aspiration rather than the lords' exactions. (As in Southern Italy, the great age of this brigandage was in the two decades following unification.) In revolutionary times, that is normally when the signal came from one of the great and perennially riotous cities of the island – Palermo, Catania, Messina –, they would launch blind and savage insurrections, occupying the common lands, sacking town halls, excise stations, communal archives, and the houses and clubs of the gentry. Verga has described one such Jacquerie memorably in his short story 'Liberty'.† The 19th century is a succession of such risings: in 1820, 1837, 1848, 1860 and 1866. The movement of the Fasci is not only the most widespread of these, but also the first which can be described as organized, with a leadership, a modern ideology and programme, in fact as the

---

* The prevalence of blood vengeance contributed to the extremely high homicide rate. Cf. N. Colajanni, *La Delinquenza in Sicilia* (1885), 39. An indication of its importance in earlier periods is given by the following list of motives for the homicides tried in the island in 1834 (C. J. A. Mittermaier, *Italienische Zustaende* (Heidelberg 1844), 128–9): total number of homicides: 64; robbery or other economic motive: 18; jealousy, adultery, etc.: 16: vengeance: 30.

† Denis Mack Smith, 'The peasants' revolt of Sicily in 1860', in *Scritti in Onore di Gino Luzzatto* (Milan 1950); S. F. Romano, *Momenti del Risorgimento in Sicilia* (Messina-Firenze 1952).

first peasant movement as distinct from spontaneous peasant reaction.*

The precise reasons why yet another outbreak of peasant unrest occurred in 1891–4 do not concern us here, for our business is less with the causes of the Fasci than with their forms of Sicilian peasant revolutionism within their framework.† It is enough to observe that the habitual effects of the introduction of capitalist relationships were intensified by the world agrarian depression of the 1880s, and not yet even partially alleviated by the massive emigration which was to become so characteristic of the island. In fact, the period of the Fasci marks the beginning of mass emigration, a fact which may explain why the next major bout of peasant revolt did not take place until the aftermath of the First World War. The movement took the form of the founding and expansion of peasant Leagues (the so-called Fasci) mainly under Socialist leadership, of riots and agricultural strikes on a scale which frightened the Italian government into special military measures which easily suppressed it.

It was not, in fact, a consciously insurrectionary movement at all. Unlike the risings of 1820, 1848, 1860 and 1866 which had at their core liberal and Italian or Sicilian national attempts to depose governments and seize power, the Fasci remained throughout a movement for specific economic improvements, though in the minds of its participants it had far

---

* This account of the Fasci is based mainly on N. Colajanni, *Gli avvenimenti in Sicilia* (Palermo 1894), Adolfo Rossi, *L'agitazione in Sicilia* (Milan 1894) and the special number of *Movimento Operaio* (N.S. Nov.–Dec. 1954) on the Fasci Siciliani.

† Of the literature on the cause of the Fasci, I note only the three articles in the *Giornale degli Economist* I, 1894, esp. the excellent one 'I Moti di Sicilia', by E. La Loggia, cf. also F. Voechting, *La Questione Meridionale* (Naples n.d.), 204–11.

wider objectives. But it would be as wrong to think of it simply as 'reformist' as it would be to think of Chartism as simply a movement for parliamentary reform. Indeed, in Sicilian history it occupies a position somewhat analogous to Chartism.

The leadership of the movement came from the towns and the town workers. As is well known, the years after 1889 saw the rapid growth of socialist influence and propaganda everywhere in Europe and the theory and propaganda of the Second International reached Sicily both through radically-minded intellectuals and artisans, who set about organizing left-wing societies, unions and mutual defence organizations in the cities: in fact, *Fasci*. But in a situation of endemic revolution these spread all over the country and became the all-purpose organizations for every discontented section of Sicilians, including the peasants, though peasant Fasci were almost invariably founded much later than the urban ones. Organization as such was not unfamiliar to Sicilian peasants, who still live mainly in large agglomerations and not villages, in which each class had long had religious fraternities – if only for burial purposes – except the middle class which did not require them economically and perhaps also found that they conflicted with its individualism. Small peasant associations had also come into existence here and there in the 1880s, though normally these earlier types of organization proved incapable of being converted into Fasci.*

We note, therefore, that there is no question in the Fasci of a priority of religious or social interests. They were economic organizations and came to the peasants as such, inspired

---

* F. Renda, 'Origini e caratteristiche del movimento contadino della Sicilia Occidentale', in *Movimento Operaio,* N.S. May–Aug. 1955, 619–67. The author describes the fraternities in his own home town as late as the Fascist period: the Confraternity of Purgatory, which recruited master artisans, that of the Immacolata, which recruited mainly peasants.

by Socialist propaganda. Their demands themselves were anything but millenarian. Almost invariably they demanded municipal reform and the abolition of taxes and excise – partly for the reasons already discussed in the chapter on the Lazzarettists, partly because of the abnormal prevalence of a municipal spoils system in the hands of whichever middle-class faction controlled local government.* In the least advanced areas the peasants demanded the division of the *latifundia*, in the more advanced ones a reform of agrarian contracts, whether for labourers, share-croppers or other tenants. The strikes which took place, and were largely successful, were on this latter issue. The less advanced riots and demonstrations, which took place mostly in the less organized centres, were overwhelmingly on municipal or tax issues.† There is absolutely no evidence that the leaders of the movement aimed at the immediate seizure of power.

There was thus nothing which specifically encouraged millenarianism among the peasants. Yet we must remember that the people who went into these movements were essentially 'medieval' in their outlook. If they shouted 'Down with taxes' they also very often shouted 'Long live the King and Queen', holding the traditional view that if the king only knew what injustices were done in his name, he would not tolerate them.‡ It was equally natural for them to carry crucifixes and saints' images before their processions; to have crucifixes with candles lit before them in the Fascio

---

* Of the large denunciatory literature on Sicilian municipal politics, note sp. G. Alongi, 'Le condizioni economiche e sociali della Sicilia', in *Archivio di Psichiatria* XV, 1894, 229, esp. 242 ff.
† See the useful table of riots in La Loggia, *loc. cit*. For the absence of riots in centres with strong Fasci, *ibid.*, 212.
‡ Colajanni, *op. cit.*, 186.

headquarters; to treat visiting Socialist leaders as though they were bishops – men and women throwing themselves on the ground and strewing flowers in their path.* All the more natural because one of the most striking phenomena of the Fasci as of every revolutionary movement was the active participation of masses of peasant women. It is thus not surprising that the vast and moving revolutionary hopes which the peasants placed in the Fasci should find expression in traditional millenarian terms.

There is no doubt at all that revolution was what the peasants hoped for, a new and just, equal and communist society. 'What do you understand by Socialism?' a northern journalist asked the peasants at Corleone, a strong centre of the movement. 'Revolution,' said some in chorus. 'To put all property together and all eat the same,' said others. And a peasant woman in Piana dei Greci put their aspirations with remarkable clarity.† All should work. There should be neither rich nor poor. All should be equal. There was no need to divide estates and houses. All should be put in common and the income should be justly distributed. This would not give rise to quarrels or selfishness, because there would be brother-hood – the Fasci called their members 'brothers' – and those who broke brotherhood would be punished. Not that these sentiments were new. But what had hitherto been a hidden, hopeless aspiration seemed capable of realization because the peasants had had a revelation, brought to them by good and noble men, whom one peasant in Canicatti described as 'angels come down from Paradise. We were in the dark and they have

* Rossi, *op. cit.*, 7, 10.
† Rossi, *op. cit.*, 86, 69 ff. The views of the peasant woman are more fully reproduced in Appendix 5.

brought us light.* The revelation said that unity was strength and organization could bring a new society. No wonder that the peasants went to the Fasci not only for organization, but to learn:

> 'We don't go to church any more,' said a peasant woman from Piana dei Greci, 'but to the Fascio. There we must learn, there we must organize for the conquest of our rights.'†

To describe the movement as millenarian either in the Lazzarettist or the anarchist sense, is therefore not wholly accurate. What the Fasci taught was not millenarianism but modern politics. But under Sicilian conditions it was bound to have strong millenarian characteristics simply because it was revolutionary. It was, as observers were never tired of repeating, a new religion: 'these are primitive people made fanatic by a new faith,' Rossi remarks. The official Parliamentary Enquiry was later to write:‡

> and the peasant (listening to the Socialist preaching) was struck by it and believed in truth that a new religion had come, the true religion of Christ, which had been betrayed by the priests in alliance with the rich. And in many villages they abandoned the priests . . .

For it stood to reason that what the Socialists said could not conflict with the true faith of Christ. Jesus, said the peasant woman of Piana, was a true Socialist and wanted precisely

* Rossi, *op. cit.*, 38.
† Rossi, *op. cit.*, 10.
‡ *Inchiesta Parlamentare* (1910), vol. VI, 1–2, G. Lorenzoni: *Sicilia*, 633.

what the Fasci were demanding, but the priests did not represent him properly, especially when they practised usury. When
the Fascio had been founded the priests used the confessional
to oppose it and said Socialists were excommunicated. But the
peasants answered that the priests were mistaken and boy-
cotted the Corpus Domini procession in protest.* Moreover,
dissident Christian rebels came to reinforce the Fasci here
and there. In Bisacquino Father Lorenzo, the chaplain of the
church of the Madonna del Balzo, was called 'the Socialist'
because he openly – in the intervals of giving the peasants
tips on the lottery – said that joining the Fascio did not mean
excommunication, and that St Francis had been one of the
first and greatest of Socialists, who had, among other things,
abolished money. In Grotte among the sulphur-miners a local
middle-class man and ex-priest, S. Dimino, had founded an
evangelical church some decades back, which had established
itself in the teeth of bitter ecclesiastical opposition. Now all the
evangelical miners became Socialists and founded a Circolo
Savonarola where Dimino taught them Christian Socialism.†
It was not surprising that a few churchmen should recognize
that the word of God which the Socialist intellectuals preached
was also the word of religion.

Unlike Andalusia the new religion thus did not mean an
open breach with the old, though it is probable that, had the
Socialists concentrated on anti-religious propaganda, they
might have de-christianized sections of the peasants as the
anarchists did. There were examples of peasants who, instead
of bringing their babies to be baptized in church, brought
them to the Fascio. But religion was fundamentally irrelevant

* Rossi, *op. cit.*, 70.
† Rossi, *op. cit.*, 55, 89–90.

to the movement, except insofar as the peasants' aspirations were automatically expressed in its terminology. What was important was the new world:

> The advent of a new world without poverty, hunger or cold was a certain fact, because it was God's will. And it was an imminent fact. As though by magic Fasci arose all over the province. A single speech by Barbato or by Verro was sufficient to arouse minds out of the lethargy of centuries. How then could men doubt that the great event would soon come to pass?*

And the spread of the new gospel took place in the same atmosphere of 'mania' which we have already observed in Andalusia. Rossi's phrase might apply to the Cordovese country as well as to Sicily:

> In some regions it spread like a sort of epidemic contagion; the masses were invaded by the belief that a new reign of justice was imminent.†

As in Andalusia, the precise way in which the new world would come about was uncertain, and, as we have seen, the leaders of the movement had no immediate insurrectionary plans for bringing it about, though neither they nor the Fasci were at all committed to millenarian waiting, or to a refusal to demand and to accept the lesser concessions which might alleviate the lot of the peasant here and now. The movement was defeated. But here the Andalusian and the Sicilian stories

---

* M. Ganci, 'Il movimento dei Fasci nella provincia di Palermo', in *Movimento Operaio, loc. cit.*, 873.
† Rossi, *op. cit.*, 6–7.

diverge. For in Spain the cycle of waiting, of preparing and of new millenarian outbursts began again, only slowly and hesitantly allowing the infiltration of politics and organization. But in certain parts of Sicily the non-anarchist teachings of the Socialists saved something from the wreck of defeat. Permanent peasant movements, capable of outlasting oppression and utilizing even non-revolutionary periods, came into existence here and there. It may be convenient to illustrate this process by the example of a particular revolutionary peasant township, Piana dei Greci (now called Piana degli Albanesi).*

Piana was founded at the end of the 15th century when a number of Albanian clans fled from the Turkish conquest and were received in Sicily. The settlement, which is to this day the most self-consciously Albanian centre in the island, retaining its language and the Greek (Uniate) rite of the Catholic Church, is still populated by the descendants of the original settlers, for a handful of surnames, some of which can be traced as those of 'noble Albanian families' – i.e. clans – to the 15th century, still virtually monopolize the local population: Matranga, Stassi, Schiro, Barbato, Loyacano.† The Albanians in Italy have been much given to revolution, probably because the constant efforts of local lords to whittle away the privileges they received

* This fragmentary account of the movement in Piana is based largely on local information gathered in the town, thanks to the courtesy of the mayor and deputy On. Michele Sala, and on various references in newspapers and the secondary literature. Fortunately Piana, being fairly near Palermo, has been much described by visiting journalists and investigators.

† The Matrangas, Schiròs and Barbatos are mentioned as original 'noble families' in P. P. Rodota, *Dell' rito greco in Italia* III (Rome 1763), and in V. Dorsa, *Su gli Albanesi* (Naples 1847). On the early settlement see also Amico and Stratella, *Lexic. Sicul.* II ii, Piana Graecorum, p. 83. Also: Breve Cenno storico delle colonie greco-albanesi di Sicilia, in *Roma e l'Oriente* III, 1911–12, 264. For a bibliography, see S. Petrotta, *Albanesi di Sicilia* (Palermo 1966), 200–17.

at the original settlement, the constant efforts of the Church to turn them into Roman Catholics, and the peculiarities of their land-grants, which put their villages into an unfavourable position after the abolition of feudalism, exacerbated their relations with the authorities. Perhaps the tenacity with which they maintained national cohesion also helped. At all events, Piana had a reputation for rebelliousness long before 1893. 'The nature of the inhabitants,' a local moderate told Rossi, 'is so prone to rebellion that every time there are revolutions or tumults in Palermo or on the continent there are excesses at Piana.'* Indeed very often before then. Trevelyan described the place as 'the hearth of freedom in Western Sicily' because the Pianesi were already in revolt well before Garibaldi and the Thousand landed at Marsala; and several years earlier the Lieutenant-General had been constrained to report to the King at Naples that Piana, among other places, contained a population 'ferocious and always ready to make revolutions'.†

As to the causes of revolution, there was no disagreement among observers, among whom Villari in his *Lettere Meridionali* has described the appalling conditions of the inhabitants, and their economic deterioration by 1878. Piana was and is in the latifundist grain-growing uplands. Its population was by the 1890s composed mainly of landless labourers and proletarianized tenants – by the outbreak of the Fasci 'sharecroppers and day labourers had become confused in a single stratum of poverty' and, to judge by La Loggia's figures, wages were even lower than in Villari's day.‡ The town had no marked tradition of peasant organization, though it had a feeble association in

---

* Rossi, *op. cit.*, 32.
† F. Guardione, *Il dominio dei Borboni in Sicilia (1830–61)* (Turin 1907), II, 56.
‡ La Loggia, *loc. cit.*, 215–16.

1890 of about 100 members.* Local Politics, except at times of revolution, were dominated by the *stasis* of the local middle-class families who fought for the control of the municipality, the terror of the *mafiosi* and *campieri* and the dumb class hated of the '*caps*' for the '*hats*'.

The Fasci swept through the town like a tidal wave. Fortunately one of their national leaders – perhaps the ablest – was a Pianese, Dr Nicola Barbato, a medical man in his early thirties. 'Within a fortnight,' Rossi's moderate informant told him, 'Barbato became the real boss (il vero padrone) of the district.' When the Fascio arrived, rather late, in April 1893, it recruited virtually the entire adult population, 'except for the wealthy', men and women included. The police estimated its membership at 2800, which was more than twice as high as that of any other Fascio in the province except that of Palermo itself.† So completely was the place organized that there was no important rioting at all, in spite of one or two murders of leading members of the Fascio, presumably by the landlords, who threatened to kill the militants. The organization survived Barbato's arrest.

Though, as we have seen, the expectations of the Pianesi were millennial enough, and the spirit in which they entered the Fascio one of tremendous exaltation – the women were particularly active in it – the movement which received them was quite hard-headed, and taught them the lessons of non-millennial politics to good effect: organization and – for the time being – elections. As in other places the Fascio promptly put up municipal candidates, and elected several. When Rossi asked how they thought Socialism would come about, the

* F. Renda, Origine e caratteristiche, *loc. cit.*, 637–8.
† Ganci, *loc. cit.*, 861–2.

peasant woman whom we have already quoted on several occasions had, as usual, a clear idea of the process. At the next elections the Fasci would capture the majority in Piana, for all voters except the ex-lords were for them. Obviously this would only mean that the municipality could protect the citizens a little against the abuses and excessive powers of the *signori*. But in time the Fasci would elect provincial councillors, and deputies, and when there was a Socialist majority at Rome all the bad laws would go.* So far as lies within its power Piana has carried out this programme. The local council and deputy became Socialist before the First World War, and Communist subsequently – in 1953 it had an absolute majority of votes for the Communist Party, not counting the Nenni Socialists.

What is more important, the Pianesi retained and even extended their organization. A peasant league survived the Fascio, with a fluctuating but never negligible membership: 600 in 1906, 1000 in 1907, 400 in 1908.† The Socialist leaders after 1893 also strongly favoured the establishment of collective farms, which they saw not only as ancillaries to peasant agitation but as the nuclei of the new society within the old, and this form of co-operation naturally appealed greatly to the peasantry, indeed more so than less ambitious forms of agricultural co-operation: they leased land from the *gabellotti* and cultivated it in common, sharing out the proceeds.‡ Piana, naturally, had one from the beginning and has maintained it throughout all the political and economic vicissitudes since the 1890s, a fantastically impressive achievement. In 1953 it had

* Rossi, *op. cit.*, 74.
† Lorenzoni, *op. cit.*, 663.
‡ 'Italy: Collective Farms', in *Int. Review of Agric. Economics*, VIII, 1918, 617–30, esp. 626.

about 750 members – out of 2000 or so families – exclusively composed of Socialists and Communists.

Ever since the Fasci, therefore, the Pianesi have retained their attachment to their triple loyalty: to Communism, to the Albanians and to Greek Christianity; an attachment which has naturally been reinforced by the conversion of Scanderbeg's homeland to the cause which the Pianesi had adopted so long before Enver Hoxha. Since May 1893 they have never once – not even under Fascism – omitted to go in procession to a remote mountain pass, the Portella della Ginestra, there to hold a May Day meeting and to hear speeches given from 'Dr Barbato's Stone', a rock on which the great man once stood to address them. No doubt during Fascism there were only token processions, but the Pianesi insist that someone always celebrated May Day there. In 1947 the *Mafia* hired the bandit Giuliano to shoot down this demonstration, which he did, killing fourteen people or so, and creating a national political scandal which only ended in 1956 with the conviction of the surviving members of his band for this massacre. For left-wing politics in this area has never been an activity without considerable physical hazard, even though, as we saw in an earlier chapter, the *Mafiosi* have been notably less powerful in Piana than elsewhere in the province since the Fascio. The Pianesi have not ceased to be revolutionaries, even though their ideology can now hardly be called millenarian or even spontaneously riotous, and even though, while still very poor, they are by no means as desperately off as in the 1890s. The mere strength of their organization has won them many advantages. But the old spirit has not been weakened into mere reformism. It may take unsuspected forms, as in 1943 when the fall of Fascism caused them to declare themselves an independent republic for a few days, until the Communist Party pointed out that this was not advisable. To this day, if there is any news of agrarian demonstrations, direct occupations of estates and the like anywhere in Sicily, it is certain that the Pianesi will be involved in them. Their original millenarian enthusiasm has been transmuted into something more durable: permanent and organized allegiance to a modern social-revolutionary movement. Their experience shows that millenarianism need not be a temporary phenomenon but can, under favourable conditions, be the foundation of a permanent and exceedingly tough and resistant form of movement.

We have discussed the causes and nature of peasant mille-narianism, and its connexion with modern social movements. It remains to consider its function in peasant movements, for in fact it had a practical function, which may explain why a 'millenarian atmosphere' surrounds even many revolutionary movements which are not otherwise given to it. It helped to organize masses of hitherto unorganized people on a national scale, and almost simultaneously.

All social movements expand in jerks: the history of all contains periods of abnormally, often fantastically rapid and easy mobilization of hitherto untouched masses. Almost always such expansion takes the form of contagion: a propagandist arrives in a locality, and within a short time the whole region is affected; someone establishes or re-establishes a union in a disorganized trade, and within weeks members swamp the new organization; a strike breaks out, or perhaps even better, a strike is won, and within days hundreds of factories in contact with the original strikers are also out.* Within a

---

* I have discussed some aspects of this discontinuity in 'Economic Fluctuations and some Social Movements', in *Econ. Hist. Rev.,* 2d Ser. V, 1, 1952:

village or town such contagion is easy, since men and women are in close personal contact, and in advanced countries news is spread by press, radio and TV, and communications are easy. In backward countries they are slow and patchy. The difficulties of organizing a movement on a national scale are ironically underlined by the Sicilian experience in organizing the first May Day in 1890: had it not been for the nervousness of the authorities who warned local officials of the need to prevent disorder on that day – information which gossip rapidly spread – the local Socialists would often not even have known that the International expected them to demonstrate. But an atmosphere of high exaltation greatly facilitates the spreading of news. It provides teams of men and women who will spread the joyful tidings wherever they can, for at millennial times, as we have seen in Andalusia, everyone becomes a propagandist. 'Peasants from Piana and San Giuseppe Iato', wrote a newspaper in Trapani province, 'have come here for the harvest, describing the enthusiasm in those parts and inflaming our peasants'.* It invests even the smallest organizational advance with an aura of invincibility and future triumph, and nothing is more contagious than success. By these means a movement can almost simultaneously mobilize masses over a wide area, and nothing is more important politically than to do this, for six villages developing a movement at the same time make a vastly greater impact, and generate incomparably more political effectiveness than the same villages developing the same sort of movement separately at intervals of, say, a year. Millenarianism, in fact, is not merely a touching survival from an archaic past, but an extremely useful phenomenon, which

---

* Salvatore Costanza, 'I Fasci dei Lavoratori nel Trapanese', in *Movimento Operaio, loc. cit.*, 1028 n.

modern social and political movements can profitably utilize to spread their range of influence, and to imprint the groups of men and women affected by it with their teaching. For, as we have seen, without being imprinted with the right kind of ideas about political organization, strategy and tactics and the right kind of programme, millenarianism inevitably collapses. Alone it can maintain itself at best as an underground current of belief among a sect, as with the Lazzarettians, or as a body of potential leaders and a predisposition to periodic revolt, as in Andalusia. It can be, indeed it will always be, intensely moving to anyone who cares for the fate of man: but, as we have seen, it will certainly be perennially defeated.

However, when harnessed to a modern movement, millenarianism can not only become politically effective, but it may do so without the loss of that zeal, that burning confidence in a new world, and that generosity of emotion which characterizes it even in its most primitive and perverse forms. And no one can read the testimony of such people as the anonymous peasant woman of Piana without hoping that their spirit can be preserved.

Chapter VII

The City Mob

We have so far dealt almost entirely with social movements which are primitive in both their outlook and their members. It is, as it were, a historical accident that the bandits, the *mafiosi*, the Lazzarettists, Sicilian peasant socialists or Andalusian peasant anarchists found themselves living in the 19th and 20th instead of the 14th century. They were geared to an earlier way of life; it was their tragedy that a new world, which they did not properly understand, whirled them into a future with which they attempted to cope by dreams and violence. We must now consider primitive forms of social movement among groups of people who belonged to the new world of towns and industry, of modern capitalism. Naturally we shall not expect to find so many traces of primitivism here, though we must expect to find some, for the first generation of the modern industrial population were as yet far from adjusted to a way of life which was novel and revolutionary. Eventually – in Britain I should put the crucial turning-point somewhere about 1850 – they learned what we may call the 'rules of the game' of modern industrial society, and the modern labour

143

movements are the most striking and universal results of their 'education'. But it must never be forgotten that the bulk of industrial workers in all countries began, like Americans, as first-generation immigrants from pre-industrial societies, even if they never actually moved from the place in which they had been born. And like all first-generation immigrants, they looked backwards as much as forwards.

However, before discussing primitivism among the characteristic classes of modern capitalist society, it may be as well to consider some movements which stand between the old and the new: those of large pre-industrial cities. The most characteristic movements of such centres were and are *artisan gilds*, a type of organization which appears to be quite universal wherever and whenever there are pre-industrial cities. The nature of such gilds and the part they played in urban politics is sufficiently well known to make a discussion of them unnecessary. The links between such gilds (and analogous organizations) and the subsequent movements of skilled urban wage-workers are also fairly familiar.* Broadly speaking, social differentiation within or between crafts produced organizations modelled on the pattern of the older gilds or fraternities, but expressing the specific interests of particular sections, notably the journeymen, and a good deal of the traditional pattern was subsequently taken over – the exact ways are still occasionally in dispute – into the early trade unions of skilled wage-workers in the industrial period. Alternatively, some of the older journeymen organizations – the French *Compagnonnages* or the German *Gesellenverbaende* – took over certain trade union functions in the early industrial period before giving way to

---

* G. Unwin, *Industrial Organisation in the Sixteenth and Seventeenth Centuries*, remains the best discussion of this subject for this country.

the more up-to-date trade union pattern.* Some aspects of the
survival of such traditions will be discussed in the chapter on
the ritual in social movements.

Similarly, the political activities of urban journeymen and
skilled pre-industrial workers are fairly well known; or to be
more exact, the fact that they were politically extremely active
and conscious is familiar to everyone. Who says cobbler says
Radical, and much the same went for many of the other small
crafts and their journeymen. Their movements may indeed
have shown signs of 'primitivism', but on the whole they must
be regarded as the most 'modern' and advanced section of the
labouring poor, and the one most likely to adopt new ideologies – generally variants of Jacobinism.

However, this central current of organization and politics
among town workers is not what interests us here. I should
rather prefer to discuss something that is better described as
a perennial eddy in city life than as a current. We may call it
for short, using the classical English phrase, '*the mob*', for that
fickleness which struck observers about it was one of its more
obvious superficial characteristics.† The *mob* may be defined as
the movement of all classes of the urban poor for the achievement of economic or political changes by direct action – that

* Schoenlank's article 'Gesellenverbaende' in early editions of the
Handwoerterbuch d. Staatswissenschaften and M. St. Léon's *Le Compagnonnage* are
the most useful introductions. For a specially traditional craft, also discussed
by Unwin, see G. Des Marez, *Le Compagnonnage des Chapeliers Bruxellois* (Brussels
1909), and J. Vial, *La Coutume Chapelière* (Paris 1941). For *compagnonnages*
taking over some trade union functions, see e.g. E. Todt and H. Radandt, *Zur
Fruehgeschichte d. deutschen Gewerkschaftsbewegung 1800–1849* (Berlin E. 1950).

† I trust it will be clear from what follows that not every city riot is a 'mob riot'
nor every large assembly of townsmen a 'mob' in the sense of the word as used
in this chapter. Since few words have been used more indiscriminately than
'mob', this disclaimer may not be out of place.

is by riot or rebellion – but as a movement which was as yet inspired by no specific ideology; or, if it found expression for its aspirations at all, in terms of traditionalism and conservatism (the 'church and king mob'). It was a 'pre-political' movement, and as such a primitive one in our sense. Oddly enough, though the mob and its riots have been much talked about through the ages and even more condemned, it has been surprisingly little studied. However, serious study of riots is now being undertaken in various countries, notably by Dr George Rudé, who has worked on both French and English material, and to whose knowledge of the 18th-century riot I am much indebted. And the riot must be studied today, if it is to be understood, for it has, in many parts of the world, long ceased to be the commonplace, and even the accepted method of popular action which it once was.* The 'mob' as a social phenomenon has tended to disappear, to give way in many places to the industrial working class. Further, since the French Revolution and the rise of Socialist movements public authorities have become far more sensitive to crowds and disorder, especially in large or capital cities, than they were previously; and lastly, perhaps in consequence, the apparatus of public order has become increasingly large and efficient in the past one and a half centuries, even in the countries most suspicious of State action. Only outside Western Europe can the ordinary citizen of large towns still be expected to have experience of the pre-industrial riot and the pre-industrial mob.

The fact that the mob is a pre-political phenomenon does not mean that it had no implicit or explicit ideas about politics. Indeed, it often rioted 'without ideas', that is to say, normally

---

* Cf. Halevy, *A History of the English People in 1815* (Pelican edn.) 1, 193 ff. for the 'right of rebellion'.

against unemployment and for a cheap cost of living – famine prices and unemployment normally tending to coincide in pre-industrial periods* – and consequently markets, dealers and local taxes such as Excises were in all countries its obvious and almost invariable targets. The Neapolitans who sang, during the 1647 revolution

> On the foodstuffs there used to be no charge,
> There used to be no excise and no customs†

were expressing an aspiration which almost all urban poor anywhere would have echoed. And in view of the fact that large masses of the urban poor lived on the verge of subsistence even in normal times, and were precipitated into catastrophe by any increase in prices or in unemployment, their riots were often no more than automatic and inevitable reactions to such changes. The movement of food-prices, it is now well-known, is an almost infallible indicator of popular unrest in Paris during the French Revolution. However, simple food-riots do not exhaust the activities and ideas of the 'mob'.

At least two – perhaps three – other ideas were normally present in its manifestations. First, there was the claim to be considered. The classical mob did not merely riot as a protest, but because it expected to achieve something by its riot. It assumed that the authorities would be sensitive to its movements, and probably also that they would make some sort of immediate concession; for the 'mob' was not simply a casual collection of people united for some *ad hoc* purpose,

* E. J. Hobsbawm, 'Economic fluctuations and some social movements', *Econ. Hist. Rev.* 2d Ser. V, 1 (1952), p. 5.
† M. Schipa, 'La cosidetta rivoluzione di Masaniello', in *Archivio Stor. delle Provincie Napoletane* 2d ser. 11, 75.

but in a recognized sense, a permanent entity, even though rarely permanently organized as such. It sometimes was, though the forms of permanent organization of the *plebs* – apart from artisan gilds – remain to be investigated; e.g. religious fraternities in European cities, or the various 'Pangs' in China. Second, the mob's activities, whatever their ostensible object, ideology or lack of theory, were always directed against the rich and powerful (though not necessarily the official head of the State or city). In the Gordon Riots – of the great English late 18th-century riots the only one to be adequately described – the parishes with the largest Catholic population escaped relatively easily. The greatest numbers of houses destroyed were, with one exception, in parishes with quite small Catholic colonies. Of the 136 citizens who claimed compensation after the riots, and whose professions can be discovered, 33 were peers, ambassadors and gentlemen, 23 members of the professions and priests, 29 publicans and the like, 33 merchants, dealers and shopkeepers, 15 probably artisans and only four wage-earners.* The Viennese who rioted against the execution of the French king in 1793 directed their fury against the French emigrant nobles.† The *lazzaroni* of Naples, the quintessential 'mob', were passionate defenders of Church and King, and even more savage anti-Jacobins in 1799. Yet they sang songs against all the upper classes who, in their view, had 'betrayed the king', notably 'knights and monks', sacked the houses of royalists impartially, and defined as Jacobins and enemies of the king any owners of property,

---

* George Rudé, 'The Gordon Riots', *Trans. Royal Hist. Soc.* 5th Ser. VI (1956). The Liverpool riot of 1778 and the Birmingham Riots of 1791 have not so far been adequately analysed.

† I am grateful to Dr Ernst Wangermann for this point.

or more simply, anyone with a carriage.* This proclivity has time and again tempted unsympathetic observers – and almost all observers, of whatever politics, have been far from complete sympathy with the classical 'mob' – to present it as a collection of *lumpenproletarians* and criminals out for loot.† And indeed there is no doubt that the demoralized and the criminal, who abounded in great cities, seized their opportunities which, as anyone who has ever spent even a few hours in Naples or Palermo knows, these destitute populations need only too sorely. However, as we shall see, the 'mob' was not primarily a body of such people.

The third constant factor is perhaps the hostility to foreigners; that is to non-townsmen. An instinctive kind of municipal patriotism seems to be a constant characteristic of the classical 'mob'. The popular comedies of Vienna from 1700 to 1860, which being addressed to the 'suburban' and common audience, provide a magnificent mirror of the views held by people who are normally inarticulate, reflect this underlying pride of the city man extremely well. The Neapolitan *lazzari* were even prepared to defend the glory of the city against the despised provincials at the cost of supporting the Jacobins.

Who, then, were the 'mob'? Its main strength lay in the strata commonly described on the continent as the 'little people' (*menu peuple, popolo minuto* or *popolino*), particularly those of certain cohesive and ancient quarters of the city like the Faubourg St Antoine in Paris, the Trastevere in Rome or the

---

* B. Croce, *Curiosità Storiche* (Naples 1919), 136–7, quotes some verses, Croce, *Storia del Regno di Napoli* (Bari 1925), 224, *La Rivoluzione napolitana del 1799*, Maffei, *Brigand Life*, for the sacking of royalist houses in 1860.

† F. Brancato, 'Origini e carattere della rivolta palermitana del 1866', in *Arch. Storico Siciliano* 3d Ser. V (1952–3), I, 139 ff., for some French consular reports specifically contradicting this interpretation.

Mercato in Naples. It was a combination of wage-earners, small property-owners and the unclassifiable urban poor.* In Naples, where it was perhaps more conscious of its collective existence under the name of *lazzari* or *lazzaroni* and where it has been most often accused of consisting primarily of beggars and *lumpenproletarians*, we happen to be fairly well informed about it. Goethe thought of the *lazzari* simply as the *menu peuple* or the unemployed. A diarist writing during the 1799 revolution, whom Croce paraphrases, gives a more precise analysis of them. They consisted of the porters, a riot-leading class even in other cities,† – presumably they include the dockers – and the apprentices and journeymen of the lower trades and crafts such as rope-makers, smiths, brass-workers, tin and locksmiths, tanners, tailors and shoemakers. The wool and silkworkers, woodworkers, gold and silversmiths and the jewellers as well as the servants in well-to-do houses regarded themselves as superior to the *lazzari*.‡ We must obviously also add the mass of hawkers and unclassifiable small dealers and people making ends meet which filled pre-industrial cities. The *lazzari* were thus fundamentally much the same as the *menu peuple* of other cities except for their superior cohesion, for they elected some sort of *capolazzari* annually, and were fanatically attached to the city cult of St Januarius, as their equivalents in Palermo favoured the cult of that city's saint, Sta. Rosalia. They emerged as a recognized class in the revolution of 1647 which brought one of them, the fish-seller Masaniello, to temporary power; neither the first nor the last, but certainly the most

* G. Rudé, 'The motives of popular insurrection during the French Revolution', in *Bull. Inst. Histor. Research* XXVI (1953), 55 n.

† G. Rudé, 'La taxation populaire de Mai 1775', in *Annates Historiques de la Revolution Francaise* (Apl.–June 1956), 38.

‡ Croce, 'I Lazzari', in *Varietà di Storia Letteraria e Civile* (Bari 1935) I, 189 ff.

striking of the many rebellions of the city.* At least the name first appears in 1647 as a description of Masaniello's partisans, and, though little used from 1650 to 1750, it reappears later and is firmly established by their counter-revolution of 1799.† In Rome the native plebs appears to have been – perhaps from long tradition – more disinclined to the crafts. There they seem to have followed such occupations as those of butchers, boatmen, carters, fishermen, porters, tanners, paviours or hawkers and costermongers of various kinds, leaving the crafts – it is reported – to foreigners who had come to Rome in search of fortune.‡ No doubt the proportion of *lumpenproletarians* among them was high. On the other hand in a large northern city like Milan it was low, for out of its male inhabitants there were perhaps 27,000 workers and small shopkeepers and only 2500 'beggars, idlers, vagrants, prisoners and their women'.§

At all events it is clear that the 'mob' consisted of the ordinary urban poor, and not simply of the scum. And often enough even the 'respectable' sections of the city, such as the artisan corporations, co-operated or merged with it, as in the Palermo riots of 1773 or the Bolognese riots of the 1790s, in which 'persons of low and vile extraction, but also those of artisan profession' took part.¶

Such a body of potential, and often actual, rioters existed in every city of importance in which police and military

---

* On this see M. Schipa, *op. cit., loc. cit.*, N.S. vols. II and III and his 'La Mente di Masaniello', *ibid.*, 1st Ser. XXXVIII, XXXIX.
† Croce, 'Varietà intorno ai "Lazzari",' in *Napoli Nobilissima* XIV (1905), 140, 171, 190.
‡ Silvagni, 'La Corte', qu. L. Dal Pane, in *Storia del Lavoro in Italia 1700–1815* (Milan 1943), 102.
§ Dal Pane, *op. cit.*, 100.
¶ *Ibid.*, 279, 323.

were slack. However, there was a group of towns in which 'the mob' was of particular importance and developed a peculiar sub-political complexion of its own: the classical pre-industrial metropolis – normally a capital – living on a resident court, state, church or aristocracy. Most of these occurred in Southern Europe, for this combination of characteristics was most likely to be found in towns with a continuous existence dating back to beyond the High Middle Ages, and which had never been republics. At all events the purest examples of this urban tradition are to be found in places like Rome, Naples, Palermo, and perhaps Vienna or Istanbul – towns which have long been great cities and always ruled by a prince.

In such cities the *popolino* lived in an odd relationship with its rulers, equally compounded of parasitism and riot. Its views – if that is the right word – may be set out fairly lucidly. It is the business of the ruler and his aristocracy to provide a livelihood for his people, either by giving employment himself, for instance by patronizing local tradesmen and general free spending and tipping as befits the status of a prince or gentleman, or by attracting employment, as for instance the tourist and pilgrim traffic. This is all the more necessary since such princely centres are not normally industrial towns, being often too large for the local manufactures to provide employment, since it has often been observed that the largest pre-industrial cities were normally so huge precisely because they were administrative and court centres. Of course, as we have seen in Rome, the *popolino* might come to resist industrialization as being below its metropolitan dignity, preferring casual work. However, if for one reason or another the usual livelihood of the people was jeopardized or broke down, it was the duty of the prince and his aristocracy to provide relief and to keep the cost-of-living low.

Provided he and they did their duty, they received active and enthusiastic popular support. Indeed, ragged and miserable as it was, the populace identified itself with the splendour and greatness of the city, which it naturally often – but not necessarily – identified with the ruler. Vienna *was* the Imperial Court, Rome the Papacy, and the French Bourbons may have been ill-advised to exchange the riotous but important loyalty of their Parisians for the peace of Versailles, where riots were more manageable, but royal residence gained far fewer political advantages. Nothing was easier than for the *popolino* thus to identify itself with city and rulers. Miserable and destitute though it was, it was not directly exploited by the Bourbon or Papal court, but was on the contrary its parasite, sharing, however modestly, in the city's general exploitation of the provinces and the peasants – the root of all Mediterranean pre-industrial city economy – and of the rest of the world by trade, tourists or pilgrims. The rulers and the parasitic poor thus lived in a sort of symbiosis. There was not even much need to keep the two classes apart, as in modern cities. The traditional medieval or absolutist metropolis has no *beaux quartiers*: slums and street markets adjoined the palaces as we may still see them doing in parts of Rome or Palermo, and in the older parts of Paris – but not in the post-revolutionary ones. The city was a cultural unit. It may well be that the convention by which the aristocracy in Vienna, Venice or Naples patronized the dialect theatre and spoke a slightly modified version of the prevailing popular idiom and not a special 'U' language, reflected this fundamental community of interest of the whole city against the exploited outsiders. It is not easy today to conceive of an Emperor and his archdukes conducting their conversations in the Viennese equivalent of a modified cockney, as the Habsburgs did until the end.

Provided the ruler did his duty, the populace was prepared to defend him with enthusiasm. But if he did not, it rioted until he did. This mechanism was perfectly understood by both sides, and caused no political problems beyond a little occasional destruction of property, so long as the normal attachment of the *menu peuple* to its city and rulers was not replaced by some other political ideal or so long as the rulers' failure to do their duty was no more than temporary. The threat of perennial rioting kept rulers ready to control prices and to distribute work or largesses, or indeed to listen to their faithful commons on other matters. Since the riots were not directed against the social system, public order could remain surprisingly lax by modern standards. Conversely, the populace was quite satisfied with the effectiveness of this mechanism for expressing its political demands, and required no other, since these demands were for little more than a bare subsistence and a little entertainment and vicarious glory. An admirable picture of this situation has been drawn for Parma, where the unskilled dole-drawing proletariat who lived on ducal bounties always had its 'holy' rebellions of barricade-raising and brick-throwing, while remaining sincerely attached to its dear Duchess.* Consequently the Parmesans had the utmost difficulty in adjusting themselves to the new political techniques of the late 19th century, such as elections and trade unions, which they regarded as unnecessary. Thus as late as 1890, while all around them took to the new ways, the Parmesans still rioted in spite of their Reformist labour leaders, and in 1895, while Milan and the Romagna voted left, Parma did not. The ballot had not yet come to be considered a serious weapon for the people.

* B. Riguzzi, *Sindacalismo e Riformismo nel Parmense* (Bari 1931).

Significantly, in 1898 it was the countryside which organized strikes as well as riots: Parma only rioted. However, the national wave of riots in that year, a crucial one in the development of Italian Socialism, brought even the Parmesans into the left-wing fold, though even then Parma remained a Radical-Masonic island in a Socialist countryside, that is, its swing to the left was directed by the petite-bourgeoisie rather than the labouring classes.

This political lag of the (non-industrial) city behind the countryside was and is not confined to Parma. It is a fairly widespread phenomenon in Southern Italy to this day, though the leftward shift of the big-city vote has begun to take place in the last ten years. Thus, as we have seen in the chapter on *Mafia*, in the first post-fascist elections the left-wing vote in Palermo, Messina and Catania was less than half that in the rural provinces, though it has approximately doubled since. In the same elections (1946) the non-political, including monarchist, vote in Rome was considerably higher than in any other province of Latium, in Naples somewhat higher than elsewhere in Campania.* In the Calabrian province of Cosenza the Left in 1953 polled more than twice as many votes as the Monarchists-Neofascists; but in the City of Cosenza they only polled about 15 per cent more.† Nor is it an accident that Monarchism of a sort, represented mainly by a demagogic

---

* Monarchist, Qualunquist (Neofascist) votes are rightly considered by students of the Italian South as signs of a lack of political consciousness rather than as political votes. A low vote for Demochristians or Socialists-Communists marks what has been called the 'grey zone' of political awakening as does a capricious shifting between one lunatic fringe candidate and another. See Rocco Scotellaro, *Contadini del Sud* (Bari 1955), 31–2.

† I am indebted to Mr Nino Cavatassi, Secretary of the Cosenza Federation of the P.C.I., for the provincial election figures, broken down by towns and villages.

millionaire ship-owner and big-city boss, has remained more influential in Naples than in any other great city of Italy. In 1956 it polled almost three times as many votes there as the Communists. However, this lack of interest in modern politics among the big-city poor – which expresses itself as some sort of conservatism, when they do vote – is not only the result of such peculiar symbioses, but may also be due simply to helplessness and to the absence of anything – such as large factories, craft or village solidarity – which helps them to crystallize their political opinions. One of the best-known facts about the political history of London is the a-political voting of the East End until the 20th century, when it made the transition to the Labour Party without passing through the earlier stage of political consciousness, Liberal-Radicalism. The old boroughs of artisans and small shopkeepers – notably those South of the Thames – took to political consciousness, i.e. to Radicalism, much earlier, and remained loyal to it much longer, switching their allegiance to Labour only in the 1920's.

Nevertheless, such a symbiosis of the 'mob' and the people against whom it rioted was not necessarily the fundamental factor about its politics. The 'mob' rioted, but it also sometimes made revolutions, even if they were camouflaged as counter-revolutions. It was poor; 'they' were rich; life was fundamentally unjust for the poor. These were the foundations of its attitude, which may be found in countless street-ballads ('It's the same the whole world over, it's the poor wot gets the blame' in London, or in Seville 'I am a prisoner in jail/because I have not enough money./With a key of gold/There is no gate which does not open.'), in the idealization of the anarchic rebellion of highwaymen and bandits, always outlawed because of trouble with a great lord or the State, always betrayed, always taking their revenge. The implicit revolutionism of the 'mob' was primitive; in its way it was the metropolitan equivalent of the stage of political consciousness represented by social banditry in the country-side. Like banditry, when it emerged as a frankly political phenomenon, it generally did so as what can best be described as a legitimism of the barricades, e.g. in absolutist countries as the 'Church and King Mob'.

It is worth analysing this populist legitimism for a moment, for the assumptions which underlay it were not confined to the big cities, but were widely held among pre-political populations. Peasant movements in Tsarist Russia until the early 20th century are deeply imbued with it. Its main assumptions are perhaps the following.

First, the ruler (or an institution like the Church) in some sense symbolizes and represents the people and its way of life as uninstructed public opinion sees it. He may be evil, corrupt and unjust; or rather the system of government which he represents may be all these things; but insofar as the society over which he presides is stable and traditional, he represents the norm of life. This norm is not particularly happy for the common people, unless they are very lucky indeed: famine, plague and pestilence, battle, murder and sudden death, poverty and injustice are always present or round the corner; but then, that is man's fate. But if this stable order, poor though it should be, should be threatened from outside or inside then, unless the ruler has produced or tolerated more than the expected measure of poverty, injustice and death (unless, to use the Chinese phrase, 'the mandate of Heaven has run out'), the people will rally round him, since he is in a symbolic and magical sense 'themselves', or at least the personification of the social order. Thus the Castilians rallied round the Bourbons against the foreign invaders. This is not in itself a social movement, but if the challenge to the old order takes the form of new and disruptive social forces 'legitimism' may cover a mass revolt against the injustices of the new order, a sort of political Luddism. Legitimate monarchs or institutions like churches may not welcome this. The Emperor Francis I of Austria took a poor view of the revolutionary legitimism of his people, observing correctly: 'Now they are patriots for me; but one day they may be patriots against me.' From the point of view of the genuinely conservative institution the ideal is obedience, not enthusiasm, whatever the nature of the enthusiasm. Not for nothing was 'Ruhe ist die erste Buergerpflicht' (Tranquillity is the first duty of the citizen) the slogan of every German princeling.

Second, the ruler (fortunately for himself a remote institution) represents justice. Though it is patent that local lords, officials, clergymen and other exploiters suck the blood of the poor, this is probably because the monarch does not know what is done in his name. If the Tsar or the King of France only knew he would doubtless sweep through the country to shrivel up the unjust officials with his eagle eye, and to dispense justice to his loyal commons. A score of folk-myths express this attitude, for instance the wishful dream of the king who goes about his country incognito discovering injustice and dispensing justice, from Harun-al-Rashid to the Emperor Joseph II. The king's (or the pope's) remoteness preserves his reputation. But conversely, as soon as the injustices and sufferings of the people are laid *directly* at his door, his reputation vanishes. Not a cock will crow for an 'unjust king', however legitimate – for a Nicholas II after three years of slaughter – for an unjust king is the negation of kingship. The less personal institution of the church resists the discovery of fallibility better, but, as we have seen in the discussion of the Millenarians, it is subject to the equally damaging discovery that it is not the 'true' church, but a conspiracy of the oppressors to keep the poor in ignorance. The devout but fiercely anti-clerical Christian is a familiar figure in European revolutionary history.

'Church and king' movements are therefore social protests, though revolutionary ones only in what I have called their 'Luddite' phases. Generally their object is to preserve the traditional norm of social relationships, which implies an acceptance of the traditional hierarchy; though the secular dream of a genuinely and completely free society in which there are neither 'hats' nor 'caps' (to use the Sicilian phrase) occasionally bursts out in wild massacres. They become the 'revolutionism of fools' only in revolutionary periods. If they had a constitutional theory, we might explain their difference from royal legitimism by saying that the king's legitimism implies above all a monopoly of obedience; the people's, some real or fancied services to justice which the king renders, or might render if not otherwise prevented. Popular Church and King movements are therefore neither uncritical nor unconditional, and indeed, since they are not fundamentally concerned with what Church and King think, they take little notice of it. The Parisians in 1588 did not care whether Henry III approved the insurrectionary commune which they set up in his name. The Neapolitans and Parmesans had not the slightest hesitation in rioting against their ruler when he appeared to fail in his duties of providing them with the modest living they felt to be their right. Sean O'Casey's Dubliners are not really troubled about whether the Church approves of the rebels – in fact, the Church's relations with the Irish Republican Brotherhood, whose origins are in 18th-century secularism or deism, were always rather distant. It is not really conceivable to them that the Church could *not* stand for Ireland. There is thus no mystery in the sudden defection of legitimist subjects from their king which has, in the past forty years, turned the monarchism which was almost universal in Central, Southern and Eastern Europe in 1914 into an unimportant political anomaly.

The populace therefore riots for justice under the banner of King or Tsar, as in the terrible urban *jacquerie* of Naples in 1799, or in many rural risings in which the peasants, whether in Sicily or on the Volga, cannot believe that the State's forces have come to suppress them, for they are, they *must* be, carrying out the ruler's desires. 'Don't open fire on us,' cried the peasants of Bezdna to General Apraxin, making the sign of the Cross, 'you are shooting on Alexander Nikoleyevitch, you are shedding the blood of the Tsar.'* They were not thinking of a real Tsar, *any* real ruler, but of the ideal legitimate people's Tsar who can never exist. When, as in Naples, the king is not so remote as to be personally unknown and unrecognizable, the lack of commitment to legitimacy as understood by the rulers is more obvious. The *lazzari* were committed only to a king – for an impersonal republic was something they could not understand –, not to a Bourbon king. Indeed, after their conquest by the French they were quite ready to transfer their loyalty to the French general Championnet, whom they compared favourably with 'the king that went away', because of his more democratic demeanour. A good deal of the mob's reputation for fickleness is due to this empiricism. It wants a king who does his duty, as it wants a saint who does his duty: anyone will do. It was only logical for the *lazzari* after their defeat to demonstrate against St Januarius, and to transfer their piety temporarily to St Antonius.†

* For this most interesting rising, R. Labry, *Autour du Moujik* (Paris 1923) and F. Venturi, *Il Popolismo Russo* (Turin 1952) vol. I, which is based on the latest Russian researches.
† Croce, 'I lazzari', *loc. cit.*, 197–8.

But at bottom the 'mob' was not committed to any king, ruler or system at all, and political labels were merely attached to movements which had no positive programme except the hatred of the rich and a certain sub-anarchist egalitarianism. For not even anarchism provided a positive solution. A peasant village could hope to function as a village, by the simple consensus of the community, if only the State, the law and the rich who exploit and interfere are abolished. But a city cannot hope to be run in this way. The only solution for cities, which primitive anarchism has to propose, is their destruction, a proposal which (as we have seen) anarchist peasants may welcome, but which by their very situation the city poor cannot entertain. Somebody must organize the city and provide its livelihood. If there is 'equality' in it, it can only be the sophisticated equality of the vote, or of equal opportunity, or something of the sort, not the simple equality of all men cultivating the land in common in brotherhood and perhaps redistributing it periodically. The 'mob' could rebel. It could do so remarkably effectively, because, living in cities and capitals, it had a far more precise conception of what 'government', 'power' and the 'seizure of power' meant than peasants in remote villages. But it could do no more than rebel periodically against man's fate, and then relapse, and it preferred the tacit acceptance of government and the providers of employment – some government, any government – and riots for limited or short-range objectives. It did not greatly matter under whose banner it rioted. I know of no millenarian movement among classical big-city 'mobs' in the past two centuries, for the conception of a new and perfect world was exceptionally difficult for them to gain.

Nevertheless, gradually the 'mob' changed sides, if the phrase is not too precise or too question-begging. If we confine ourselves, for the sake of comparability, to the populace of absolutist or formerly absolutist cities of the southern type, the transition may be observed at various stages from the French Revolution onward. Whatever the Parisian *menu peuple* rioted about, from the Revolution onward it did so under the auspices of the Left. The Viennese populace, loyal and anti-Jacobin in the 1790s (with the characteristic exception of the cobblers who were pro-French because the French were against religion*) was revolutionary in 1848. By a study of the suburban comedies we can even place the change in the popular political atmosphere more precisely: between the early 1830s and 1848.† In Spain the heroes of the cafe-singers of Seville and Barcelona after the middle of the 19th century were Liberal generals, if we are to judge by the contents of their *coplas* (songs) and the experiences of the singers.‡ Even in Naples itself, the fortress of pauper Bourbonism, the Bourbons in 1860 waited in vain for another edition of the *lazzaroni* rising of 1799. The *lazzari* remained quiet. Indeed, the Camorra had for some years come to terms with the Liberals, and Garibaldi captured the Neapolitan poor as he captured the hearts of all other poor men. And if the Palermo rising of 1866 was still 'for Sta Rosalia', it was also 'for Garibaldi and the Republic', for Palermo had long got into the habit of rising with, or ahead of, its Liberals. This does not mean that the purely 'pre-political' or right-wing 'mob' ceased

---

* Dr Ernst Wangermann has extracted this information from the archives.

† O. Rommel, *Die Altwiener Volkskomoedie* (Vienna 1952), is the standard work; Johann Nestroy the typical actor-author of the pre-1848 suburban stage.

‡ Silverio, the father of the – normally unpolitical – *flamenco*, had an elegy on the Republican hero Riego in his early repertoire: Demofilo, *El Cante Flamenco* (Seville 1881), 194. The minstrel Fernando el de Triana explains (*Arte y artistas flamencos* (1952 edn. Madrid), 85–9) how he captured the Barcelona public, which was unsympathetic to Andalusian song, by inventing a *tango* on the subject of General Prim.

to exist, though now, more often than not, it functioned less as a consciously traditionalist force than as one moved by an ostensibly left-wing demagogy – anti-semitic, as in Vienna, anti-clerical and anti-rich, as in Barcelona – which happened to suit the book of the conservative elements. It was under such slogans that Alejandro Lerroux, the 'emperor of the Paralelo', brought out his men from the Barrio Chino, the purulent quarter of slums and brothels in the centre of old Barcelona, for the *Tragic Week* of anarchic mob-rule in 1909.*

Why did this change take place? Partly, no doubt, because the 'mob' was empiricist, and Church-and-King regimes were on their way out. The stubborn lost-cause traditionalism of Vendéan peasants or the Carlist Navarrese and Aragonese is not to be sought in the slums of the big cities. But partly it was, no doubt, because with the revolutionary movements of the new age, a new sort of hero who stood for the people and was perhaps sprung from the people, appeared, a champion, and perhaps the glimmerings of a free society and not merely a regulated one. Garibaldi, whose capacity to incarnate the popular ideal of the 'people's champion' bordered on the miraculous – he remains to this day the man who has single-handed collected probably the largest mass demonstrations ever held in London – is perhaps the most vivid example. Long before South Italians had abandoned traditional revolution-ism, he broke through their incomprehension of the actual causes to which he lent his name, perhaps – as Mr Mack Smith has persuasively argued – because he was himself a simple pre-ideological man who had an instinctive understanding of the way to deal with pre-political poor men and women. The

---

* Brenan, *op. cit.*, 34. His movement had been tacitly tolerated by the govern-ment as being anti-Catalanist.

'mob' was traditionalist only for want of something better, and this is what the new movements, Jacobin, national, Socialist, seemed, however vaguely, to provide.

Admittedly they could absorb it only incompletely. The 'mob's' readiness to riot has made the tasks of revolutionaries easy on the first days of revolutions, but had been offset by an almost total inability to understand that social agitation does not end when a riot has achieved its immediate objectives, and by its lack of discipline. Almost every modern socialist or communist movement would take the disciplined stolidness of any small coalfield in exchange for the ebullience of three cities like Palermo, if it could. And indeed, with some exceptions, the real strength of modern labour movements almost from the beginning lay not in the non-industrial capital cities, but in the provinces: in the Nord and the Pas-de-Calais, in Central Germany, in Wales and the North, in Turin and Milan. The classical age of the revolutionary metropolitan populace was that of Jacobinism and early Radicalism.

But even in its strongholds, the classical 'mob' has declined. In the first place industrialization substituted for the *menu peuple* the industrial working class, whose very being is organization and lasting solidarity, as that of the classical 'mob' is the intermittent and short riot. In the second place the change in economic conditions removed periodic famine combined with high unemployment, and substituted a form of economic crisis which did not produce the food-riot as an almost automatic and inescapable reaction. Lastly, the increasing sensitiveness of governments to rioting in capital cities after the French Revolution, and perhaps also the 19th-century evolution of urban structure, which tended to remove the rich from the poor into their specialized quarters, and to remove both from the main business and government districts, made the classical spontaneous riot or rising less easy, even where the material for it still existed. The observer who only knows the London, Paris or Berlin of the late 19th century will find it difficult to grasp what the 'mob' was about. Only when he walks through, say, Palermo, where the Quattro Canti are still the nerve-centre of the city, within rifle-shot of the palaces, the government offices, the slums and the markets, will he feel in his bones what the call 'the populace have risen' meant in the days of the classic 'mob'.*

Few will regret its passing. Defenders of the *status quo* have rarely bragged about the sound traditionalism of the 'mob' as they have done about that of peasant conservatives, even when they have benefited from it. For the labour movement it has, on balance, been a force delaying its conquest of great non-industrial cities, and where it has been on its side, they have tried to explain it away. Even the anarchists, the most logical champions of primitive and spontaneous, even of negative, rebellion, have hesitated to idealize it. The transformation of the *menu peuple* of large capital cities into a modern working class has meant a loss of colour, but whoever has seen the hor-rifying spectacle of the Neapolitan sub-proletariat, will treat even Stoke-on-Trent with indulgence. But with all its faults, the 'mob' has been a fact in history. It is perhaps the form of social agitation with the longest record of continuous existence, for it is not too fanciful to recognize its lineaments in the Blues and the Greens of the circus factions of antiquity. And because it has – perhaps only half-consciously – played an important part in the political evolution of the modern world, before giving

* For the fear of revolution influencing town-planning, cf. the work of Haussmann in Paris and, for Vienna, H. Benedikt, *Die wirtschaftliche Entwicklung in der Franz-Joseph-Zeit* (Vienna-Munich 1958), 46–7.

way to better movements, and other groupings of the poor, the historian must make the attempt to understand how it worked, even though it can rarely rouse his sympathy, like some other primitive social movements.

Chapter VIII

The Labour Sects

The American and French Revolutions of the 18th century are probably the first mass political movements in the history of the world which expressed their ideology and aspirations in terms of secular rationalism and not of traditional religion. The fact marks a revolution in the life and thought of the common people so profound that its nature is difficult even to appreciate for those of us who have grown up in an epoch when politics is agnostic, whatever the private beliefs of politicians and voters. The modern labour movement is the product of this epoch in two distinct ways. First, because its leading ideology, Socialism (or Communism or Anarchism, which belong to the same family), is the last and most extreme descendant of 18th-century illuminism and rationalism; and second, because the working classes themselves, its supporters, the children of an unprecedented era, were probably as a class less affected by traditional religions than any other social group of men, except for certain limited strata or elite groups such as middle-class intellectuals. This does not mean that workers were or are predominantly agnostic or atheist. It merely means that

167

the historical or individual step from village to town, or from peasant to worker, has in general led to a sharp reduction in the influence of traditional religions and churches. The enquiries which have been made into the religious affiliations and practices of the working classes from the 1840s to the 1950s have almost without exception observed that they are characterized, compared with other classes, by an abnormal degree of religious indifferentism.* Even the exceptions are often more apparent than real for the abnormally religious groups among the working class – in Western Europe they are normally Roman Catholic – are frequently national minorities, such as the Irish in Britain and the Poles in imperial Germany, for whom their specific religion is a badge of nationality as much as anything else. And even they, though more markedly religious than their colleagues, are normally very much less so than their co-religionists at home, who are not members of the working class. As for the leaders and militants of the Socialist movements, they have been almost from the start not merely religiously indifferent, but in general actively agnostic, atheist and anti-clerical.

The characteristic 'modern' form of working-class move-ment is thus purely, if not militantly, secular. However, it would be incredible if the forms and fashions of traditional religion, which had enclosed the lives of the common people from time immemorial, were to have suddenly and completely dropped away. In the early stages of even the strongly secular social and political movements we often observe a sort of nostalgia for the old religions, or perhaps more accurately, an inability

---

* The *Religious Census* of England and Wales in 1851 is the first of the great enquiries; the works of Le Bras and the French Catholic school of 'religious sociology' since 1941 have produced the best recent studies.

to conceive of new ideologies which do not follow the patterns of the old; perhaps with attenuated or transformed gods, perhaps with echoes of the old cults and rituals. The illuminist middle classes themselves had their Masonic Deism, the French Revolution its cults of Reason and the Supreme Being. What is more to the point, as Albert Soboul has lately shown, the rank-and-file revolutionaries re-created cults of Saints and Martyrs, including miracle-working ones, on the old model: Perrine Dugué in the Sarthe, who rose to Heaven with tricolour wings and whose tomb healed the sick, Marat, Lepeletier and Chalier among the Paris *sansculottes*.* The early forms of Socialism in the epoch of the Utopian communities often took the form of new religions (such as the Saint Simonian) or of prophetic sectarianism (such as Wilhelm Weitling's). The 'cult-creating' capacity of secular movements persisted for a considerable time. Even Auguste Comte's Positivism still had its religion of Humanity. However, except in the very early stages, these are curious rather than important phenomena. The new Socialist movements did indeed fulfil many of the functions of the traditional religions for its members, and developed analogous phenomena to theirs. Spanish Socialists even addressed one another in correspondence as 'coreligionario'. But such sociological similarities are beyond the scope of this discussion. In its secularism the labour and socialist movement is distinctively 'modern'.

The major exception to this generalization are the labour sects in the Anglo-Saxon countries.† The ideological history of

---

* 'Sentiment religieux et cultes populaires pendant la Revolution', in *Archives de Sociologie des Religions* (Jul.–Dec. 1956), No. 2.

† I do not imply that similar bodies did not exist elsewhere. However, for the sake of convenience, I shall discuss the British phenomena almost exclusively. They are in any case the most important.

the British labour movements is not, of course, totally different from that of continental countries. British labour and socialist movements, like those on the continent, were dominated by the secularist-radical tradition, which provided the most influential pamphleteers from Tom Paine to Bradlaugh and Blatchford, virtually all the theorists of the movement from the Spenceans, 'labour economists', Owenites and O'Brienites to the Marxists and Fabians, and most of its political impetus. There are localities – mainly London, but also some of the other cities whose history of artisan and labour agitation goes back continuously to beyond the Industrial Revolution – in which the religious or labour-sectarian labour militant has always been a curiosity. Secularism is the ideological thread which binds London labour history together, from the London Jacobins and Place, through the anti-religious Owenites and co-operators, the anti-religious journalists and booksellers, through the free-thinking Radicals who followed Holyoake and flocked to Bradlaugh's Hall of Science, to the Social Democratic Federation and the London Fabians with their unconcealed distaste for chapel rhetoric. In London even so quintessential a religious rebel as George Lansbury had to make his career in the atheist and Marxist S.D.F, for not even the chapel-tinted Independent Labour Party ever got much of a foothold there. But there is no denying that in Britain as a whole the links between traditional religion and labour movements were close, and far more important than in most other countries until a far later date. As late as 1929 out of 249 Labour M.P.s whose religious affiliations were investigated by a German scholar, only *eight* declared themselves to be agnostics or atheists.* There has been no similar enquiry since.

* F. Linden, *Sozialismus und Religion* (Leipzig 1932).

The precise relations between traditional religion and labour movements have been much debated, though generally on the basis of insufficient information or with a somewhat crippling denominational or political *parti-pris.** It may be convenient, before dealing with labour sectarianism as such, to summarize briefly what we know about the general relations between religion and the British working classes in the period since the Industrial Revolution.†

The period of the industrialization of Britain – *c.* 1790–1850 – was one of major religious change, for it saw the creation of Protestant nonconformity as a mass religion. The sects had been large and influential in the revolutionary 17th century, but in the course of the 18th they had lost considerable ground. The 'Old Dissenters', Independents, Baptists, English Presbyterians/Unitarians and Quakers were little more than smallish communities of the respectable middle and lower-middle class, somewhat eroded by the forces of Deism and rationalism. The Methodist Revival had made no large body of permanent converts before the French Revolution, when its adherents numbered rather less than 60,000. By 1851 the situation had changed fundamentally, for the Religious Census of that year demonstrated that the official Church of England

---

* Halévy's thesis that the rise of Methodism prevented revolution in Britain has been the foundation of most of these discussions. For a critical discussion, see my 'Methodism and the threat of revolution in Britain', in *Labouring Men* (London 1964). The bulk of the material has been collected by Methodist historians anxious to show the contribution of their groups to the labour movement, esp. R. Wearmouth, who has published a series of volumes on the subject, on which this chapter has drawn heavily. In recent years the slogan 'British Labour owes more to Wesley than to Marx' has spread obscurity rather than light.

† This summary is based mainly on the Religious Census of 1851 and on the statistics of membership of various religious denominations.

barely maintained its lead over the dissident Protestant sects in the country as a whole and was, with one exception, clearly outdistanced by them in the towns and industrial regions. Most of this astonishing mass conversion to Protestant sectarianism took place in the period between 1805 and 1850. Thus the Methodists grew from about 107,000 in 1805 to near on 600,000 in 1851, not counting an additional 125,000 of Calvinistic Methodists in Wales.* Conversion was clearly correlated with periods of economic and social strain. The most rapid years of Methodist expansion were in the Jacobin era (1793–5), the increasingly tense last years of the Napoleonic Wars (1805–16, especially 1813–16), the years of the Reform Bill and Poor Law (1831–4) which saw the highest annual rate of growth, and so on. What is equally significant, the expansion slackened and temporarily ceased for all sects in the first half of the 1850s, the only years in the century which saw a net decline in their numbers. These were the years of the decline of Chartism and Radicalism also. It is quite evident that there was a marked parallelism between the movements of religious, social and political consciousness.

How many among this mass of new converts were workers we do not know, for neither contemporary statisticians nor the records of the sects are very good at providing us with figures about the social composition of their populations. However, even if we agree that – as is highly probable – the appeal of Nonconformism diminished as we ascend from the border-zone between middle and working classes into the

* Wesleyans and Kilhamites for 1805, Wesleyans, Kilhamites, Primitive Methodists, Wesleyan Methodist Association, Wesleyan Methodist Reformers for 1851. The absence of useful statistics in the more decentralized Dissenting sects makes it difficult to give comparable figures for them; but see the 1851 Census for estimates.

upper bourgeoisie, or as we descend from it to the lower depths of wretchedness, it is clear that a great many workers were affected by this vast religious movement. Certainly many of them were swept into Nonconformity in the course of the periodic and semi-hysterical 'revivals' which are so characteristic of 19th-century Protestantism, and in the course of which the main numerical advances of the sects were made or initiated: 1797–1800, 1805–7, 1815–18, 1823–4, 1831–4, 1849, 1859, 1904–5.

Virtually all these conversions were to *sects* of one kind or another; for the increase in the Roman Catholic community was due to the immigration of Irish Catholics rather than to conversions from non-Catholic groups, and the absorption of some of the wealthier Nonconformists into the Church of England was a phenomenon of social ascent, not of religious conversion. What part did sectarian Christianity play in the life of the early industrial working class?

The proletarian strata to whom it clearly appealed most, were the newest and rawest. The skilled artisan class of a pre-industrial city like London had its established way of life and political agitation – Radical and Jacobin – though of course this too was often based on a transformed version of an earlier revolutionary Protestant Sectarianism.* Industrial towns like Sheffield were Painite and Owenite: there the tradesmen and smaller manufacturers were the chief Nonconformists. But new industrial areas, villages rapidly turned into industrial towns, had no pattern of life suited to the new age, and what is more, nobody who felt a responsibility for constructing any form of

---

* The remarks about working-class religion made below do *not* apply to these older and artisan groups, even those who were labour sectarians in their fashion. For an excellent description of such a community, L. J. Saunders, *Scottish Democracy 1815–1850* (Edinburgh 1950), 127.

human community, except perhaps the publican. Some, like many early coal-fields, were inhabited chiefly by an indigenous population which expanded by its own high birth-rate, forming tight isolated and remote centres, where men and women drew on the only spiritual resources at their disposal, pre-industrial custom and religion. These were the places which developed the folk-songs of early industrialism, which were later to be drowned in the flood of urbanization and immigration: colliers', weavers', seamen's songs. Others were agglomerations of natives and miscellaneous immigrants grouped round one or two basic industries. A third group, in which social disorganization was greatest, consisted of the vast accumulations of immigrants in cities like London and the port towns, in which men lived by an unclassifiable jumble of occupations, especially the unskilled ones. In such towns, medium or large, there could be no real question of recreating pre-industrial life on an adapted basis, as in the industrial villages.*

In all these areas life was, for the working class, miserable, poor, nasty, brutish, short and above all insecure, and the religions they chose for themselves mirrored their situation. Their worship was above all fervent. ('Lack of social security is compensated for by fervour of congregational response', Pope.) Visions of splendour, of judgement and of hellfire for the evil men filled those who needed support to bear the burden of their suffering, and the emotional orgies of hellfire preaching, revivals and similar occasions brought diversion into their

* The best account I know of working-class religion under early industrialism is L. Pope, *Millhands and Preachers* (Yale 1942), which deals with Gastonia, North Carolina, *c.* 1900–39. Though my account is based on British conditions, the religion of these mountain-poor-whites turned millworkers is so strikingly like that of 19th-century sectarians, that I shall from time to time use Pope to illustrate it.

lives. A lady describing the Courtauld mills in Essex in the 1840s observed the need for excitement which the girls felt when not obliged to be at work: 'When no other is provided, religious enthusiasm would occasionally take its place'.* They 'want plenty of blood' a minister said of his congregation. Only the poorest and socially most disorganized were perhaps below the level at which even religion could touch them, though the Salvation Army tried to reach them.

It was also totally untheological, unintellectual and emotional. It is characteristic of working-class sects that they were designed for the uneducated, so that passion and morality, in which the most ignorant can compete on equal terms, were the exclusive criteria of faith and salvation. All the sects which appealed to new industrial workers (as distinct from the older or better-off artisans) have tended to be 'ranting' sects, and Pope's observation is true also of Britain: 'they simply accept (theological) notions coming from a wide variety of sources and weld them together without regard for consistency'. For the same reasons it was also democratic: congregations participated in worship to a much greater extent than elsewhere, by choral singing, speaking with voices and 'testifying', by lay preaching (including that of women), and in the proliferating chapel committees and offices. Chapel democracy fused with chapel community, for one of the great things about the sect was that it provided a working-class community both with its own cohesion and scale of values in which the poor could outdo the rich – poverty became a symptom of grace, austerity of virtue, moral rigour contrasted with the laxity of the reprobate,

---

* Mary Merryweather, *Experience of Factory Life* (3d edn. London 1862), 18. Cf. Pope 90–1 for revivals turning into community festivals and 'prayer meetings are about the only entertainment we have', p. 89.

and a new spiritual status system replaced that of the secular world* – and with the community institutions which were otherwise almost totally lacking.

On the other hand – and this is what makes the British labour sects so remarkable – the sect normally dealt with the problems of the proletarian by evading them, or rather by solving them not for the class, but for the individual or a chosen group of the elect (hence probably the incurable tendency of the 'ranting' sects to split into a mass of independent rival conventicles). Religion was indeed expected to help, if only by means of magic and superstition† which might somehow control the fortunes to which they were subject – for instance to affect the prosperity and policy of their factory or mine. But economic conditions were a matter of fate, rather than for struggle. What counted was individual salvation: 'In the theology of the millworkers the world is a great battlefield on which the Lord and the Devil struggle for each individual soul. The "blood of Jesus" and the reading of the Bible turn the tide of victory to the Lord' (Pope). Politically the sectarian normally got only two things out of his religion: patience and a sort of etherealized revenge, as he 'looked for the wrath to come' like the numerous sects which spread during the Depression of the 1930s in Miss Jennings' Brynmawr‡ or the 'Lookers' about whom Gwyn Thomas writes in his admirable South Welsh novels. Both have been classically expressed in

---

* In the Gastonia 'Holiness' churches it runs: saved, sanctified, baptized with the Holy Ghost, baptized with water, having the first, second, third blessing etc. Pope, 137.

† 'Their religion is intimately related to the everyday struggles and vicissitudes of an insecure life, and proves useful for interpretation and succor. It "works" and "changes things".' Pope, 86.

‡ Hilda Jennings, *Brynmawr* (London 1934), 124.

Gerhart Hauptmann's *The Weavers*, a historically accurate impression of the Silesian Luddite riots of 1844, and I can do no better than to quote two speeches by an old sectarian from this remarkable play:

> Lord, we can't thank thee enough, because in thy grace and goodness thou hast brought us through this night also . . . and thou hast had pity on us. And we have come through this night without harm. 'Lord, thy goodness is infinite' and we are poor, evil and sinful children of man, not worthy of being trodden under thy feet, we are so rotten and full of sin. But thou, dear father, art willing to look at us and to have pity on us for the sake of thy son, our Lord and Saviour Jesus Christ. 'Jesu blood and justice is my adornment and my garment of splendour.' And even if we sometimes lose faith under thy chastisement, and if the furnace of thy purification burns a bit too hot for us, don't lose patience with us, and forgive us our trespasses. Give us patience, holy father in heaven, so that we may partake of thy eternal salvation after our sufferings are over. Amen.

And again:

> I tell you, Gottlieb, don't doubt the only thing that we poor humans have. Why else should I have sat here for forty year, treading the treadmill while that man over there lived in pride and gluttony and made gold out of my sorrow? Why? Because I have hope. Because I have something in my bitter need. You play your part in this world; I in the world beyond; that's what I thought when I looked over his house. And you can chop me into small pieces, I still have that certainty. It has been prophesied to us. There will be a judgment. But we shall not be the judges, but 'vengeance is mine', saith the Lord, our God.

In fact, the phrase 'opium of the people' is a far from inaccurate description of much of this sectarianism.* The bulk of labour religions were what Troeltsch has called non-aggressive sects, whose members concluded that the true believer must turn his back upon the world and looks forward only to the glory of eternal salvation, which his conversion has guaranteed. The obviously proletarian 'Walworth Jumpers', an extreme ecstatic sect of whom we possess a description,† pushed this to the final extreme of actually believing that they died with conversion, and were thereby reborn into eternal life: they would henceforth be immortal.

II

The labour sect as such is distinct from this sort of religion, because it is primarily *active*. The membership of the group is not only drawn primarily from wage-workers, but the entire sect is closely connected with labour and trade union movements, whether doctrinally, organizationally, or through the activities of its members. More: it is a search for a religious doctrine and organization to mirror not only the fate but the collective aspirations of the new class. In this extreme form it is rare. The only clear example I know of a sect formed as such because its members were class-conscious workers is a late and transitory phenomenon, the Labour Church; though other examples may well be discovered. What is far more

---

* 'Overtly, religion in mill churches appears to be indifferent to economic conditions; actually it is in part a product of those conditions and, by diverting attention from them, is indirectly a sanction on them', Pope, 91. It may perhaps be noted that this author is a Christian who strongly disliked the 'economic interpretation of history'.

† C. M. Davies, *Unorthodox London* (1873) I, 89 ff.

common is the partial transformation of a non-aggressive sect into a labour sect under the pressure of the social agitations of its members. In a mild way this is extremely common: working-class Wesleyans and others neglected the Toryism of their connexion to take part in Luddite, Radical and Chartist activities.* In spite of their other-worldliness (which included hostility to trade unions) the preachers in the Gastonia Churches of God and Pentecostal Holiness Churches often defended the strikers in the 1929 strike, simply because their churches were completely identified with the workers. But there are few examples of such sects in which trade union militancy has become systematic rather than exceptional. The *Primitive Methodists* are the best known.†

The Primitive Methodists broke away from the Wesleyans towards the end of the Napoleonic Wars, that is at the beginning of the period of massive industrial conversions. (A strikingly similar group, the *Bible Christians* whose strength lay in the West Country and later in Kent, broke away slightly earlier.) The ostensible reasons for the breach were disagreements on what we may call religious democracy. Wesleyanism, as we know, remained Arminian in theology, centralized, hierarchical and – insofar as the preacher was sharply distinct from the layman – sacerdotal in organization, high Tory in politics. Though it had won its footing as a non-intellectual faith, appealing to all directly through the emotions, which knew no class qualification, it was not without some inhibitions even

---

* Cf. Wearmouth, *Methodism and the Workingclass Movement 1800–1850* and my article in History Today, loc. cit.

† In addition to the Reports of the connexion, I have drawn on H. B. Kendall, *History of the Primitive Methodist Church*, 2 vols. (1906), Townsend, Workman and Eayrs, *A New History of Methodism*, 2 vols. (London 1909), and R. Wearmouth's works.

in its enthusiasm. Thus when American frontier evangelists invented the device of the 'camp meeting' at the end of the 18th century, which one of them brought to England a few years later, the official Wesleyans held aloof, being suspicious of these mass demonstrations of religious ecstasy where vast crowds were reduced to collective hysteria and mass conversion, as well as – the cynics said – to less godly forms of emotional release. The Primitive Methodists, whose nickname 'Ranters' indicates their style of preaching, welcomed them. Moreover, they insisted strongly on lay preaching, including – another point of discord and an almost certain sign of instinctive radicalism – on the right of women to preach.* Throughout its existence the sect had far and away the highest proportion of lay preachers. Though politics as such probably did not consciously enter into the matter, anti-Toryism may well have played a part. We know of at least one secession in what was to be a stronghold of Primitive Methodism, on the issue of both Parliamentary Reform and the question of whether preachers should not, like primitive Christians, forgo all reward for their evangelism, and at one point the new connexion almost committed itself officially to Radicalism.†

As we might expect, theology hardly entered consciously into the preaching of the Primitives, but the tone of their religion was harsh and implacable. Whatever its precise contents, the religion of the poor and insecure seems to require a sharp contrast between the gold of the redeemed and the flame-shot black of the damned, a combination which was perhaps best met by the hellfire and predestination of Calvinism. Given

---

* Jas. Bennett, *The History of Dissenters during the last 30 Years* (London 1839), 31–4.
† *Monthly Repository* vol. V (1820), 560, Wearmouth (1800–1850), 211–12.

the choice between a gentler and a stricter sect, they would invariably choose the stricter – for instance, in Lancashire, the strict calvinizing 'Particular Baptists' rather than the moderate ones.* It is perhaps worth observing that this was not a reflection of conditions peculiar to proletarians, for others were also poor and insecure. Unyielding and tragic forms of religion appealed equally to others whose life was isolated, hard, chancy and poor – to mountain farmers in the Appalachians as in the North and West of England (where they were often Primitive Methodists), to frontiersmen, above all to fishermen who, whether as Primitive Methodists in Grimsby and Yarmouth, or as members of various other forbidding sects in Norway and Holland, take to hellfire religion with a zeal which not even the alternative appeal (in Norway and Iceland) of Communism can rival. Labour religion is normally a special variant of a much more widespread sectarianism: that of the pre-industrial labouring poor, whether proletarian or not.

The new sect – it only emerged as such gradually – was from the first recognized as predominantly a working-class cult. Indeed, one has only to look at the photographs of its early chapels in Kendall's history, and at their addresses, to abandon all doubt on this point. The religious map of Britain is rather complex, and often the Primitives failed to penetrate a region which had been previously colonized by some other sect which there fulfilled the same function – for instance, in Cornwall, Dorset, the West Riding and Lincolnshire the Wesleyans themselves. They therefore became to some extent a regional religion. Their main strength lay in the North, particularly Durham, the East, particularly Norfolk, the miserable

* R. Halley, *Lancashire, its Puritanism and Nonconformity* (Manchester 1869) II, 482–4.

zone of petty and archaic industries in the West Midlands, and the Thames Valley villages. (In South Wales, incidentally, contrary to common conceptions, no kind of Methodism was strong, there being enough hellfire in the local Baptists and Congregationalists; in North Wales a quasi-national sect, the Welsh-preaching Calvinistic Methodists, predominated.)

Like the other sects, only to a more marked extent, the Primitives advanced most rapidly in the period of maximum social discontent and rapid industrialization between 1815 and 1848. In the second half of the century they lost some of their impetus, though they made some striking progress in newly industrialized zones lacking the structure of old-fashioned skilled labour, as in the East End of Sheffield, as distinct from the old cutlery area.* As a working-class sect, they were particularly sensitive to cyclical fluctuations and the movements of unemployment, and indeed normally explained any fluctuations in their numbers primarily in economic terms.† In general, they had lost their dynamism by the last quarter of the century, if not before.

The Primitives were not simply a working-class sect; they were pre-eminently a *village* labour sect; a fact amply attested and commented upon. That is why perhaps we find them in greatest force in certain areas of miners and farm-labourers, some of whom may well have read even more revolutionary implications into them than their brethren were normally willing to admit, for it is reported from Berkshire that the 1830 labourers' rick-burning was 'due to ranting; for they all say, do what you will, it is no sin'.‡ In area after area the strength

---

* Cf. the *Beehive* 15.6.1867.
† Wearmouth: *Methodism and the Working Class Movement 1850–1900*, p. 101.
‡ Royal Commission on the Poor Laws, *Parl. Papers* XXXIV of 1834, Rural questions 53: Sutton Wick, Berks.

of this sect is not in the medium-sized industrial town, let alone in the large city, inhospitable to working-class religion, but in the semi-village. This may explain why in 1850 the Primitives had half as many chapels again as the Wesleyans had ministers – 1555 and 1034 respectively – although they had less than a third of the Wesleyans' members. Thus in 1863–4 they had under 700 members in Newcastle-on-Tyne itself, but 800 in Shotley Bridge, and 700 in Thornley, which were mere villages. One is constantly struck by otherwise quite insignificant villages which were centres of this sect: Wangford (Suffolk), Rockland (Norfolk), Docking (Norfolk), Brinkworth (Wiltshire), Motcombe (Dorset), Minsterley (Shropshire). One would conclude that labour sects are phenomena of early, relatively undeveloped industrialism, the conditions which favour them tending to disappear as the modern pattern of urbanization and factory industry develops. Perhaps this is partly because the Primitives, like all working-class sects, functioned best in small congregations in which the nearest equivalent to simple democracy of the believers could operate, and the greatest degree of lay participation could obtain. It must not be forgotten that this was a sect of activists: up to 1853 it never contained much less than 10 per cent of members who were actually travelling or local preachers.*

This tendency to individual activity may help to explain the most startling fact about the Primitives, their close connexion with trade unionism. In fact, it is not too much to think of them as primarily a sect of trade union cadres. When Lord Londonderry evicted his striking miners in 1844 two-thirds of the Durham Primitive Methodist circuit became homeless. Practically all leaders of the Northumberland and Durham

* *Religious Census of 1851*, lxxxii.

miners in the 19th century belonged to the sect: Hepburn, Burt, Fenwick, John Wilson, William Crawford, John Johnson, Peter Lee. They were disproportionately strong even in other coalfields, where they were numerically much weaker. Yorkshire miners' leaders like Parrott and Cowey, Midland leaders like Enoch Edwards, Albert Stanley, Sam Finney, Derbyshire ones like Barnett Kenyon, Clevelanders like Toyn, Cumbrians like Tom Cape, were all Primitive Methodists. The same is true of the agricultural labourers' unions: Joseph Arch, George Edwards, Edwin Gooch are the obvious names which spring to mind, but there were areas, as in Norfolk, where the union emerged virtually as a direct offshoot of the Chapel. This trade unionist bias of the sect is all the more striking, since other sects – for instance the Wesleyans – were far less successful in producing union leaders; indeed the only important-19th century union leaders of Wesleyan provenance seem to have been Henry Broadhurst, the mason, Ben Pickard of the Yorkshire miners, and Arthur Henderson, although the Wesleyans were about five times as numerous as the Primitives. Only in remote places like Dorset did they play the same sort of role: three of the six Tolpuddle martyrs were Wesleyan lay preachers.

It may be noted that the *direct* connexion between Primitive Methodism and the labour movement was small. Primitive doctrine, though sympathetic to the cause of Radicalism, Reform, total abstinence and various other movements of the Left, was not notably more so than the rest of Nonconformity and rather less so than some groups among the Old Dissenters – e.g. the Congregationalists and Unitarians. The leaders of the sect were, as is obvious, favourable to trade unions and under certain circumstances to strikes, but no more so than one would expect of a sect whose members took to both so enthusiastically. It is difficult to see any trace of collectivist political or economic ideas among them, though their historian points out, correctly I think, that the rise of the temperance movement, and its more intensive form, total abstinence, 'began to breathe upon the society and the Churches, softening the hard outlines of individualism and blending men together in a conscious community of interest'.* In fact, if we did not know how close the connexion between the Primitives and organized labour was, we should not easily guess it from an inspection of their doctrines and organization.

What, then, made them into so marked a labour sect? *First*, I suggest, the general suitability of their kind of evangelistic technique and doctrine to their kind of working class. *Second*, the Hebraism of old Testament preaching which made all who took to it like the ancient prophets a stiff-necked people unwilling to bow down in the House of Rimmon. It is perfectly evident that nothing in Primitive Methodist teaching discouraged organization for working-class defence, and much encouraged it. *Third*, their organization. Dr Wearmouth has described the numerous borrowings of labour movements from Methodism at length, and though he overstates the case, it remains strong. Chapel, and particularly the small self-contained village chapel, provided a school of organization for all purposes, and among both miners and farm-labourers we can often see the union borrowing the very formulae of the sect.† Above all, the anti-sacerdotal nature of the sect provided a first-rate mechanism for selecting and training leaders and cadres. Without education, and without any social sanction

---

* Kendall, *op. cit.*, I, 474.
† One such document, from the Norfolk farm-labourers, is reprinted in my *Labour's Turning Point* (London 1948), 89.

against 'making himself prominent', the lay preacher could
come forward among his fellows; and the practice of preaching
gave him self-confidence and facility. The trade union leader
who is also a lay preacher is still fairly common, especially
among miners. Primitive Methodism was thus not specifically
made to the measure of class-conscious workers: few sects of
importance were, and even those were normally evanescent.
But where it took root among workers, its remarkable technical
suitability could hardly fail to turn it into a school of cadres.*

But the sect and the labour movement were – especially
among the cadres and leaders of the movement – connected in
another way; by the process of *conversion*; that is to say, by the
sudden, emotionally overpowering realization of sin and the
finding of grace which Methodism, pre-eminently a doctrine
of the adult man's 'New Birth', encouraged. (It may be significant that another 'New Birth' sect, the Baptists, were perhaps
second only to the Primitive Methodists in their appeal to
the manual workers.) Among a remarkably large number
of labour leaders political consciousness and activity began
with or shortly after such a conversion. Arthur Henderson
found religion at the age of 16. 'Life began with his conversion'.† Fenwick, Batey (secretary of the Colliery Mechanics),
Reid (agent for the Northumberland and Durham Miners'
Permanent Relief Fund), Peter Lee of the Durham miners,
Parrott of the Midland miners, Samuel Jacks of Dewsbury,
Bloor of the Staffordshire Underground Firemen, Kenyon of

* 'Natural leaders among the workers find in Church almost their only vehicle
for expression of leadership; this fact helps to explain the continuing popularity
of "testimony meetings" in which a number of worshippers are given opportunity to speak, and the comparatively large number of officers and committees
found in mill churches.' Pope, 89.
† Wearmouth (1850–1900), 174.

the Derbyshire miners, George Edwards of the Norfolk farm-labourers, are among those who experienced conversion in their 'teens (i.e. who were not, as many other unionists were, born into a sect). J. H. Thomas of the railwaymen became a Baptist in his 'teens, Fred Messer, a Labour M.P., at the age of twenty-one. Later conversions, such as that of John Wilson of the Durham miners, seem to have been rarer. On the other hand very early ones, and so-called 'boy-preachers', were not uncommon. George Dallas, a farm-labourer and later leader of the Workers' Union and M.P., taught Sunday school at 17. C. Simons, an M.P., was a lay preacher at 16; W. J. Brown of the Civil Service Clerical Association, A. J. Cook and Arthur Horner of the South Wales Miners and Communist Party, all began as boy-preachers. I may perhaps add that representative statistics are hard to come by. Even the only good enquiry into the religion of Labour M.P.s, Franz Linden's, is not quite satisfactory, and there is no representative survey of trade union leaders. Hence these impressions may well be mistaken, but the figures are all the more impressive when we remember that many labour people were in fact born into a sect and thus either had no need for conversion or did not specially record it.

In the absence of further biographical data one hesitates to analyse these conversions too closely. All one can say about them is that they indicated a sudden change in a man's attitude to life in general, that is to say to his everyday activities as well as to his spiritual exercises; for the characteristic attitude of the labour sectarian was this-worldly and non-mystical, or if mystical, disciplined to this-worldly activity. It is therefore not surprising that conversion indicated, reflected, or perhaps stimulated the kind of unselfish activity which labour militancy inevitably implied. For then as now, the man who takes his labour activity seriously is to some extent a dedicated man, who renounces other and often superficially more attractive activities, including the making of money. Conversion of some kind is, of course, a commonplace in labour movements. British ones, however, are peculiarly archaic insofar as the conversion was normally a traditionally religious one, or a political one which took religious form.

We may, in passing, ask the question whether there was any difference between labour cadres and the rank and file in religious matters. One would expect it, but we cannot tell. The analysis of the 1929 Labour M.P.s is inconclusive. Of the 249 who gave information about their religion only 47 were Anglicans – obviously a much smaller percentage than the national one, 51 Methodists of various kinds, 42 Old Dissenters (Independents, Baptists, Unitarians, Quakers), 17 Presbyterians, 3 Jews, 18 Catholics, 8 agnostics or atheists, and the balance non-denominational Christians, mainly, one would say, tending towards Nonconformity. But Labour M.P.s were drawn largely from areas where the Anglicans were abnormally weak, such as the North, Wales and Scotland, and do not therefore reflect the religious composition of the population accurately. There is some reason to believe that labour cadres have always tended to take to ideologies, religious or otherwise, more than the rest. Thus in late 19th-century Britain Secularism, in mid-19th-century France Positivism, became for a while something like a religion of activists or craft union leaders, though their mass following was small.* But the matter must be left in suspense.

The Primitive Methodists were the product of the earliest

---

* R. Goetz-Girey, *La Pensée Syndicale Française* (1948), 24. Keufer of the printers, Isidore Finance of the housepainters, the chief pillars of Reformism, were Positivists.

stage of industrialization. How late the forces tending to create labour sects remained active is demonstrated by the history of one of the few labour sects deliberately created as such, John Trevor's Labour Church,* founded in Manchester in 1891. Characteristically, the Labour Church did not last. Its chief function was to lubricate the passage of Northern workers from Liberal Radicalism to an Independent Labour Party, and having done this it disappeared, except insofar as it continued in a few towns to provide a useful neutral meeting-place of non-denominational Socialism for the various groups on the left. But the interesting point about the Labour Church is not that it failed, but that a phenomenon of its kind should still have appeared natural in Britain at the end of the 19th century.

The founder of the Church, John Trevor, has described his and its evolution in a verbose but interesting autobiography.† Briefly, he had been born into an ambitious lower-middle class family and into a small sect of extremely hellfire-conscious Baptists of the kind which tends to split off from larger bodies in order to ensure the purity of the real believers and to separate the true elect from the damned. After a period of childhood pietism he lost his faith in the middle 1870s, but regained it, after a period of doubt, in the form of an extremely attentuated deism. The 1880s added a social conscience to his other theological perplexities. He tried, with the help of Philip Wicksteed, to find a niche in Unitarianism, but grew dissatisfied with all organized religion and founded the Labour

---

* The most convenient account of this odd movement is in K. S. Inglis *The Churches and the Working Classes in Victorian England* (London 1963). The present sketch is based on the Churches' journal, the *Labour Prophet (1892–8)*, the MS. records of the Birmingham Labour Church, and various contemporary biographical materials.
† *My Quest for God*, 1898.

Church. Its theology is difficult to describe, because it hardly existed. It was certainly not Christian in any traditional sense. Trevor himself believed that

> God is in the Labour movement. This is the word of our prophecy ... The great religious movement of our time is the movement for the emancipation of labour ... Labour is saving the churches far more than the churches are saving labour. And just as it is necessary for labour, if it would secure its own salvation (which involves the salvation of all society) to be independent of either political party, so it is necessary for labour, if it would be strong with religious life, to realize that it has a religion of its own which can make it independent of the particular doctrine of any church, be it never so 'liberal'.*

So long as the Labour Movement had a religion of its own, it did not greatly matter what it was, and Trevor, who believed it should 'stand securely alone, without priest, without parson, without creed, without tradition, without Bible' was not the one to define its dogmas. But, as the principles of the Labour Church Union stated, it was 'not a class religion, but unites members of all classes working for the abolition of commercial slavery'.†

In fact, the Churches which spread rapidly in practice shared neither Trevor's theology nor his rejection of class religion. They consisted overwhelmingly of workers, grown up in the atmosphere of protestant sectarian dissent, who found it impossible to conceive that a political and economic break with capitalism should not also lead to a religious breach. In Bradford, where there had long been talk of setting

---

* *Labour Prophet* (1892), p. 4.
† Pelling, *Origins of the Labour Party* (1954), 143.

up a separate church, this was not done 'until several of the
Nonconformist leaders in the town had manifested a marked
antipathy to the candidature of [the Socialist] Ben Tillet'.* In
Plymouth the question was asked: 'Why have [the Labour
Church congregations] not been to hear the gospel preached
by some denomination or other? Because Nonconformists as
well as the State Church in their preachings have been blas-
pheming and libelling the Nazarene Carpenter, telling men to
be content with that position which it has pleased God to place
them in.'† Seth Ackroyd, of the Hull Labour Church, an ex-
Wesleyan machine-sawyer of great moral energy, put it clearly:

> The workers feel that the Christian Churches have been (like
> the public Press) captured by the capitalist; and the minister
> who speaks out, has speedily to move on, and make way for one
> who will sell his office and his soul. We see that ecclesiastical
> organizations have thus become part and parcel of the com-
> petitive capitalist system; and as they are run in the interests
> of the employers, it is needful that the employed should have
> their own Church, their own service which shall be to them
> a Sunday home, and the influence of which shall develop all
> that is best and noblest in their characters. Combination is the
> only salvation of the workers. But for successful combination,
> character is necessary. Hence a Labour Church, as the maker
> of character, is necessary to the true interests of the workers.‡

To those brought up in a dissenting atmosphere, nothing
would seem more natural than to form another sect on the

---

* *Labour Prophet* (1892), p. 64.
† *Labour Prophet* (1893), p. 8.
‡ Seth Ackroyd, 'Labour's Case for a Labour Church', *ibid.*, (1897), 1–3.

traditional model, and the Labour Church, with the familiar dissenting forms of worship – the sermons, hymns, brass
bands, children's outings – expressed the new socialist ideology in the familiar terms of their experience. It was never
more than a minor phenomenon, though the Churches spread
quite rapidly in the North. I estimate their full membership
at perhaps 2000 in the middle 1890s, and rather more previously. Attendance was not, however, confined to members;
congregations of several hundreds are reported by quite
small Churches in the early 1890s, and the Birmingham
Church ordered 100 hymn-books in 1892. At the peak of
the movement there were such churches in 24 places, 16
of them in Lancashire and the West Riding. Manchester
and Bradford, with perhaps 300 members, were the largest,
though the former declined rapidly, Halifax, Leeds, Hyde
and Birmingham with 100–130 the next largest. Several
of the churches were prolongations of some secular labour
body, normally the Independent Labour Party – Bolton,
Bradshaw, Farnworth and Morley were actually governed
by the local I.L.P. executive, and Plymouth was an offshoot
of the Gasworkers' Union.* Most of them declined as the
energy of their active members was absorbed by a primarily secular socialist body; for even on the ideological plane
the propaganda of other socialist organizations and of the
Clarion – whose editor, Blatchford, was to become a propagandist of free-thought – counteracted that of traditional labour
sectarianism. By the end of the century the Churches were
no longer a serious movement. The I.L.P. was their chief heir,
but, though a whiff of the dissenting chapel continued to hang
round its oratory, it was no longer a labour sect, but a secular

* *Ibid.*, (1894), 127.

political party. The chief historic interest of the Churches is thus as one of the forms of organization developed by northern workers in the process of separating themselves, politically and ideologically, from the Liberal Party.

III

The reasons for the abnormal development of labour sectarianism in the British Isles are not far to seek. It was the achievement or the penalty of the social pioneer, for it is the irony of history that the pioneer revolutionary preserves far more of what he revolts against than later comers. The ideology of political labour movements descends from that of its bourgeois-revolutionary predecessors – most socialist movements passed through a stage of left-wing Jacobinism before developing their independent theories. But in the British Isles alone was bourgeois revolution fought and won before secular ideology had reached the masses or the middle classes. The declaration of the Rights of Man established itself among the British people, not in the Roman toga and the illuminist prose of the late 18th century, but in the mantle of the Old Testament prophets and in the biblical language of Bunyan: the Bible, the *Pilgrim's Progress* and Foxe's *Book of Martyrs* were the texts from which English labouring men learned the A.B.C. of politics, if not the A.B.C. of reading. It was thus as natural for the common people to use religious language to express their first aspirations, as it was natural for American orators and judges to continue re-echoing the balanced periods of 18th-century prose long after they had passed out of currency elsewhere. For nothing marks a people more deeply than the major revolutions it has undergone.

Moreover, though the revolution of the dissenting sectaries

of the 17th century was defeated, and indeed the social basis of their sectarianism was largely destroyed, the fact of Dissent was officially recognized. There was henceforth in England a sort of religion which was not identified with the State and the powers that be, if not actually in opposition to both. Even revolutionary anti-clericalism, an almost universal phenomenon of the period of middle-class revolution and the earlier labour movement, was thus not compelled to be either schismatic or anti-religious. What was Voltairean in 19th-century France, was Nonconformist in 19th-century Britain, a fact which has led superficial observers to overlook the remarkable similarities between the political phenomena of anti-clericalism in both countries. Moreover, the sect was not merely an expression of institutionalized dissent, but a flexible form of popular organization for all purposes, including that of agitation on practical matters. Nothing was more natural than that groups of early industrial workers should adopt so obvious a form, and one which lay so close to their hands, if nobody taught them a better one.

And who would? The groups of artisans and journeymen craftsmen in the pre-industrial cities – London, Sheffield, Norwich and the like – had slowly developed their specific forms of craft unionism out of the older journeymen's societies, and their specific form of agnostic Jacobinism out of the relics of 17th-century sectarianism; or else they maintained among themselves the hard core of passionate and intellectual Leveller puritanism, as Mark Rutherford has painted it in the figure of Zachariah Coleman in *The Revolution in Tanner's Lane*: not a ranter or revivalist but a moderate Calvinist, a great reader of Bunyan and Milton, a great arguer and Republican. Or perhaps, out of all these such small groups of the educated and militant developed such sects as the 'Rational Society' of the Owenites who founded Rochdale co-operation.* But beside such groups, with their long and continuous tradition of political and trade unionist awareness, there were the masses of workers who flocked into the towns from the country, and the masses who grew up as an agricultural proletariat, or an industrial proletariat or semi-proletariat in villages remote from the world of radical politics, helpless, ignorant – indeed often more illiterate than their predecessors before industrialization. Theirs was a pre-political discontent, and the propaganda of the radicals and freethinkers from the cities could often as yet hardly affect them, even when it reached them: the Northern miners in England remained largely remote from Chartism, even when their peculiar rhythm of discontent happened to be in phase with that of the general movements. The operatives in Northern France were remote from the 1848 revolution and struck or rioted merely for wages and against Belgian immigrants: not until 1851 did Republicanism make a little headway among them. Normally such groups were proselytized by apostles from the outside, who showed them the way at a time when they were ready to follow, but would not have been ready to develop ambitious labour organizations on their own. Thus the men of the First International in the early 1870s, the Marxian Socialists in the late 1880s, and (as in the Gastonia cotton mills of 1929) the Communists, became the pioneer organizers, and often the result was that the masses to whom they brought the new teaching were solidly and permanently converted to the new faith. The rise of the Socialist union and the Socialist vote in many an area of remote and neglected industrial villages and mines could be startlingly sudden: in the Liege area in 1886 the workers were reported 'to abhor

* G. D. H. Cole, *A Century of Co-operation* (1944), cap. III–IV.

Socialists', but by the early '90s 80 per cent – in the Vesdre valley 90 per cent – of them voted for Socialists.* But this could only happen where industrialization took place so late that backward areas could be absorbed into an already existing and active 'modern' movement before too long. In Britain, where industrialism was far older, some sort of labour movement had often to be constructed long before 'modern' bodies were available to provide leadership, ideology and a programme.

In such conditions the labour sect had to fill the gap, for want of anything better.† It had few political obstacles to overcome, for its political approach did not differ from that of secular working-class and Radical movements, and where it did, the sectarians soon assimilated it to the general pattern of radical democracy. Sectarianism did not inhibit co-operation with, or learning from, the secular Radicals and Socialists: Zachariah Coleman co-operated readily with his godless contemporaries, as the South Wales miners, dissenting sectarians almost to a man, followed the freethinker Zephaniah Williams in the Newport rising.‡ Those who fought for the same cause fought together, a fact which made it easy subsequently for the Labour Churches to try to unify all sections of the political labour movement, a body always given to its own sectarian

* A. Swaine, 'Heimarbeit in der Gewehrindustrie von Luettich', *Jahrb. f. Nationaloekonomie* 3d. Ser. XII, (1896), p. 218.

† 'With my study of theology, I soon began to realize that the social conditions of the people were not as God intended they should be. The gross injustices meted out to my parents and the terrible sufferings I had undergone in my boyhood burned themselves into my soul like a hot iron. Many a time did I vow I would do something to better the conditions of my class.' George Edwards, *From Crow-Scaring to Westminster* (1957 edn.), 36. Edwards, the leader of the Norfolk farmworkers union, was converted to Primitive Methodism in 1869 and became a militant unionist as soon as Joseph Arch appeared.

‡ David Williams, *John Frost* (1939), 150, and 324 for religions of rioters.

quarrels. The labour sect was thus easily absorbed into the general current of left-wing activity, and it had the inestimable and treble advantage of clothing the social protest of the workers in the familiar and powerful language of the Bible, of doing so by methods within the reach of the least educated and qualified workers, and of providing them, as we have seen, with invaluable schooling and experience.

However, it also had its limitations. Sociologically, it tended, like all groups of its kind, to lose its character as a single-class sect of labouring men, all the more easily for not being theoretically committed to a community of a class, but to one of true believers irrespective of class. Unless it kept itself pure by periodic secession, as many tiny but uninfluential sects of labourers did in many towns, it inevitably tended to produce its crop of brethren who did well in the world, and adopted the views of the middle classes; and these normally tended to occupy leading positions in the congregations and nationally. Only the most unified communities, in which social ascent was virtually impossible except through the united action of labour, remained partly immune to this: pit villages for instance. Theologically, it suffered from the drawback of all Christian groups, which are committed by their Scriptures both to rebellion and (through St. Paul) to accepting existing government as morally good. The ambiguity of Christian teaching is not beyond the power of suitable exegesis or casuistry to spirit away, but it remains an obstacle to the construction of a consistently social-revolutionary doctrine. Lastly, it suffered from the fragmentary nature of its teaching; for, as we have seen, it rarely – in its activist forms – produced a comprehensive programme of political and social action, but chiefly gave effective expression to such programmes elaborated elsewhere. Labour sects produced no theorists of importance.

What radical or socialist theory emerged from them, came out of the rationalized and Jacobinized 'Old Dissenters' of 18th-century vintage – the Unitarians, the Quakers and perhaps some Congregationalists – and was lost in the main tradition of Rationalism and Jacobinism. There was no working-class Christian Socialism of importance; merely the standard kind of Socialism, elaborated by the secular thinkers, and translated into the familiar Biblical terminology.

The labour sect therefore contributed much less than one might have expected from its numerical importance to the evolution of the British Labour Movement; so much so that its practical contribution can be reduced to little more than a few organizational and propagandist devices, and to some invaluable pioneering work among certain groups of miners and farm-labourers. As we have seen, it lost its importance by the end of the 19th century, except perhaps – and for the reasons given in the preceding paragraph – as a tradition which helped to reinforce the already very strong moderate and reformist bias of the British Labour Movement. It long remained a training-ground for labour cadres; and as Seth Ackroyd of Hull correctly saw, this was its chief practical function. These cadres were by no means necessarily moderate: we have seen that so native a revolutionary as Arthur Horner of the Welsh miners came out of the sectarian atmosphere. However, even this function has declined. The Marxist organizations since the 1880s, the adult education movements since the early 1900s, took over most of those functions, except for one or two specialized groups. Labour sectarianism has withered away, even though its spirit is still far from dead in areas like Southwest Wales or in some remote agricultural villages. It was perhaps best suited to the early radical-democratic phase of the labour movement, and it has declined with working-class Radicalism.

Chapter IX

Ritual in Social Movements

All human organizations have their ceremonial or ritual sides, but modern social movements are surprisingly lacking in deliberately contrived ritual. Officially, what binds their members together is content and not form. The docker or doctor who takes out a card of his union or professional organization (assuming that this is an act of free choice) knows, without special formalities, that he is committing himself to certain activities and forms of behaviour, such as solidarity with his colleagues. The prospective member of a Communist Party commits himself or herself to an intense and demanding set of activities and duties comparable, for some members at least, to that accepted by religious orders. But he or she does so with no greater ceremony than the taking of a piece of paste-board of purely utilitarian design, on which stamps are periodically stuck.

Obviously this does not eliminate ritual from trade unions and political parties. Where the plans of their founders or leaders take no account of it, it has a knack of developing

spontaneously, if only because human beings like to ritu-
alize and formalize their relationships with one another.
Demonstrations, whose original purpose in labour movements
was utilitarian – to demonstrate the massed strength of the
workers to their adversaries, and to encourage their supporters
by demonstrating it, become ceremonies of solidarity whose
value, for many participants, lies as much in the experience
of 'one-ness' as in any practical object they may seek to
achieve. A set of ritual furnishings may arise: banners, flags,
massed singing and so on. In organizations whose spontaneous development is less inhibited by rationalism than labour
movements, the urge to create ritual may flourish like tropical
undergrowth. American party conventions are perhaps the
most striking instances. But the fact that men give ritual significance to their actions, so that the annual card-exchange
in some Communist Parties is a much more solemn occasion
than a simple acquisition of a new piece of paste-board, is
of secondary importance. What holds Communists together
is the content of the party they join; what holds American
Democrats together is not the antics at their quadrennial
Conventions.

In primitive social movements in Europe form plays
a vastly more important part, though of course the clear
modern distinction between form and content hardly occurs
to their members. Neither can properly exist without the
other. Students of the Middle Ages are familiar with such
phenomena. Subjects owe allegiance to the King, but if the
King does not fulfil certain formal demands, e.g. of having
been crowned and anointed at Rheims, his rights and their
duties are much more questionable. Only a journeyman smith
can join the society of journeymen smiths, but unless he has
joined it in due and proper form at the appointed time and

place, and with the correct answers and responses, he is not 'really' a member and may be refused his rights or refuse his duties. Not to have been baptized or married in the correct ritual way or at the correct ritual moment may, even today, jeopardize a man's membership of religious communities. Such excessive legalism can be, and has been, rationally justified, at least insofar as it permeates legal systems, especially those based on a common law tradition. It may be argued that the meticulous adherence to technical procedures guarantees the rule of law, even though individual criminals may have their convictions quashed because of ritual inaccuracies in their prosecution. It may also be argued, in illiterate societies, or in organizations run largely by rather stupid people such as many armies, that even very slight departures from a rigorously fixed traditional procedure lead either to increasing divergences from customary practice, or to chaos and confusion. Nevertheless, a good deal of the insistence on literal accuracy in ritual observances is not in fact rational in our sense. The argument that Jews are circumcised because there may be medical advantages in circumcision is not the one which has made Jewish parents circumcise their sons throughout the ages.

We may distinguish a number of elements in this formalism of primitive social movements. First, there is the importance of binding forms of *initiation*. In voluntary bodies such as social movements this normally takes the form of a ceremony, undertaken by men and women capable of making a conscious choice (i.e. not before puberty); hence the stress on adult as against infant baptism among revolutionary 16th-century sects. The initiation may, by the terms of its ritual, serve to bind the member closely to the organization, e.g. by causing him or her to break normal taboos, as in the case of the fraternities of conscious social outsiders like robbers.* Again, more commonly, it may establish a particularly solemn and magic atmosphere designed to impress the candidate with the seriousness of the step he is about to take, or – though this may be a later, degenerate stage – by impressing upon him the sanctions to which a breach of loyalty will expose him. The candidate may be 'tested' or examined in various ways. The actual initiation may culminate in a ritual act such as the laying on of hands, but will normally contain some solemn oath or declaration by the candidate which binds him by his personal choice.

Next, there are *ceremonials of periodic meeting*, which from time to time reaffirm the unity of the members: meetings, processions, joint acts of worship or the like. Third, there are what we may call the *practical rituals* which permit the members to carry out their functions effectively, such as secret and formal recognition signs – the 'Mason Word',† the Freemason's handclasp, passwords and so forth.

Lastly, most important and most pervasive, is *symbolism*. In primitive organizations this is what united form and content. The symbolism to which we are accustomed in modern movements – the badge, the flag, the symbolic figure, etc. – is a pale and degenerate version of the real thing. It is true that for the Socialist or Communist today a red flag, a five-pointed star, a hammer and sickle (symbolizing, I take it, the unity of worker and peasant), may be a shorthand expression for his movement: its programme and aspirations, its achievements,

---

* F. C. B. Avé-Lallemant, *Das Deutsche Gaunerthum*, 4 vols. (Leipzig 1858) gives some interesting, and in the nature of the case, distasteful examples. See also Chapter II.

† D. Knoop and G. P. Jones, *The Genesis of Freemasonry* (Manchester 1947), 96–107.

its collective existence and emotional power, and may evoke them all. But in primitive movements, as in Gothic cathedrals, an entire universe of symbolism and allegory may exist, each piece corresponding to, and indeed 'being', a specific piece, small or large, of the entire ideology and movement. The elaborately allegorical banners and letterheads of 19th-century British trade unions* are a somewhat enfeebled version of this. Masonic symbolism is perhaps the best-known type of such a universe outside the established religions and – for our purposes – the most influential. The amount of misplaced ingenuity which in the past went into the elaboration of such universes of symbolism, each item of which might have a different meaning to members of different 'grades' in the organization, is quite staggering. Most of it had little bearing on the function of an organization, as a social movement, for these were and are, at any given moment, concrete and limited. When taken over from past organizations and traditions, most symbolism therefore remained chiefly as a sort of emotional furniture which social movements used for much less elaborate purposes than those for which it had originally been built.

II

Where should we expect to find primitivism of this sort in 19th-century social movements? First, in organizations which because they were or had to be secret, or because their revolutionary aims were extremely ambitious, imposed an exceptional degree of cohesion on their members; second, in

* The 'emblem' of the Dockers' Union (1889) is fully described in my *Labour's Turning Point* (London 1948), 87–8. There is room for a discussion of the symbolism of early British trade unions, some of whose banners may still be admired.

organizations which, because they derived from older bodies and traditions, retained exceptionally lively links with the primitive past. In other words, on the one hand in secret revolutionary societies and orders, on the other in trade unions and friendly societies, especially those descended from skilled independent artisans. The family of societies which we may call 'masonic' provides a link between the two groups. This does not, of course, exhaust the possibilities.

The early trade union organizations, friendly societies, or even the unofficial customs and conventions of the workers at their place of work, do indeed show numerous traces of primitivism. Since practically all of them ended in drink, in Britain our fullest catalogues of such ceremonies – but one somewhat lacking in nonalcoholic detail – comes from zealous temperance advocates like John Dunlop* who were anxious to acquaint the public with the multiplicity of obstacles facing the sober Briton.

Let us consider *initiation*, which might be initiation into a trade (as when the apprentice became journeyman), into an organization (as when the journeyman became a member of his *compagnonnage* or society, often as the automatic corollary of the first initiation), or into a new job or lodge (as when a journeyman arrived in a foreign town). Such ritualization of 'beginnings' remained almost universal in Britain in the first half of the 19th century. Thus among the coachmakers the new apprentice was ceremonially bound; each new kind of work he attempted was celebrated; the new journeyman must ceremonially get his 'footing'; the change from one bench to another in the workshop, the first visit of a man's wife to the

---

* *Artificial and Compulsory Drinking Usages of the United Kingdom*, various and increasingly full editions.

shop, his marriage and the birth of each child were commemorated, and a new partner of the employer was 'kicked' in a
supper to the men. At the beginning of the winter season the
men received a 'waygoose'. On the delivery of a coach the cus-
tomer's coachman received a present. The journeyman most
recently arrived in the shop became 'constable' and received
a staff, ceremonially presented. New clothes were sometimes,
though not always, 'wetted'. And so on. These usages were
fairly standardized throughout the crafts.

If we bear in mind this widespread practice of ceremonially
celebrating any beginning, or indeed any formal change in
the life of man, it will be easier to understand the heightened
ceremony which surrounded the initiation of a man into the
special group of his fellows, one designated to demonstrate its
utter difference from other groups and to bind him to it by the
strongest conceivable links. It combined awe, the element of
testing the candidate and that of instructing him in the mys-
teries of the group, and naturally culminated in some form
of most solemn declaration – normally an oath – and some
ceremony symbolizing adoption into the group. The most
elaborate rituals of this kind seem to have been the ones of
the French journeymen's associations (*compagnonnages*), though
they only follow a pattern which becomes increasingly familiar
to the student of the ritual society.* The *compagnonnages* were
peculiar in being not merely associations of particular trades,
but wider fraternities including a variety of crafts, though originally they appear to have grown out of the building trades,
and thus have much in common with the early stages of free-

---

* For a good description, 'Office du Travail', *Les Associations Professionelles
Ouvrières*, 4 vols., esp. vol. I (1894), cap. ii, pp. 90 ff. For full references, see R.
Lecotté, *Essai Bibliographique sur les Compagnonnages de tous les Devoirs du Tour de
France et Associations Ouvrières à forme initiatique* (Paris 1951).

masonry. There appear to have been originally two main rival fraternities, the *Enfants du Père Soubise* (originally carpenters, later also certain other building crafts) and the *Enfants du Maître Jacques* (originally stonemasons, carpenters and joiners, and locksmiths, later a wide variety of crafts); a third, the *Enfants de Salomon*, though claiming great antiquity, may have been a very late breakaway, which did not fully develop until the 19th century, and was confined mainly to builders of various sorts.* The secret initiation ritual of such bodies were remarkable ceremonies indeed. The candidate first passed the 'épreuve de travail' – presumably to show his knowledge of the craft. The actual ceremony began earlier in the evening, but had to take place at midnight. Before that time the candidate was three times led into the initiation chamber for various formal purposes, and three times led out again. In the chamber he was surrounded by a circle of the brethren, and faced the three officials. He was introduced by the *rouleur* with three taps of his stick. The chamber was decorated with a white canopy and contained an altar, on which stood a crucifix and six torches. (The reader may be spared the symbolic significance of all this.) A dagger lay on the altar, its point tied to a red ribbon which symbolized the candidates' blood which he was ready to shed rather than revealing the brotherhood's secrets. The 'table-cloth', which, as we shall see, played an important part in the ceremonies of periodic meeting, lay in front of the altar carrying on one plate the candidate's future brotherhood 'colours', on another the selection of his society 'names', one of which he would choose – normally a ritual combination of his place of origin with some moral or other quality –, and a bottle

---

* The very well-informed article *Compagnonnage in the Larousse du XIX Siècle* gives the exact ranges of membership.

with the wine to baptize him. The candidate then declared his willingness to join in a ritual exchange of question and answer. He was thereupon tested, being at the same time blindfolded.

The tests included ordinary 'hazing', painful ordeals, or humiliating and ridiculous practices of one kind or another (those of the Soubise carpenters were particularly brutal) and moral tests such as the request to abandon his family or religion, to commit a crime for the brotherhood or to kill a man, a test which was reproduced with so much fidelity that the blindfolded candidate often remained for some time in the belief that he had actually plunged his knife into someone. Having passed the tests, he took the oath faithfully and for ever to keep the brotherhood's secrets:

> I should prefer and deserve to have my throat cut, my body burned, my ashes thrown to the wind; I promise to plunge a dagger into the breast of whoever becomes a perjurer; let the same be done to me if I become one.

Sometimes there was also a blood-test: the candidate's blood was tapped and he signed in it, or at least a nominal drop was taken and he pretended to sign in that. Sometimes the test by burning was made: a lighted candle was stubbed against the candidate's left nipple.

The oath was repeated three times, after which the candidate received his society name, chose a godfather and a 'godmother' and a 'priest'* from those present, and was baptized with wine.†

---

* By the 19th century he was merely called a 'witness'; but mid-17th-century reports – shortly before the official theological condemnation of the *compagnon-nage* initiation in 1655 – shows him to have been a 'cure'.
† *Ass. Prof. Ouv.* I, 117–24.

The only element missing in this initiation is that of instruction in the general nature of the society, as distinct from its secret recognition signs and the like. The German craftsmen's initiations, though generally preserving the other elements in a less elaborate and formalized way, retained this one very tenaciously. Thus among the printers the 'baptism' had, by the later 19th century, become little more than the jocular ritual of 'crossing the line' on ships; among the joiners the testing had become no more than horse-play, the giving of a new name was a fairly simple affair, and the secret signs were also less complex. However the 'Hobelpredigt' became, if anything, longer as the rest of the ritual atrophied, and similar sermons are reported from most of the other crafts.* Such sermons were mixtures of speech and catechism, often very corrupt, since the old testing ritual on which they were based had been forgotten, and the practical advice to the journeyman which was grafted onto it, had often been turned into semi-jocularity. At their best they read like something out of the Brothers Grimm, at their worst – and no doubt when pronounced by a rather drunken 'sponsor' they were often at their worst – they are as tiresome as the protestant sermons from which they may well have derived their popularity, at least as parodies. Thus among the German coopers the new journeyman is told that upon leaving town he must blow three feathers, of which one will fly to the right, one to the left, and one straight ahead. He must follow the middle one. He will then come to a pond in which a lot of green men will sit saying 'arg, arg, arg' (bad, bad, bad'). In spite of this warning he must go on; presumably it echoes a much more

---

* W. Krebs, *Alte Handwerksbraeuche,* Basel 1933, cap. IV. Several such sermons are reproduced in R. Wissell, *Des alten Handwerks Recht und Gewohnheit,* 2 vols. (Berlin 1929–30).

serious ritual encounter than one with frogs. He will then come to a turning millwheel which will say (onomatopoeically, at least in German): turn back, turn back, and so on past three gates, three ravens, encounters with millers, farmers, their wives and the like. In each case the candidate is asked what he would do, and advised what he ought to do.*

With the rise of freemasonry, which was itself an offspring of the same family of craftsmen's brotherhood rituals, the tendency for artisan societies to come under masonic influence was naturally very great. In Britain at least, where the pre-industrial *compagnonnage* had almost certainly not been developed into as specialized a set of bodies as on the continent, the masonic colouring is very marked, even where we are not actually told, as by the Oddfellows, that they were 'originally instituted on the Masonic principle'.† The oaths and ceremonies of early labour organizations obviously in some cases borrowed from it, as in the woolcombers' initiation.‡ The British initiations were generally much less horrific than the French ones, and even one of the more brutal which comes, oddly enough, from the wholly legal and harmless Oddfellows is pretty small beer besides the testing of the candidate Compagnon:§

The candidate for membership, on being led into the lodge-room, was carefully blinded, and after passing the outside

* K. Helfenberger, *Geschichte der Boettcher, Kuefer und Schaefflerbewegung* (n.p. 1928).
† *Oddfellows Magazine* I (Manchester 1829), 146. I owe the references to Friendly Societies ritual mainly to Mr P. H. Gosden, who has kindly allowed me to quote from his unpublished dissertation on them.
‡ Quoted in G. D. H. Cole, *Attempts at General Union* (1953), Appendix 5.
§ S. T. Davies, P.S., *Oddfellowship, its History, Constitution, Principles and Finances* (Witham 1858).

and inside guardians he felt a peculiar and mysterious awe steal over his senses, in consequence of the solemn and death-like silence that prevailed at the time. Anon the perverted sense of hearing became fearfully awakened by the rattling of huge iron chains, and the unmeaning sounds of men's voices. If at this stage of the inauguration (that is) he was not tossed and tumbled among the brushwood, or soused over the head in a large tub* the bandage is removed from his eyes, and the first object that his visual organs discovered was the point of a naked sword close to his seat of love. As soon as he could draw his attention from the worthy warden and his blade, ten to one but his eyes would rest upon a large transparency of the Old Mortality, whose ghastly grin would be sufficient to freeze the warm blood in his veins; while every part of the room was filled with symbols both of holy and profane things, the meaning of which few could explain.

It is perhaps worth observing, in passing, that the belief of early 19th-century British governments in the necessarily subversive nature of initiations and secret oaths, was mistaken. The outsiders against which the ritual brotherhood guarded its secrets were not only the 'bourgeois' and not always the governments. In France they were generally the members of the rival *compagnonnage*, with whom the brethren were in a permanent state of war, in British Friendly Societies anyone not in the in-group, whose membership was indeed largely defined by the possession of the 'secrets'. Only insofar as all working men's organizations by virtue of their class

---

* Knoop and Jones, *op. cit.*, 209, 249–50, for similar hazing – presumably the descendant of former 'testing' rituals – among early Freemasons.

membership, were likely to engage in activities frowned upon by employers or the authorities, did the initiation and oath bind their members specifically against these. There was thus no initial distinction between, as it were, legitimately and unnecessarily secret societies, but only between the fraternal activities in which their members were ritually bound to show solidarity, some of which might be acceptable to the law while others were not.

The *rituals of periodic meeting* have also been much more completely preserved on the continent than in Britain, where they had become pretty vestigial by the 19th century, except for those surrounding the central piece of furniture of every craft society, the 'box' or 'ark' in which the records and other implements of the society were kept. We have a few traces of meeting rituals, as among the Irish carpenters, where the 'father of the shop' presided over them, and 'rang the holdfast' three times (i.e. struck a tool so as to make a sound) as a sign that the 'court' was convened; or among the printers, where the 'father of the chapel' summoned members round him to impose justice at the *imposing stone* in the shop. But these are poor things beside the German smiths, who drew a 'journeyman's circle' – a figure something like a diagram of a lifebelt or tire, except that the outer circle was left open –, inscribed the names of all present between the two circles and then 'closed' it, to mark the presence of all brethren at each meeting. After dues had been paid another circle would be drawn and the chalk – normally kept in the 'box' *(Lade)* – was placed within it.* And the ritual furniture of the smiths was less elaborate than that of the French *compagnons* who took a holy oath to meet (*faire la montée de chambre*) when there was a quorum of

---

* E. Basner, *Geschichte der deutschen Schmiedebewegung* (Hamburg 1912).

men in any town at 2 o'clock precisely each Sunday, except in Paris, where the available distractions may explain why they were permitted to meet only twice a month. The ritual requirements of such meetings were so numerous and strict that they probably represent a stage in the societies' evolution when they had nothing better to do. The *compagnons* had to be properly clothed, their coats buttoned by the third button on the left side, as was the brotherhood's wont, but unadorned. The 'napkin' was placed before the 'premier en ville', the senior journeyman in the town, in a precisely aligned position. It was garnished with a bottle of wine in the centre and two glasses placed to the right and left of the president, the right one half-full of wine and containing a circular piece cut from the upper crust of a loaf (it had to be the upper crust), which was called the *pavilion*, the one on the left, the 'fraternal cup', empty. Between the two glasses there had to be a knife, its point hidden in a button of bread. Other crusts – this time cut square, but also from the upper crust – were placed at each angle of the napkin.*

All brotherhoods had general public ceremonies in addition to the specific and esoteric ones of periodic meeting. Normally these were religious, at least in Roman Catholic countries, where there were invariably processions of some kind on the days of the fraternity's saint – St Joseph for the carpenters, St Anne for the joiners, St Eligius in summer for the farriers, St Eligius in winter for the smiths, St Peter for the locksmiths, St Crispin for the shoemakers etc. – and generally also on high days and holidays. Annual processions and ceremonies of this kind on fixed days remained universal in Britain, and the Rules of village Friendly Societies normally make the most elaborate

---

* *Ass. Prof. Ouv.* 103 n.

provision for them. To what extent they still reflect the old saints' days is a question which local antiquaries might well pursue. However, in France the public religious rituals came to be less strictly insisted upon as the 19th century advanced.

The *practical rituals*, that is to say normally the secret recognition signs such as the 'grip, password, sign, countersign or travelling password'* had a much more obvious rational foundation. The brethren were generally illiterate in the early stages of the fraternity, and where they were not, the prohibition of keeping written records to safeguard secrecy – the *compagnons* burned them annually, stirring the ashes into the wine which they drank – obliged the society to rely on unwritten signs. Even if there had been no other reason, the constant risk that outsiders might abuse the society's facilities, made a system of recognition of 'legitimate' brethren imperative: the records of British craft unions are full of the fight against fraudulent claimants on the hospitality of local branches. It must be remembered that all such bodies assumed that journeymen travelled from place to place. Brethren in one town therefore had to have reliable means of recognizing strangers. As usual recognition ritual ranged from the utilitarian to the fantastic, from the simple to the complexities of the *compagnonnages*, which take three large pages to describe, and from the prosaic to the colourful and poetic. There is no need for elaborate description of them here. Nor need we say much about the symbolism, regalia and 'theology' of such organizations. Members were pleased and edified by them, non-members impressed and entertained. So far as wider social movements are concerned they transmitted or invented a vast store of devices, tested for emotional appeal, from which such movements could draw

* *General Laws of the Ancient Order of Foresters*, Bolton 1865.

supplies as and when needed.* Only one aspect is worth special mention: the practice, doubtless derived from ancient craft tradition, for members to scale the rungs of a hierarchy analogous to, though often more elaborate than, that of apprentice, journeyman and master.

Though ritual in one form or another was universal, highly ritualized working-class organizations were probably rarer than one might think, except among artisans in traditional crafts and in bodies which had no primary purpose as organizations for collective political or economic action, such as Friendly Societies, convivial orders of a semi-masonic kind, and the like. Even among the pre-industrial crafts they were not universal, though they tended to occur wherever journeymen's societies with quasi-trade union functions flourished. In France in 1791 only 27 trades were in *compagnonnages*, and – with the exception of such specialist craftsmen as shearmen, or in Britain, woolcombers, – they were apparently weak among the more nearly proletarian groups such as textile workers. 'Modern' social movements outside such old-fashioned circles tended to adopt ritual chiefly for the more utilitarian purpose of security against the blows of their enemies. That is why, apart from the vast non-political ritual Friendly Societies and similar bodies, the characteristic and highly ritualized organizations were probably small. The climate of the 19th century was not propitious to ritual, unless non-political. Among the British trade unions secret oaths and the like declined very rapidly, and were already much scarcer by the 1830s than hostile observers cared to admit.† Among the traditional crafts

* See e.g. O. Karmin, 'L'influence du symbolisme maçonnique sur le symbolisme revolutionnaire', in *Rev. Hist, de la Rev. Française* I (1910), 176 ff.
† See the Reports from the *Select Committee on Combinations of Workmen 1838* for the paucity of oaths.

ritual declined, perhaps with urbanization: at the end of the
19th century it was observed that the *compagnonnage* in Paris
was strongest among craftsmen recruited in small provincial
towns, such as coachbuilders.* The *compagnonnages* themselves
were shaken by a rationalist secession which gained ground
after 1830, the call of common sense being reinforced by a
revolt of young craftsmen against the attempt of the established
full brethren to monopolize the *compagnon's* privileges. An open
journeymen's fraternity was formed from dissidents of all the
Devoirs, and the inspirers of this body 'have eliminated all
the customs which, though they had their justification in the
Middle Ages, have lost it today'.† By the end of the century
something like 40 per cent of journeymen organized in *compagnonnages* rather than trade unions – a small band of less than
10,000 altogether – were members of the open organization.
In fine, the ritual labour organization was a fast-disappearing
survival.

III

If the ritual brotherhood had been no more than this, it would
not be worth lengthy discussion. However, the period between
1789 and 1848 saw a development of the ritual organization
which is of considerable importance in the history of social
movements, not to mention world history. Throughout the
period of the three French Revolutions the secret revolutionary
brotherhood was by far the most important form of organization for changing society in Western Europe, and it was
often ritualized to the point of resembling an Italian opera

---

* *Ass. Prof. Ouv.* II, 802.
† *Larousse du XIX Siècle, loc. cit.,* p. 769.

rather than a revolutionary body. Similar brotherhoods have remained politically important elsewhere and some are still important. Their ritual aspects are therefore of more than antiquarian interest.

This is not the place for a brief history of the secret brotherhoods, a complex and difficult subject for which I am not qualified. However, it is clear that they all tended to belong to a single family, partly by descent from masonic groups of the 18th century, partly because they copied one another,* and partly because the world of the conspirators, particularly in the international places of asylum in which *emigrés* congregated – Geneva, Brussels, Paris, London – was a small, coherent, and to some extent cooperative world, in spite of its ferocious and interminable dissensions. Such informal institutions as the 'Court of Honour' before which *emigrés* brought personal quarrels, and the practice of passing information about known police-agents to rival groups of revolutionaries, indicate this.†

The relations between Freemasonry, or quasi-masonic fraternities, and revolutionary movements have been much debated, particularly by those in search of a paranoiac view of history, and the problem is therefore not one which the serious historian tackles with enthusiasm. Eighteenth-century Masonry appears to have been less a single organization

---

* Cf. F. Venturi, *Il Populismo Russo* (Turin 1952) I, 587, for Russians inspired by Buonarotti's *Conspiracy of the Equals*, the *Report of the Sedition Committee 1918* (Calcutta 1918), better known as the Rowlatt Report, for Bengali terrorist indebtedness to the Russian Narodniks, and Kalpana Dutt, *Chittagong Armoury Raiders: Reminiscences* (Bombay 1945) for their indebtedness to the Irish Republican Army.

† For an example of the Court of Honour, E. H. Carr, *The Romantic Exiles* (Penguin edn.), 127.

with a fixed doctrine and programme, than a complex of groups, difficult to define beyond the statement that they all shared a common pattern of organization and ritual, and a common belief in the values of the 'Enlightenment'. It is therefore difficult to maintain theories of masonic conspiracy of the more lurid type. On the other hand the very sympathy of the Masons (or other bodies formed on their model) for the ideas which found expression in the American and French Revolutions, made many of them revolutionaries, and masonic organization made it easy for lodges or higher groupings to turn into political centres or pressure groups, to hatch or protect revolutionary brotherhoods, and to be in turn 'infiltrated' by them. Masons were prominent in the American and French Revolutions, and in Ireland so many lodges were linked with the United Irishmen in 1798, that the authorities assumed a close organic connexion between the two bodies. Where no other organization existed, as after the defeat of a revolutionary movement, masonic lodges were very likely to become the refuge of the rebels. Thus in the French provinces after 1834 the Republican opposition retired largely into the lodges, to the disgust of the Grand-Orient.* When revolutionary agitation revived or expanded, Masonry was quite likely to give birth to more specialized revolutionary orders, as like as not with some variation in their ritual and symbolism. These remained in a peculiar relationship with the Masons, partly drawing away from them – though retaining many links with them – partly using them as a recruiting ground for their members and seeking to convert their lodges. Thus Weishaupt's *Illuminati*, who had grown up in the masonic environment, appear to

---

* G. Perreux, *Au temps des societés secrètes* (Paris 1931), 365 ff.

have converted parts of Masonry to their revolutionary ideas (mainly, it seems, by means of the 'Scots Templar' rite), and thus to have given life to a succession of secret brotherhoods in the Napoleonic and Restoration period, most of which showed a tendency to make themselves independent of Masonry: the Filadelfi (who in turn became a notable nursery for secret societies and infiltrated *compagnonnages* also), the Tugendbund, the Adelfi, the Carbonari.* Napoleon's attempt to bring Masonry under government control, which drove many Masons into political opposition at the beginning of the 19th century, naturally facilitated such tendencies. It is certainly evident that many, perhaps most, of the persistent revolutionaries and conspirators of the period from 1789 to 1830 had a masonic background, and continued to think, organizationally, in something like masonic terms. This is notably true of the quintessential conspirator of that generation, Philip Buonarroti (1761–1837), about whom we are beginning to be well-informed.†

This common background and environment of the secret brotherhoods may account for their persistent tendency to breed international super-conspiracies, or secret co-ordinating leaderships standing above the individual brotherhoods or lodges, and technically composed of 'higher degrees' of initiation than the ordinary run. This practice may have contributed greatly to the establishment of the strong internationalist tradition of

---

* I follow C. Francovich, 'Gli Illuminati di Weishaupt e l'idea egualitaria in alcune società segrete del Risorgimento', in *Movimento Operaio* (Jul.–Aug. 1952) for reservations about whom, see E. L. Eisenstein, *Filippo Michele Buonarroti* (Harvard 1959), 176–7.

† Thanks to the recent works of Samuel Bernstein, Galante-Garrone and especially A. Saitta, whose two volumes throw a flood of light on the entire conspirational world of this period.

later socialist movements, i.e. of the belief that all such movements should be ideally co-ordinated in or directed by an
International; though the ideal of an International composed
of all varieties of rebels was soon abandoned.* Buonarroti in
his time was actively involved not only in Masonry, Babouvism
and Carbonarism, but dominated one of the best known of
these shadowy super-conspiracies, the *Sublime Perfect Masters*
(said to be the result of a merger between Adelfi and Filadelfi
in 1818), which had three degrees, the highest being the 'sublime elect', a *Grand Firmament* in Paris, and agreements for
accepting the degrees of some affiliated brotherhoods. Italian
Carbonari, some French Masons, the German Tugendbund
and the Russian Decembrist societies were said to be linked
with it.† Possibly this is the same body as the *Universal Democratic
Charbonnerie* which occupied his energies a few years later. A
more purely masonic body of this kind, with headquarters in
Gibraltar, appears, as D. Dakin has shown, to have been active
in the Philhellenic movement in the middle 1820s and to have
engaged in a variety of colourful cloak-and-dagger pursuits. A
wider and less esoteric internationalism absorbed and transmuted the energies of the international rebels subsequently,
and only notably archaic and romantic revolutionaries like
Bakunin continued to found 'Secret Alliances' of this kind.
How effective they were even at their peak, must remain a
matter for speculation.

* The First International (1864–73) almost represented this ideal, though the
Blanquists held aloof; but the difficulties of running Marxists, Mazzinians,
Proudhonists, Bakuninists, and a variety of other revolutionaries and left-
wingers in harness proved insuperable. All subsequent internationals, except
specialized ones, e.g. of Cooperators, have been ideologically exclusive.
† Francovich, *loc. cit.*, 584, Bernstein, *Buonarroti* (Paris 1949), 167–8, 178; Jean
Witt, *Les sociétés secrètes de France et d'Italie* (Paris 1830), 6–7, 9.

The classical secret brotherhood was a hierarchical élite group, with a tremendous paraphernalia of initiation and other rituals, symbolism, ritual nomenclature, signs, passwords, oaths and the rest. The candidate was carefully selected and, after admission, progressively advanced through a succession of degrees, each bringing higher responsibility and a more esoteric knowledge until, with luck, he joined (or rather, was co-opted into) the innermost of whatever inner directing circles there were. Marx, who had no fondness for this sort of thing, described it as 'superstitious authoritarianism' and the phrase may stand. The actual political function of the brotherhood was twofold. First, each of the initiates, who was also a member of various uninitiated and 'broad' organizations, attempted to influence these in the direction favoured by the brotherhood. The brotherhood itself did not always, or even normally, operate through a broader movement specifically identified with its policies, but 'permeated' – to use a Fabian phrase – all suitable bodies. Second, in insurrectionary situations, it aimed at making risings with small groups of devoted initiates who would, it was hoped, draw the masses behind them or succeed in seizing power in some other way. While waiting for insurrectionary situations the brotherhood would agitate, undertake individual terrorism, or any other suitable activity to prepare revolution. The best illustration of the (non-ritual) operations of such a brotherhood is furnished by the longest-lived of them, the *Irish Republican Brotherhood*, better known as the *Fenians*, which has functioned since the 1850s.*

* There appears to be no good history of it. See D. Macardle, *The Irish Republic* (London 1937), 64, for the IRB oath. Its similarities with the continental pattern have often been noted, e.g. by the (biased) B. C. Pollard, *The Secret Societies of Ireland* (London 1922), 46, 49, but the precise filiation, if any, has not so far been established.

Secret revolutionary organizations persecuted, for good reasons, by governments, must naturally take steps to preserve Security, and nothing is more natural than that bodies descended from the artisan-masonic family of brotherhoods should adapt their rituals for this purpose. There is, as we have seen, a utilitarian case to be made for 'practical rituals', and naturally also for a hierarchical organization of underground movements, in which members of one group do not know members of others, and lower ranks do not know the identity of more than their immediate superiors. But it is reasonably clear that the requirements of illegality, as understood today, account only for part of the remarkable fancy-dress display which the classical brotherhoods put on, and indeed militated against secrecy. The police agent De la Hodde observes in passing that the French brotherhoods only became genuinely secret when their membership became proletarian, that is from the policeman's point of view, anonymous, and met in the back rooms of pubs and not in elaborate lodge-chambers, whose equipment was in any case too cumbersome and elaborate to be within the reach of the poor. The lengthy and elaborate rituals of the Carbonari, of which we have descriptions,* were standing invitations to policemen. The fantastic nomenclature of the brotherhoods was totally non-utilitarian unlike later revolutionary organizations which have normally attempted to pick names indicative of their ideology or programme. The list of the brotherhoods functioning in Apulia may inspire the amateur of operatic librettos, but hardly the serious rebel: Carbonari of various descriptions, Supreme Masters, Perfect Masons, Filadelfi, Edennisti, Hellenists, European Patriots,

---

* E.g. in Perreux, *op. cit.*, 371 ff.

The Men of Decision, The Men of the Dagger, the Shirtless Ones, the Unnamed Ones, Illuminati, White Pilgrims, Three Colours, Four Colours, Seven Letters, Eight Letters, Sect of Five, St John the Baptist, Society of the Venerable Souls in Purgatory, The Onion, The Central Tomb, the Society of the Seasons, the Bella Constantina etc.* The most serious of the professional revolutionaries, Blanqui, perpetrated a Society of the Seasons whose basic unit was the 'week' – six men and a leader called *Sunday* – four weeks being combined into a 'month' led by *July*, three months a 'season', led by *Spring* and four seasons a 'year' led by the surprisingly colourless *revolutionary agent*.† Clearly the ritualization of the brotherhood had a sociological function distinct from the practical needs of illegal agitation. The brotherhood was something like a religious sect as well as a political group.

IV

Before we consider the reasons for their excessive ritualization we may briefly sketch the decline of the ritual brotherhood. The great age of the brotherhoods as a single, at least theoretically united, family probably ended with the 1830 revolutions. The conspiracies of 1830–48 may have partly retained the original Carbonarist pattern, but the rise

* A. Lucarelli, 'I moti rivoluzionari del 1848 nelle Puglie', in *Arch. Stor. delle Prov. Napoletane* N.S. XXXI, (1947–9), 436–7. The fullest description of the atmosphere of Carbonarism, the best-known phenomenon of the kind, is in the anonymous *Memoirs of the Secret Societies of the South of Italy particularly the Carbonari* (London, John Murray 1821). The author, reputed to be a certain Bertholdi, is said by experts in the subject and period to be extremely well informed and the book abounds in documentation.

† De la Hodde, *Histoire des Societies Secretès et du Parti Republicain* (Paris 1850), 217.

of nationally and socially specialized groupings weakened their cohesion. Outside Western Europe the secret revolutionary brotherhood remained important, or indeed rose to importance in whatever corresponded to the 1789–1848 period in the history of the countries affected. Some of the finest examples come from Asia in the 20th century, e.g. the Bengali Terrorist movement, which owed little if any of its ritual to the West European tradition, but drew its inspiration from Hindu religion, stressing the cult of the goddess Kali and combining the advocacy of revolution with that of the construction of a temple in a spot 'far from the contamination of modern cities and as yet little trodden by man, in a high and pure air steeped in calm and energy' and of a new order of devotees, some of whose members should be *sanyasis* and most unmarried men who would return to an ashram when the allotted work of Indian liberation was accomplished.* However, a general decline of ritualization is to be observed in all, or almost all, revolutionary groups, especially in those which gravitated towards the Labour and Socialist Movement, as some of the most determined and revolutionary have tended to do: the Bengal terrorists were largely converted to Communism in the 1930s, and what Communism exists in Ireland seems to have been largely the result of left-wing breakaways from the Irish Republican Army. And the decline in ritualization in turn automatically weakened the appeal of the brotherhoods.

This decline may be discovered in many different ways. For instance, it is significant that Blanqui's *Society of the Seasons,*

---

* *Rowlatt Report*, quoting the *Bhawani Mandir* pamphlet of 1905. The link between revolutionism and ritual chastity remained strong. Kalpana Dutt, *op. cit.*, observes that the terrorist Suriya Sen had a holy man present on his wedding night, and never cohabited with his wife (1918–28).

after its first defeats, reorganized under a much more sober nomenclature (revolutionary agents, *chefs de groupe, hommes*). The illegal ceremonial of the later Blanquists, or of most of the Russian *Narodnik* groups, seem to have been no more than what one might expect of hard-headed, though perhaps politically mistaken, groups of professional revolutionaries in illegality, though it is difficult to speak with any certainty on so obscure a matter.* But the clearest example of the actual decline of a ritual organization is also the most significant, for it concerns the origins of Marxism.†

In 1834, when legal revolutionary activity in France had once again to cease, a *League of Outlaws* (Bund der Geaechteten) arose in Paris out of the debris of a German Popular Society, a broad mass organization for German emigrants, without, so far as we know, any special ritual aspects. (However, it should be born in mind that the bulk of German emigrants were travelling journeymen, steeped in the *compagnonnage* tradition.) The League had the usual pyramidal structure, and a carbonaro-influenced nomenclature: *Huetten* (i.e. the carbonarist *Ventes* or *Vendite*), *Berge* (mountains), *Dicasteries* and the *Nationalhuette* (National Hut). (Later these were renamed on semi-military lines as *tents, camps, district camps* and *foci* (*Brennpunkte*).) A sharp line separated the two lower from the two higher grades. There was certainly some ritual initiation, at least into the *Berge*, but ritual was already growing less important. Thus while candidates were blindfolded in Paris, the sections in Germany dropped the practice. Recognition signs and passwords were naturally used. They were either

* For the very cursory form of initiation see *Les Conspirateurs* par A. Chenu (Paris 1850), 20, and Appendix 13.
† Details from Wermuth and Stieber, *Die Communistenverschwoerungen des neunzehnten Jahrbunderts* (Berlin 1853) and various biographies of Marx.

ritual questions and answers, probably borrowed from the *compagnonnage* or masonic store, or simple ideological words like 'civic virtue'. There was an oath, though some observers doubted whether it was more than a solemn declaration, for it was not in religious form.

The *Outlaws* eventually gave birth to the *League of the Just*, which in turn, under the influence of Marx and Engels, became the *League of the Communists* for which the famous Manifesto was written. The Communists were no longer a brotherhood of the old type. Marx, whose dislike for the brotherhoods was marked – he had always refused to join any of them – saw to this, and specifically stipulated the elimination of all superstitious authoritarianism from their rules. The new body, democratic but centralized, elected all its officers and made them subject to recall. For practical purposes it was a wholly modern revolutionary organization. Thus we have here an instance of the fairly complete transition from the quasi-Carbonarism of the *Outlaws* to complete rationalism in organization. The entire process was completed between 1834 and 1846.

Why did the ritual brotherhoods decline and fall? The simplest explanation would be that they discovered that ritual was unnecessary and might even get in their way. It had two main practical functions, to bind the member closely to the brotherhood and to preserve its secrets, but was necessary for neither. Shakespeare's Brutus had long since said:

> No, not an oath: if not the face of men,
> the sufferance of our souls, the time's abuse, –
> if these be motives weak, break off betimes,
> and every man hence to his idle bed ...

> What need we any spur, but our own cause,
> to prick us to redress?

Strong and devoted men kept secrets anyway; weak men betrayed them in spite of oaths. What kept men together was not the oath but the cause, and – though one can only speak with caution – it looks as though the oath had become little more than a solemn declaration even in many classical brotherhoods, and that they dropped that element of ritually breaking taboos which we have noticed from time to time. The practical rituals were useful for security, but the real strength of security rules such as those of conspiracy lies in their *common sense*. To learn them as ritual may actually interfere with their efficient use. It is thus not surprising that among the Indian terrorists of the early 1900s the rules for underground activity, which they borrowed from the Russians, were quite matter-of-fact and that the religious ideas underlying such publications as the *Bhawani Mandir* pamphlet soon faded into the background, only oaths and vows being retained.

Nevertheless this purely utilitarian explanation of the decline of ritualism is hardly adequate. Another explanation may be suggested.

The classical ritual brotherhoods were overwhelmingly composed of what de la Hodde calls unemployed intellectuals and other 'impuissants' members of the middle and upper classes.* They also appealed strongly to another half declassed group – and one with its own fondness for fancy-dress and ceremony – army officers and n.c.os. The revolution these men stood for was, to some extent, an artefact imposed from outside on those whom it would benefit. The masses as such played

* *Op. cit.*, 13.

next to no role in their calculations.* They were nationalist, at a time when the masses of their fellow-citizens were not yet so: the isolation of the urban Carbonari and Mazzinians from the bulk of the Italian peasantry is legendary. They were rationalist – in ideology, if not in organization – at a time when the potentially revolutionary masses were held by traditional religion. (Paradoxically, free-thinking was perhaps most widespread among moderate conservatives or whigs.) The liberation of humanity from tyranny, vaguely conceived as it was, did not, and was not supposed to, emerge directly from the interests of any particular class or group. If we regard them as 'standing for' or 'representing' some class or other, it is not because they did so consciously.

The strategy and tactics of the classical brotherhoods were therefore those of self-selected elite groups, imposing the revolution on an inert, but grateful mass, or at best drawing a passive mass into activity by their example and isolated initiative, as in the Easter Rising in Dublin. Men who thus operated in isolation would find rituals symbolizing their emotional one-ness and cohesion not only convenient, but essential. The greater the real or imaginary separation of the group from the rest of the people the more likely it was to create such conventions for itself.

But the crucial development of the 1830s – at least in one

* This view is naturally subject to various qualifications, particularly since different lodges of various brotherhoods had widely varying policies and success. Exceptions to the generalization will come to the mind of any specialist, especially of the South Italian societies. However, there can be no doubt of its general validity. The revolutionary projects of such brotherhoods, as detailed in e.g. Appendix VI to the *Memoirs of the Secret Societies*, were essentially those of the classical pronunciamento; and indeed the traditional army coups of the Iberian countries, which have remained largely based on semi-secret officers' and soldiers' brotherhoods, still reflect this pattern.

section of the revolutionary movement – was the decline of the middle-class and the rise of the working-class conspirator, and the rise of a 'proletarian' theory of revolution. The Blanquists illustrate this well. Their initiation catechism, as recorded by de la Hodde for 1834, was already quite unambiguous. What was government? It consisted of traitors who acted, in the interests of a small group of exploiters, aristocrats, bankers, monopolists, large proprietors and all exploiters of men. What was the people? The body of labouring citizens, whose lot was slavery. What was the lot of the proletarian under the government of the rich? That of the serf and the slave. Was a social revolution necessary or only a political one? A social one. And shortly after, the composition of the societies changed. 'Le recrutement qui s'était fait dans les mauvaises couches de la bourgeoisie va s'opérer exclusivement dans les bas-fonds de la classe populaire.'* The *League of the Just*, in its turn, was a working-class breakaway of the Outlaws' (if the German journeymen artisans can be so described). Tailors, printers and shoemakers dominated it.

Now one might argue that such a shift of membership would intensify ritualism, because uneducated and politically

---

* De la Hodde, *La Naissance de la Republique en Février 1848* (Bruxelles 1850), gives the professions of the four Revolutionary Agents of the Society of the Seasons after 1839 as *cabinet-maker, gilder, copper-turner* and himself, journalist (and, we may add, police spy). 'Albert' the worker who entered the provisional government of February 1848 came there *via* the *Société des Nouvelles Saisons*, the heir of the Saisons. The *Societe Communiste Révolutionnaire* (according to de la Hodde) had as its chief militants a barber, a tailor, a mechanic and a stonecutter. The *Dissident Society* (of the New Seasons) had among its leaders two tailors, a former soldier, a maker of straw covers, as well as a wine-merchant and doctor (pp. 10, 15–16). The subsequent attraction of Blanquism for intellectuals, especially students, should not blind us to the fact that it was originally much more plebeian than the secret brotherhoods of the 1820s.

undeveloped men would take to the crude colours of secret oaths and ceremonies. Indeed – at least in the Blanquist organizations – the phrases of the initiatory catechism became sharper and more vivid as the (proletarian) Society of the Seasons replaced the (middle class) Society of the Families; but as we have seen the catechism was a perfectly rational political document. Such minor variations in the style of secret organizations do not alter the fact that their proletarianization marked a decline of ritual, because they no longer needed it so much. For the proletarian revolutionary (or the intellectual who identified himself with him) had no need of romantic formulae. He was, by revolutionary definition, swimming in and with the stream of history and the proletariat. If a worker, he merely carried out in a more efficient way what he and other workers – provided they were 'class-conscious' – felt to be the obvious strategy of their social situation. For such class-conscious workers *not* to belong to, or to sympathize with, 'the movement' would have been the difficult thing. If an intellectual, he had only to look at the workers to feel himself, though individually declassed, to be part of a 'natural' collective. Elite groups ceased to be self-contained combat units and became, in the Leninist phrase, 'vanguards' of a large army. The vanguard might have to be created, but the army was already there. History had shaped it, would strengthen it, and ensure its triumph. Marx did not merely oppose the secret brotherhood because he had a natural and understandable distaste for ham acting in politics, and thus for people like Mazzini, but because his kind of movement created stronger emotional commitments among a larger number of people than the quasi-masonic conspiracies.

It would be unwise to pursue our hypotheses further in the present state of our knowledge. A great deal of work remains to be done by scholars, as distinct from cranks, on the secret revolutionary societies of the past 150 years all over the world before we can do more than speculate about the phenomenon as a whole. Their relationships with national as distinct from social liberation movements, their links with various local traditions or their borrowing from western traditions, their contacts with primitive movements of the types discussed in earlier chapters, remain to be investigated. What has been said here applies to the brotherhoods which were eventually, directly or indirectly, absorbed into the modern labour and socialist movements, but not necessarily to other and similar bodies.

Their absorption proved fairly easy. Many of the individuals who composed them, insofar as they were serious revolutionaries, moved over into the non-ritual movements and occupied leading places in them, as can be seen by following the fortunes of such original members of the *League of the Just* or the Blanquist bodies as we have record of. The conspiratorial form of organization, which they pioneered, continued to do good service, shorn of its ritualism, wherever the situation required utter devotion and dangerous illegal activity. Lenin's Bolsheviks owe more than they have sometimes admitted to the experience and methods of work of the Buonarrotist-Narodnik tradition, though Marxist anti-ritualism has done its best to establish an atmosphere of deliberate and extreme matter-of-factness and colourlessness even in cloak-and-dagger activities which, as their popular name shows, tend to compensate for the extreme tension in which participants are involved by a certain amount of romanticism. The older brotherhoods declined, because politics ceased to be a matter of conspiracies, except in the limited situations which still provide scope, here and there, for activities such as the brotherhoods had in mind. In fact, time has by and large solved the problem of the brotherhoods. They were 'primitive', because they represented an early and immature form of revolutionary organization, which had to compensate in various ways for its lack of clear political strategy, tactics and perspectives. Insofar as revolutionary movements have advanced beyond this stage, they became unnecessary and were sometimes, like the Blanquists after the Commune, lost sight of in the wider parliamentary and non-parliamentary activities in aid of their cause. But their primitivism was largely adventitious: a combination of a particular form of isolated elite activity and a particular, historically given, supply of ideological and organizational devices. Unlike the other primitive movements discussed in this book, they belong to the history rather than to the prehistory of modern social movements, though to a very early stage of that history.

Appendix:

In Their Own Voices

1. A letter from Pasquate Tanteddu, outlaw and bandit (Sardinia 1954).
2. The brigand Vardarelli helps the poor (Apulia 1817).
3. A Bourbon brigand examined (South Italy, early 1860s).
4. Donato Manduzio confutes a false apostle (San Nicandro, early 1930s).
5. A peasant woman on the good society (Piana dei Greci 1893).
6. A peasant commune unpoisoned by cities (Ukraine 1918).
7. The peasants distrust governments (Ukraine 1917).
8. The Will of the Tsar (Ukraine 1902, 1905).
9. The conversation of Giovanni Lopez, cobbler (Calabria 1955).
10. Two strike sermons (North Carolina 1929).
11. A Lincolnshire unionist: Joseph Chapman (Alford 1899).
12. The 'Men of Decision' recommend a brother (Lecce, Apulia, 1817).
13. Some secret oaths (Britain 1830s, Naples 1815–20, Paris 1834).

The documents collected together here are not intended to illustrate all aspects of the text, but to help readers – if they have any
need of such help – to think and feel themselves into the skins
of such 'primitive rebels' as have been discussed in this book. I
have made no systematic attempt to discover such 'case-papers',
confining myself in the main to reprinting suitable documents I
have come across in the ordinary course of reading about and
around the subject. One document is the record of an interview,
as taken down within an hour of the conversation.

Readers may find it useful to read these documents for
atmosphere, or to make their own analysis of them in the light
of the argument of the text, which they illustrate in various
ways. Numbers 1, 5, 6–9 and 11 probably repay close study
best. No. 1 illustrates Robin Hood activities, and the egocen-
tricity and flamboyance of the individualist champion and
avenger of the poor; No. 3 'church and king' beliefs and magic.
No. 4 takes us into the world of religious ferment out of which
millenarianism and labour sects spring. No. 5, in many ways
the most important of the documents, is a clear exposition of
the ideal of peasant revolutionaries, No. 6 a description of its
application. Both 6 and 7 illustrate the profound distrust of
'cities' by peasant revolutionaries. 8 shows us the belief in the
'just king' and the millenarian device of the long-awaited 'new
law' or 'manifesto in letters of gold' instituting freedom. It also
throws light on the destructiveness of primitive revolutionaries.
In 9 the reader will observe the social interpretation of the
Bible, anticlericalism and the profound feeling for equality,
but also the characteristic combination of brotherly love and
implacability (compare also 5 and 11). 10 shows extremely
undeveloped political consciousness and an interpretation of
religion, basically other-worldly – arguing the all-importance
of salvation and the superiority of God to earthly riches – but

diverted into social protest. 11 contains the implication of the millennium (cf. also 5 and 9), the hostility to priests and 'barren and fruitless professors', the exclusion from the millennium of those not led by the spirit of God, and the resentment of social inequality. But here these are softened into what is in practice a modest reformism. 12 illustrates the operatic aspect of the secret brotherhoods at its most flamboyant. 13, finally, gives examples of secret oaths and shows the eventual curtailment of ritualism.

1. A Letter from Pasquale Tanteddu, Outlaw and Bandit

Source: F. Cagnetta, 'Inchiesta su Orgosolo', in *Nuovi Argomenti* (Sept.–Oct. 1954), pp. 209–11. Pasquale Tanteddu was born in Orgosolo, 1926. He has been an outlaw since 1949. In 1953 he was sentenced *in absentia* by the Court of Assize in Cagliari for the massacres of Villagrande and 'sa verula', being accused of six homicides of *carabinieri*, nine attempted homicides against *carabinieri*, two robberies, the formation of criminal bands, etc. He has been provisionally acquitted (*in absentia*) of the murder of Nicolo, Giovanni and Antonio Taras, alleged to have been police informers. The reward for his capture in 1954 was 5 million lire. The letter was sent to Rome, where it arrived on August 8th 1954. Dr Cagnetta, who has done much sociological field-work in the village, describes Tanteddu as 'a very popular bandit in Orgosolo, because it is the general opinion that, unlike for instance Salvatore Giuliano, he has never committed crimes against "the poor" and has never allowed himself to be a servant of the "lords"'.

Mario Scelba, mentioned in the letter, was Italian minister of the interior and subsequently Prime Minister. Salvatore Giuliano is the famous Sicilian bandit.

I have deliberately retained the clumsiness and semi-literacy of the document.

Dear Cagnetta,

Having been informed that you have been to Orgosolo with the object of denouncing to public Opinion by means of the newspapers our tragic situation, and since it was not possible for you to interview me personally, because I must avoid spies and similar trouble-makers, I am having this letter written for me by some others, since I cannot even sign my name, and I address this Letter to you in order to clear up all those lies which are printed over and over again in the newspapers – I that have never seen a single journalist, what clowns they are! – and the lies which circulate in the mouths of so many idlers who try to profit from my sad condition of being an outlaw and illiterate. Above all I want you to give a fine literary form and a correct one to the facts which I am now about to underline.

I want to begin with the first persecution. The first time I was charged was for fighting. I was then sixteen years old and a shepherd lad. While we were in the sheep-pen one of my mates, I don't know on what pretext, abused his strength and dragged me by the legs into the middle of the room: I found myself with the knife in my hand and I wanted to frighten him to let me go, so I moved my hand, as he shifted his position, the point of the knife went into his spine. I was arrested and acquitted after six months in jail by the Juvenile Tribunal in Cagliari.

In 945 [sic] I was accused of stealing some horses by another lad who, after being tortured by the *carabinieri* was obliged to give my name and that of another mate.

In 947, while I was present at a debate in the Court at Nuoro, I was suddenly given a push by a *carabiniere*, who said I was making a row. I tried to insist, saying I was calm enough, but when he saw me arguing back the *carabiniere* threw himself upon me. When I pushed him back he was seen to fall off the railings. Then I was seized by the scruff of the neck by a whole bunch of policemen who took me to the cells. I was accused of the crime of outrage and violence and after four months in jail I was condemned to fourteen months.

When I had served my sentence I worked at home with a flock of sheep belonging to us and I looked after a garden which we had leased together with my big brother Pietro. He had been a Partisan, he had understood the true situation of the exploitation and oppression by the rich against us, who are poor. And the fact that he was a man of this sort made the owners and the spies of our country wild as beasts against him. And in 1949 both I and my brother were wanted for sending to the *Confino*, simply on account of this. We tried to escape because we knew that we were innocent. But once you are a bird of the forest, the *marescialli*, supported by the rich, try to fasten every crime that takes place on to you. The most faithful 'Benjamin' was the *maresciallo* Loddo, who for two or three years had full powers in Orgosolo to play the holy Inquisitor, sending all those who wanted to escape from his yoke to *Confino*, and threatening *Confino* to those with a record and no character and bribing them to collaborate with them. They made so many criminal machinations until in the end

there occurred the famous massacre of 'sa verula' where
all those poor *carabinieri* lost their lives, who perhaps knew
nothing of the crazy plans of the *marescialli* Loddo, Ricciu
and Serra, the chief Inquisitors of the Nuorese country.
And the brothers Tanteddu were accused of this, as of all
the other homicides. And even though all the other charges
brought against me by Loddo to the number of ten were
thrown out by the courts, this last one was not, thanks to
the most infamous accuser that the history of Sardinia
has record of, the notorious Mereu Sebastiano, a worthy
servant of those *marescialli* that were thirsting for injustice
and disorders. And I was to get hard labour and he was to
get the 'good conduct' prize from the Sicilian assassin Mario
Scelba (the same as he gave to the Lucas after they had
betrayed and killed their dear friend and the murderer of
workers, Salvatore Giuliano). This shameless informer, who
succeeded in incriminating so many honest citizens, said
that he recognized me from a snapshot that had been taken
of a group of us when I was a boy, and at a time when I was
ill with pernicious fever and so wasted away that nobody in
Orgosolo could even recognize me. I am amazed that the
Judges could have wanted to believe such a broken-down
individual, and I hope the Court of Appeal will give me
justice.

That goes for both 'sa verula' and Villagrande because I
am Innocent and I do not want to pay for things which have
been infamously put down on my account.

And it is just because of the filthy actions of the vile and
criminal methods of the *carabinieri* that the country is living
in a silent and terroristic conflict. And every crime they try
to put it on my name.

In fact this so-called police, who do nothing but 'filthy

tricks', are trying to trace me by all possible means. And because they cannot get at me they get at my Kinsmen. Perhaps they think that I am induced to give myself up after the arrest of my Brother, a lad against whom no accusation has ever been made who looks after the flock, and my Sister, who was at home alone after the death of my poor Mother, and my poor Father, an old and paralysed man.

Or perhaps they expect me to turn into a lamb on seeing so much injustice, from being a criminal, which I am not.

The proof that I am not an assassin is given by the fact that if I were one, seeing what has been done to me I ought to kill at least ten policemen every day, or perhaps some of that ridiculous pack which Scelba has sent into our countryside, that needs agricultural improvement, technique, tractors and not policemen, priests and spies. And if it is not my fate to die, they will never take me, not if they put ten thousand after me.

I hate the life of the outlaw, but I would a hundred times sooner be dead than in the galleys. My head suffers terribly when they shut me up, and then I should certainly die.

My only desire is to see the *Confino*, the police rewards, the unemployment and the exploitation of the workers abolished, and so to see our martyred country living a life of serene peace and civil Progress.

Pasquale Tanteddu.

2. The Brigand Vardarelli Helps the Poor

Source: A. Lucarelli, *Il Brigantaggio Politico del Mezzogiorno.*
(*a*) De Matteis, judge of Andria, reports to the Procurator of the High Court in Trani, 11.2.1817:

On departing Don Gaetano Vardarelli on horseback called the Bailiff and ordered him instantly to give bread to the quantity of one *rotolo* (between 3 and 4 lb.) to each labourer on the estate. It was impossible to make this distribution immediately, for there were a hundred workers and not enough bread in stock. Don Gaetano therefore told the Bailiff to carry out his orders as soon as possible, and if upon his return there was one labourer who had not received his bread, he would kill the Bailiff as he had already killed two Bailiffs on other estates.

(b) Gaetano Vardarelli to the Mayor of Atella.

I, Gaetano Vardarelli, order and command you to call together all the landlords of the Commune of Atella, and to make them understand that they shall allow gleaning to all the poor, or else I will warm their backsides, and I say what I say.

Gaetano Vardarello,
Commandant of the Lightning Troop on horseback.

(c Gaetano Vardarelli to the Mayor of Foggia.

Mr Mayor, you will be good enough to instruct all landlords in my name to stop feeding their gleanings to the cattle, but to leave them for gleaning by the poor, and if they are deaf to this my command I will burn everything they have. Do this much and I salute you with esteem, and tell you that if I have any complaints that you have not had my orders carried out, I shall hold you responsible.

The 30th June 1817
I, Vardarelli.

3. A Bourbon Brigand Examined

Source: Maffei, *Brigand Life in Italy*, II, 173–6.

Judge. – Having this conviction, why did not you and your companions give yourselves up? You must have known that, being hated by the whole population, your life was every moment in danger? You know that the village of Sturno, which was frightened by exaggerated reports of the number of brigands surrounding it, no sooner got rid of the two ruffians who had entered, than it again set up the arms of Victor Emmanuel and blessed his name and Italian unity.

Brigand. – We were fighting for the faith.

Judge. – What do you mean by the faith?

Brigand. – The holy faith of our religion.

Judge. – But you surely know that our religion condemns the thefts, the setting fire to houses, the murders, the cruelties, and all the impious and barbarous misdeeds by which brigandage every day is marked, and which you yourself and your companions have perpetrated.

Brigand. – We were fighting for the faith, and we were blessed by the Pope, and if I had not lost a paper which came from Rome you should be convinced that we were fighting for the faith.

Judge. – What kind of paper was it?

Brigand. – It was a printed paper, that came from Rome.

Judge. – But what were the contents of the paper?

Brigand. – It said that whoever fights for the holy cause of the Pope and of Francis II., does not commit sin.

Judge. – Do you recollect anything else in the paper?

Brigand. – It said that the real brigands are the Piedmontese, who have taken away from Francis II. his kingdom; that they were excommunicated, and that we are blessed by the Pope.

Judge. – In whose name was the paper written, and what signatures were attached to it?

Brigand. – The paper was a commission in the name of Francis II., and was signed by a general, who had another title, which I don't recollect, any more than his name. There was a piece of ribbon attached to it, with a seal.

Judge. – Of what colour were the ribbon and the seal, and what impression was on the seal?

Brigand. – The ribbon was white, like linen, and the seal was white, with the impression of Francis II., and letters which spoke of Rome . . .

Judge. – As it is impossible to admit, or suppose, that the Pope could bless such iniquities, or that Francis II. could degrade his dignity as King, by commanding homicides, extortions, and burnings, even though by means so dishonouring to humanity he could hope to recover his crown, what you have asserted must be false.

Brigand. – Well, as you have brought the Bersaglieri, and I am to be shot – as I know that I am to die – I tell you that I had that paper, and that all contained in it was just as I told you; and if any of my companions have been arrested, like myself, you will then be convinced that I have not lied.

Judge. – That you should keep tied on your breast with a string a crown-piece of Francis II., as a medal, is not surprising, because you believe that when you murder, and exact ransoms, and rob, you are combating for him. But that in perpetrating such wickedness you should keep, as the witness, and I might even say, if the words were not impious, as the accomplice of your crimes, the blessed Virgin, by

242

wearing, attached to your breast, that dirty figure of the
Madonna del Carmine, is astonishing. It is enough to make
me believe that your religion is more impious and wicked
than the religion of the devils themselves, if the devils have
any religion. Is not this the most infernal mockery that can
be offered to God!

Brigand. – I and my companions have the Virgin as our protec-
tress, and if I had kept the commission with the benediction,
I should certainly not have been betrayed.

On being told that the hour of execution was at hand, he
answered, 'I will confirm all the things I have said to the
confessor, who, I hope, will be granted to me.'

4. Donato Manduzio Confutes a False Apostle

Source: Elena Cassin, *San Nicandro, Histoire d'une Conversion*
(Paris 1957), 28–30. Donato Manduzio was the founder
and head of a small community of converts to Judaism in
San Nicandro, province of Foggia, Apulia. The community established itself in the 1930s and most of its members
have since emigrated to Israel. The young man who visits
him (presumably under the influence of literature distributed by protestant missionaries) believes himself to be the
white horse of the Apocalypse. ('And I saw, and behold a
white horse: and he that sat him had a bow; and a crown
was given unto him: and he went forth conquering and
to conquer.' Rev. 6, 2.) One imagines that he is appealing to Manduzio, a new Christ, to enter Rome which is
Jerusalem. The parallel with King Pippin is taken from
the *Reali di Francia*, a collection of knightly romances which
is extremely popular in Southern Italy. Incidentally, it

was the chief secular reading of Davide Lazzaretti. The incident illustrates the intense, but somewhat inchoate, apocalyptic ferment in a peasant society of medieval background.

One evening, it was a Thursday, a young man came to him and asked if this was the house of Israel. He declared himself to be 'an envoy of the Lord', come to announce the approach of the Kingdom of Heaven and he added 'I am the White Horse'. Manduzio was suspicious and on his guard, but the young man continued to talk of the Bible and of the chosen people until Manduzio could not but invite him to dine and stay the night, acting as the patriarch Abraham would have done in such a situation. The next day the young man declared that Donato was a Doctor of the Law, and that they must write to the Rabbi in Rome to send for him and take him to Rome. Donato's suspicions grew greater, and to test the young man he asked him to write to Rome himself . . . The young man wrote the letter. That evening his 'malignity' already began to show itself. Manduzio asked him suddenly 'Who is the true Son of God' and the young man – true to the saying that 'he who has gall in his stomach cannot vomit sugar' – answered without hesitation 'Jesus Christ'. Donato, trembling, then showed him Exodus 4, 22–3, Psalms 2, 1 and Hosea 11, 1 and the young man answered: 'Yes, that is true, but that one was also His Son.' Donato thereupon replied that, according to Isaiah 56, 4–5, all those who observe the Sabbath and the Law are the children of the Lord. After this incident, which took place on the Friday evening, Donato prayed to God to let him know the truth about the unknown man in a vision; and that night he saw a tree and on it a young girl with a pruning-knife. She showed him a dead branch and told him to cut off that branch, for it was rotten. Donato began to cut the branch off, and the vision disappeared. Donato meditated: the vision was clear; the young man must be sent away.

On Saturday morning, as was its custom, the small group of Brethren and Sisters met in Manduzio's house: a lamp, fed with olive oil, lit their common prayer; The young man arrived and, seeing the lamp lit, cried: 'There is no more need of lamps for the Messiah has come.' Manduzio answered him that he lied, but that God would forgive him, if he would be a good man. The young man replied that he, Manduzio, was bad, for refusing him confidence. At this moment the Brethren and Sisters intervened and asked Donato to leave the young man in peace and let him believe or do what he liked. Manduzio noted in his Journal that at this moment he understood how the children of Israel 'were capable of killing the true prophet in order to follow the bad shepherd who transgressed the Law' (I Kings, 19, 14). But the image which came spontaneously to his mind was that of King Pippin, when he saw that Elisetta, who had taken the place in his bed of Berthe-aux-grands-pieds, had deceived him, wanted to throw the traitress and the two small daughters he had by her into the fire, but was prevented by those around him.

5. The Good Society

Source: Adolfo Rossi, *L'agitazione in Sicilia* (Milan 1894), 69 ff. The speaker is a peasant woman from Piana dei Greci (province of Palermo) interviewed by a northern journalist during the peasant rising of 1893.

We want everybody to work, as we work. There should
no longer be either rich or poor. All should have bread for
themselves and for their children. We should all be equal. I
have five small children and only one little room, where we
have to eat and sleep and do everything, while so many lords
(*signori*) have ten or twelve rooms, entire palaces.'

—And so you want to divide the lands and the houses?

—No. It will be enough to put all in common and to
share with justice what is produced.

—And aren't you afraid, if you got this collectivism, some
people with confused heads or some swindlers might not
come to the fore?

—No. Because there ought to be fraternity, and if anyone
failed to be brotherly, there would be punishment.

—How do you stand with your priests?

—Jesus was a true Socialist and he wanted precisely what
the Fasci are asking for, but the priests do not represent him
well, especially when they are usurers. When the Fascio was
founded our priests were against it and in the confessional
they said that the Socialists are excommunicated. But we
answered that they were mistaken, and in June we protested
against the war they made upon the Fascio, none of us went
to the procession of the Corpus Domini. That was the first
time such a thing ever happened.

—Do you admit people convicted of crimes to the Fascio?

—Yes. But there are only three or four out of thousands
and we have accepted them to make them better men,
because if they have stolen a bit of grain they have only
done so out of poverty. Our president has said that the
object of the Fascio is to give men all the conditions for no
longer committing crimes. Among us the few criminals
feel that they still belong to the human family, they are

thankful that we have accepted them as brothers in spite of their guilt and they will do anything not to commit crimes again. If the people were also to chase them away, they would commit more crimes. Society should thank us for taking them into the Fascio. We are for mercy, as Christ was.

6. A Peasant Commune Unpoisoned by Cities

Source: Nestor Makhno, *La Révolution Russe en Ukraine. Mars 1917–Avril 1918* (Paris 1927), 297–9. The commune was one of those founded at Gulai-Polye, the capital of Nestor Makhno, in the Southern Ukraine between Dnieper and Don, north of the Azov Sea. Makhno (from whose memoirs the extract is taken) was a village anarchist of remarkable gifts as a war-leader, whose peasant forces, independent of both Bolsheviks and Whites (but allying with the former against the latter) played a crucial part in the Civil War in the Ukraine. He himself exemplifies the characteristics of peasant anarchism with remarkable accuracy. His interesting memoirs are only available in Russian except for the first volume. The history of the Makhnovsh-china has, alas, been written only by supporters who idealize and prettify it and opponents who blacken it. The standard account is still P. Arscinov, available in Russian, German and French, and in the British Museum in the most recent Italian edition (P. Arscinov, *Storia del Movimento Makhnovista 1918–1921,* Napoli 1954, first published 1922).

The *pomeshchiki* are the aristocrats and landowning gentry. The *kulaks* are the rich individualist peasants. *Skhods* (here translated as village assemblies) are the periodic meetings of the entire village community.

In every one of these communes there were a few anarchist peasants, but the majority of their members were not anarchist. Nevertheless, in their communal life they behaved with that anarchist solidarity of which, in ordinary life, only those toilers are capable whose natural simplicity has not yet been infected by the political poison of the cities. For the cities always give out a smell of lying and betrayal from which many, even among the comrades who call themselves anarchists, are not exempt.

Every commune comprised ten families of peasants and workers, i.e. a total of 100, 200 or 300 members. By decision of the regional Congress of agrarian communes every commune received a normal amount of land, i.e. as much as its members could cultivate, situated in the immediate vicinity of the commune and composed of land formerly belonging to the *pomeshchiki*. They also received cattle and farm-equipment from these former estates.

And so the free toilers of the communes set to work, to the tune of free and joyous songs, which reflected the soul of the Revolution and of the labourers who had died for it, or struggled long years for the great ideal of justice, which must triumph over iniquity and become the torch of humanity. They sowed and looked after their gardens, full of confidence in themselves, firm in the resolve never to let the old landlords take back the land which the peasants had now conquered from those who had never laboured upon it . . .

The inhabitants of the hamlets and villages bordering on the communes were still partly lacking in political consciousness, and not wholly liberated from servitude to the *kulaks*. They were therefore jealous of the communards and, more than once, showed a desire to

248

take back everything – cattle and equipment – which the communards had taken from the *pomeshchiki*. They wished to share this out among themselves. 'The free communards can always buy it back from us later, if they want to,' they said ... However, this tendency was severely judged at the general village assemblies and congresses by the absolute majority of the labourers, for these saw in the agrarian communes the happy germ of a new social life, which would continue as the Revolution approached the climax of its triumphal and creative march, to develop and grow, and to stimulate the organization of an analogous Society in the country as a whole, or at least in the villages and hamlets of our region.

7. The Peasants Distrust Governments

Source: Nestor Makhno, *op. cit.*, 166–7. Though Gulai-Polye was not exceptionally remote, the news of the October Revolution did not penetrate there until the end of November or the beginning of December. The distrust of governments reflected in this extract did not prevent the peasants welcoming the news of the Revolution, particularly in the Zaporozhe and Azov coastal regions, since they saw it as confirming their own seizures of the land in August 1917 (Makhno, 165). The chief revolutionary group in Gulai-Polye were the anarchists, hence an exceptional mistrust of the Bolsheviks was to be expected, but there is no reason to doubt that sentiments such as those expressed here must have been widely held among the ordinary 'non-political' peasantry, in whom centuries of oppression had bred a passive, but resigned, hostility to all authorities outside the village community.

As for the mass of the Ukrainian toilers, especially the peasants in the servile villages, they saw little more in the new socialist-revolutionary government (of November 1917) than another government like all the others which only came to their notice when they robbed the peasants by various taxes, recruited soldiers, or intervened by some other act of violence in the hard life of those who laboured. Often the peasants could be overheard expressing their true opinion of pre-revolutionary and revolutionary regimes. They seemed to be joking, but in reality they spoke with the utmost seriousness, and always with suffering and hatred. 'After we threw out the fool (*durak*) Nicky (Nikolka) Romanoff, they said, another fool tried to take his place, Kerensky, but he had to go too. Who will now play the fool at our expense? The Lord Lenin?' So they asked. Others, however, said: 'We cannot do without some "fool" (and by this word *durak* they always meant the government). The towns have no other purpose than this. The idea of the towns and their system is bad. They favour the existence of the *durak*, the government.' So said the peasants.

8. The Will of the Tsar

1. Poltava 1902

Source: Memories of the agrarian troubles in the Poltava Guberniya, *Istori-cheski Vyestnik* (April 1908), reprinted in R. Labry, *Autour du Moujik* (Paris 1923).

Our whole village took part in the pillage of Cs estate. It was done so quickly that by noon it was all over. The peasants returned home full of joy and songs. We were then at table.

But hardly had we swallowed the first spoonful of soup when (I received a) note ... saying we should be plundered at three o'clock ... The fatal moment had not yet arrived when my bailiff came to announce the approach of the peasants ...

'Why have you come?' I asked them.

'To demand corn, to make you give us your corn,' said several voices simultaneously.

'That is to say, you have come to plunder?'

'If you like, to plunder,' said a young lad in the crowd, who had hitherto remained silent.

I could not refrain from recalling how I had treated them for so long.

'But what are we to do?' several voices answered me. 'We aren't doing this in our name, but in the name of the Tsar.'

'It is the Tsar's order,' said one voice in the crowd.

'A general has distributed this order of the Tsar throughout the districts,' said another.

I should observe that at the beginning of the agitation there was a persistent rumour among the people that a general from Petersburg had arrived, an emissary of the Tsar, with the mission to proclaim to the people a manifesto written 'in letters of gold' ... There were stories that false police-sergeants were going round the villages distributing so-called 'decrees' to the people. The peasant is prone to believe what serves his own interests. Thus he accepted these stories about an alleged general. None of my neighbours had seen him: but this or that other man had seen him, and this was sufficient for all to believe in the reality of such impostors and of their missions.

'Anyway, *barin*,' my neighbours added, 'if you will not give anything to your peasants, strangers will come to take it. So long as they know you have been plundered, they won't come. We shan't harm you. But as for the others, who knows what they may do?'

2. *Chernigov 1905*

Source: The agrarian troubles in the Chernigov Guberniya in 1905, *Istoricheski Vyestnik* (July 1913), reprinted in Labry, *op. cit.*

At the height of violence and after the movement was over, the peasants' attitude towards the officials remained perfectly correct. These were not afraid to show themselves in the countryside, particularly the instructing magistrates and procurator's substitutes who were obliged in the course of their duties to travel throughout the province. As for the members of the police, during the pillaging they never showed their faces in the villages, with some rare exceptions. The good relations between the peasants and the judicial officials are brought out very clearly in the events of the village of Ryetsky, Gorodna district, where the pillaging of the farm of the proprietor Enko and a pogrom against the Jews took place simultaneously. During the sacking of the farm, the rioters approached the apartment of the local examining magistrate, who lived in one of this Enko's houses, but left it in peace. Voices were heard in the crowd: 'The judge is like us, he works for a crust of bread.' The apartment was not touched ...

A very large number of those who took part in these attacks refused to regard their actions as in the least criminal, since, as they put it, they had been granted rights. They even believed that in acting as they did, they were helping to transfer the lands of the landlords into their own hands, which was the natural consequence of the rights they had been granted. Only this explains why on the estates they destroyed orangeries and flower-gardens – which were useless to them – with particular fury, and in the houses pictures and furniture, in a word all that they regarded not as a necessity of life, but as a sign of comfort and luxury. On the other hand they spared the cattle and took care not to destroy stocks of corn.

Many of the peasants believed that Imperial manifestoes authorized them to take away all the goods of the gentry and the Jews. This illusion manifested itself in a particularly striking manner in the village of Kussiey, Gorodna district ... On October 26 and 27 some peasants returned to Kussiey from the village of Dobrianka, carrying the loot taken somewhere during a pogrom against the Jews. After this everybody in the village talked with conviction about the new law which allowed anyone to take what he liked where he liked. The existence of this new law was affirmed with great conviction and confirmed by two peasants who returned from work in the environs of Chernigov, Vassily Sinenko and Kirill Yevtushenko. They said it was precisely in accordance with this law that the pogroms against the gentry **and** the Jews had taken place in the Kiev *guberniya* and other provinces ...

The attitude of the pillagers towards the injunctions of the authorities is demonstrated by the following case, which was established by preliminary examination and confirmed during the actual trial. Immediately after the pogrom of Ryepki the police arrested and transported to Chernigov jail 70 peasants convicted of participation. Only two unarmed field guards were detailed to convoy the prisoners from Ryepki to Chernigov, a distance of 33 versts. Moreover, they were peasants from the same village, and very likely mixed up in the affair themselves. When the convoy halted for the night midway, at Roichensky, three of the prisoners told the guards that they still had business to arrange at home, returned to Ryepki the same night, set the house of the peasant Fyodor Ryedky on fire to pay him out for having opposed the pogrom and informed on its leaders, and then, in order not to be left behind, took a cart and caught up with their comrades. All the prisoners reported at the jail.

9. The Conversation of Giovanni Lopez, Cobbler

Source: Recorded by E. J. Hobsbawm, September 1955, in San Giovanni in Fiore, Calabria, in Mr Lopez's workshop.

Giovanni Lopez, shoemaker, San Giovanni in Fiore, about 50.

I was born in 1908. I've had fifty trades in my day, goat-herd, odd-job boy, sacristan, servant, shoemaker, I can't count them all. My father went when I was 7 or 8 months old, and we were very poor, very poor indeed. I became a goat-boy at about 6, taking it all in all boys are the slaves and serfs of everybody. Then the priests got me and I became a sacristan and stayed with them for years. Then I got fed up with the priests and left. They said, 'You'd better learn a trade.' So I found a good man who took me in and taught me shoemaking and paid decent wages. I think I was right. The Lord said 'In the sweat of thy face shalt thou eat bread' and not with clean hands like priests, that is why it is better to be a shoemaker; but I still know a bit of Latin and I can argue with the priests.

I had my military service, but beyond that I've always been here, in San Giovanni. I was an only child, now I'm

married with two children, the son's a carpenter with a
good workshop and even an electric motor, the daughter's
getting married this Christmas. Then I'll be alone with
my wife. My mother and father were both Socialists. You
must understand, in those days there was no Communist
Party. I still have their membership cards and pictures at
home, where I hid them during Fascism. Of course I'm a
Communist. The Lord said: 'Throw the money-changers
out of the temple.' I like what the priests say, but not
what they do. If you tell me this sole here is leather and
I find it's cardboard, I'll say you're a liar. Scripture is for
Communism. You know the parable of the vineyard. The
Lord said: 'I will give unto this last even as unto thee.' That
proves there ought to be equality. If it rains I say it should
rain for all. But if it rains for me, a labourer or a cobbler
and not for you, as might be a *benestante* (well-off man) or an
official, then I shall rebel. Mind you, I'm not complaining
about myself. I'm a good shoemaker, I do all the work for
the local *carabinieri* and the roadmen. The government lets
me do it because I'm a good shoemaker, not because I'm a
Communist.

Ours is a good town, San Giovanni, a well-appointed
town. We have four mills, twenty, twenty-five years ago we
got electricity and last June we even got the telephone. We
have a fine movement here and good people, our mayor
he's a good man, a building labourer. We used to be in
bondage, now we are free. Look at all those pictures I have
on my wall: Stalin, Togliatti. I cut them out of newspapers.
Under Fascism we couldn't have had that. Freedom is a
great thing. I get on well with people, even with those who
were Fascists and are now creeping back. I bear them no
grudge, because we Communists want only the welfare and

happiness of all men. We want peace because there's no good in war. The reason I argue with the priests is that they say not peace but a sword and I disagree. I'm for peace with everybody. But not with the thieves and robbers. Cut off their hands, I say.

10. Two Strike Sermons from the Loray Strike, North Carolina 1929

Source: Charlotte Observer and Baltimore Sun, quoted in Pope, op. cit.

1. 'I ain't never begged no widder for help. I ain't never asked nobody for no help. I've mighty near starved, and guess I would but somebody helped me, but hit wasn't nobody from Loray; hit was somebody on the outside.'

This brought cheers ... 'But,' said he, 'you needn't think that this here fighting to git something to wear and eat is gonna git you to heaven, for it ain't. You've got to be just as good a soldier for the Lord as you are chasing around here fighting for a living. Yes, some of youse are hot a-standin' out there, but don't you forget that there's a hotter place than this awaiting them that stays at home and goes to hell.'

The striker-preacher asked for a showing of hands of those who had been 'saved by the blood of Christ', and only about ten raised their hands. He told of his many varied experiences, and mentioned that he had seen as many as three fellows killed all at once. He made frequent references to his text, and in a very subtle manner, remarked: 'I'd hate to be in the shoes of men I know in Gaston county who are robbing God.' This brought profuse applause.

2. The strikers today went back to the fundamentals which they brought with them from the mountains. Kneeling on an old store counter salvaged out of the wreckage of the strikers' headquarters, H. J. Crabtree, minister of the Church of God, prayed for divine guidance of the strike. As the old man prayed, a group of strikers stood with bowed heads and as he came to a close fully a dozen joined in the 'Amen' . . . Brother Crabtree then preached. His text was, 'Deliver me, oh Lord, from the evil man; preserve me from the violent man.' 'I call God to witness who has been the violent man in this strike,' the preacher said. 'But we must bear it. Paul and Silas had to go through with it, and today they sit a-singing around the great white throne. In a few days you'll be a-singing through the streets of Loray with good wages. God's a poor man's God. Jesus Christ himself was born in an old ox-barn in Bethlehem. He was kicked about, speared about and finally nailed on a cross. And for what? For sin. It's sin that's causing this trouble. Sin of the rich man, the man who thinks he's rich . . .

All the wealthy men in this here crowd hold up their hands. I'll hold mine up for one. My father owns this whole world. He owns every hill in this world and every tater in them hills.'

11. A Lincolnshire Unionist: Joseph Chapman

Source: Rex C. Russell, *The Revolt of the Field in Lines.* (Lincolnshire County Committee of the National Union of Agricultural Workers n.d.), 137–8. The quotation is from a pamphlet published by Chapman in 1899. He became a Primitive Methodist in 1836 (at the age of 14).

I was among the Primitives in the Alford Circuit for over thirty years. I worked as a local preacher for the cause of Christ ... When the Labourers' Union first started in Alford I took a very great interest in it ... As an unpaid officer I worked for a living by day and went out at nights to lecture for the benefit of the Union ... The year 1872 gave birth to the Labourers' Union. I, Joseph Chapman, with Joseph Arch and William Banks of Boston, gave our tongues, our heads, our hearts, our influence in the maturing of the above Union. We don't believe in lords and ladies, priests and their wives being considered sacred and peasants being vermin. We do not think it right for idleness to sit at the banquet and the industrious gather the crust and the crumbs. I venture to say that we have done more for the emancipating of England's white slaves than all the modern priesthood put together ... I believe the time is not far distant when God will send restored apostles and prophets to his Church who will visit the aged poor and investigate how they live on three shillings a week, the annuity allowed from the parish, when rent coals and lighting is paid out of it, and enter a strong protest against such cruelty and preach with much force the gospel of God, that it will kill or cure barren and fruitless professors ... There is signs of the grand union that is coming when prince and peer and peasant shall combine and co-operate for the good of one and all. As many as are led by the spirit of God and they only. Some day it is going to be as big as the whole world, the world in union.

12. The 'Men of Decision' Recommend a Brother

Source: *Memoirs of the Secret Societies of the South of Italy, particularly the Carbonari* (London 1821), 130–2.

S.D.S.

(The Salentine Decision (Lodge). Health)

No. 5 Grand Masons L.D.D.T.G.S.A.F.G.C.I.T.D.U. etc.

(The Decision (lodge) of Jupiter the Thunderer hopes to make war against the tyrants of the universe etc.)

The mortal Gaetano Caffieri is a Brother Decided, No. 5, belonging to the Decision of Jupiter the Thunderer, spread over the face of the Earth, by his Decision, has had the pleasure to belong to this Salentine Republican Decision. We invite, therefore, all Philanthropic Societies to lend their strong arm to the same, and to assist him in his wants, he having come to the Decision that he will obtain liberty or death. Dated this day, the 29th of October 1817.

Signed

Pietro Gargaro (the Decided Grand Master No. 1)

Vito de Serio, Second Decided
Gaetano Caffieri, Registrar of the Dead.

The letters L.D.D.T. etc. and some other initials are written in blood. The four points beneath the name of the Grand Master indicate his power to pass sentence of death. The document is adorned with two skulls at the top corners, headed respectively 'Sadness' and 'Death', with two sets of crossed bones tied together with ribbon at the bottom corners, under which is written, respectively, 'Terror' and 'Mourning' and with two plaques: the fasces and the cap of liberty planted upon a death's head between two axes; and a thunderbolt darting from a cloud and striking the crowns and tiara. The lodge operated at Lecce, Apulia.

13. Some Secret Oaths

1. The Woolcombers' Union

Source: *Character, Objects and Effects of Trades Unions* (London 1834), 66 ff.

I, A.B., woolcomber, being in the awful presence of Almighty God, do voluntarily declare that I will persevere in endeavouring to support a brotherhood known by the name of the Friendly Society of Operative Stuff Manufacturers and other Industrious Operatives, and I solemnly declare and promise that I will never act in opposition to the brotherhood in any of their attempts to support wages, but will, to the utmost of my power, assist them in all lawful and just occasions, to obtain a fair remuneration for our labour. And I call upon God to witness this my most solemn declaration, that neither hopes, fears, rewards, punishments, nor even death itself, shall ever induce me directly or indirectly, to give any information respecting anything contained in this Lodge, or any similar lodge connected with the Society; and I will neither write nor cause to be written, upon paper, wood, sand, stone or any thing else, whereby it may be known, unless allowed to do so by the proper authorities of the Society. And I will never give my consent to have any money belonging to the Society divided or appropriated to any other purpose than the use of the Society and the support of the trade, so help me God, and keep me steadfast in this my most solemn obligation; and if I ever reveal either part or parts of this my most solemn obligation, may all the Society I am about to belong to, and all that is just, disgrace me so long as I live; and may what is now before me plunge my soul into the everlasting pit of misery. Amen.

2. *The Carbonaro Oath*

Source: *Memoirs of the Secret Societies of the South of Italy* (1821), 196.

I, N.N., promise and swear upon the general statutes of the order, and upon this steel, the avenging instrument of the perjured, scrupulously to keep the secret of Carbonarism; and neither to write, engrave, or paint anything concerning it, without having obtained a written permission. I swear to help my Good Cousins in case of need, as much as in me lies, and not to attempt anything against the honour of their families. I consent and wish, if I perjure myself, that my body may be cut in pieces, then burnt, and my ashes scattered to the wind, in order that my name may be held up to the execration of the Good Cousins throughout the earth. So help me God.

3. *The Abbreviated oath & ceremony of the Seasons (1834)*

Source: A. Chenu, *Les Conspirateurs* (Paris 1850), p. 20.

Copreaux, in his capacity as sponsor, blindfolded me and a formulary in the following terms was read to me:

'Are you a Republican?'

'I am.'

'Do you swear hatred to royalty?'

'I swear it.'

'If you intend to become a member of our secret society, know that the first order of your chiefs must be obeyed. Swear absolute obedience.'

'I swear it.'

'Then I proclaim you a member of the Society of the Seasons. Au revoir, citizen, and we'll meet again soon.' . . .

"There we are,' said Copreaux, 'now you belong to us. Let's go and have a drink to celebrate your welcome.'

Note on Further Reading

A few of the many publications relevant to the subjects treated in this volume are worth noting. Most of them have appeared since 1959. They should provide some guide to further reading.

Chapter I

The following discussions of issues raised in this book may be mentioned: Yonina Talmon, 'Pursuit of the Millennium: The relation between Religious and Social Change' (*Archives Europeennes de Sociologie* III, 1962, 125–48); M. I. Pereira de Queiroz, 'Millénarismes et Messiaismes' (*Annales E.S.C.* 19, 2, 1964, 330–44); L. Perini, 'Forme Primitive di rivolta' (*Studi Storici* VIII, 3, 1967, 598–606). Jean Chesneaux, Feiling Davis, Nguyen Nguget Ho ed, *Mouvements Populaires et Sociétés Secrètes en Chine au XIX et XX siècles* (Paris 1970) throws much light on the problem of archaic social movements.

Chapter II

For a fuller treatment and some bibliographical indications, E. J. Hobsbawm, *Bandits* (Harmondsworth 1972).

Chapter III

In addition to the relevant passages of D. Mack Smith, *Modern Sicily after 1713* (London 1968), see R. Rochefort, *Le Travail en Sicile* (Paris 1961) for general views. N. Russo (ed.), *Antologia de la Mafia* (Palermo 1964) reprints valuable early documents and accounts, up to and including Fascism. For the postwar era see the works of M. Pantaleone, *Mafia e political 1943–1962* (Turin 1962), *Mafia e droga* (Turin 1966), *Antimafia – occasione mancata* (Turin 1969) and D. Dolci, *Spreco* (Turin 1962). The official enquiry of the 1960s has also produced a considerable body of newspaper and periodical articles. H. Hess, *Mafia* (Tnbingeu 1970) has a good bibliography.

For the American Mafia, another increasingly documented subject, see D. Cressey, *Theft of a Nation* (New York 1969), P. Maas, *The Valachi Papers* (London 1968), Henry A. Zeiger, *Sam the Plumber* (New York 1970). The latter is particularly valuable, consisting as it does of selected transcripts of a fairly senior *mafioso's* conversations, as overheard by the F.B.I., and illustrates relationships between leaders and followers.

Chapter IV

The literature on millennialism has multiplied. Cf. the article and bibliography in *International Encyclopedia of Social Sciences* (1968) and, in particular, *Comparative Studies in Society and History* Suppl. II, 'Millennial dreams in action' (Hague 1962). W. Muehlmann, *Chiliasmus und Nativismus* (Berlin 1961), V. Lanternari, *Movimenti religiosi di libertà e di salvezza dei popoli oppressi* (Milan 1960), M. I. Pereira de Queiroz, *Réforme et révolution dans les societés traditionnelles; histoire et ethnologie des mouvements messianiques* (Paris 1968).

Since 1959 L. Graziani has published a *Studio bibliografico su David Lazzaretti* (Rome 1964) and A. Moscato and M. N. Pierini, *Rivolta religiosa nelle campagne* (Rome 1965) on both Lazzaretti and the Jews of San Nicandro.

Chapter V

Among recent publications R. Carr, *Spain 1808–1959* (Oxford 1966) provides general background, E. Malefakis, *Agrarian Reform and Peasant Revolution in Spain* (Yale 1970) is the fullest treatment of the subject, and quite first-rate; J. Martinez Alier, *La estabilidad del latifundio* (Paris 1968) investigates the mental world of the Andalusian labourers in the middle 1960s, and analyses the changes since 1936. It is also worth noting that a somewhat shortened version of Diaz del Moral's marvellous book was also reprinted as a paperback (Madrid 1967).

Chapter VI

The fullest account of the Sicilian Fasci is Salvatore F. Romano, *Storia dei Fasci Siciliani* (Bari 1959). For wider issues, see S. G. Tarrow, *Peasant Communism in Southern Italy* (New Haven and London 1967).

Chapter VII

The literature about riots and crowds is multiplying rapidly. Cf. H. D. Graham and Ted Gurr, *The History of Violence in America* (New York 1969) for samples and references. G. Rudé, *The Crowd in History, 1730–1848* (New York 1964) is an excellent introduction to the period covered here. See also R. Carr, *Spain 1808–1939*, esp. cap. V on Spanish urban revolutions.

Chapter VIII

K. S. Inglis, *The Churches and the Working Classes in Victorian England* (London 1963) is useful. E. P. Thompson, *The Making of the English Working Class* (London 1963) discusses religious aspects of the early labour movement, and J. F. C. Harrison, *Robert Owen and the Olenites* (London 1969) brings out the millennial character and the links with other millennial currents of Owenism. The proletarian sect most fully investigated is the Mormons; see P. A. M. Taylor, *Expectations Westward* (Edinburgh 1965).

Chapter IX

E. Coornaert, *Les Compagnonnages en France* (Paris 1966) supersedes earlier works in the field; E. P. Thompson, *Making of the English Working Class* (London 1963) is keenly aware of the ritual aspects of the subject; P. H. J. H. Gosden, *The Friendly Societies in England 1815–1875* (Manchester 1961) is the only modern work on its subject. On the origins of the Communist League, recent works worth noting are W. Kowalski, *Vorgeschichte und Entstehung des Bundes der Gerechten* (Berlin-East 1962) and Bert Andreas, *Gruendungsdokumente des Bundes der Kommunisten* (Hamburg 1969).

Geographical Index

Agrigento, 46n, 60n
Albania, 56n, 135, 139
Alcala del Valle, 103n
Alford, 258
Almaden, 100
America (United States), 32, 41, 44n,
    47, 47n, 58, 62–4, 95n, 96,
    144, 167, 180, 193, 200, 217
  states:
  Arizona, 48
  California, 33
  North Carolina, 174n, 256–7
Andria, 239
Angri, 73
Antequera, 103n
Arcidosso, 88, 92, 93, 94
Arcos de la Frontera, 103, 103n,
    106
Aspromonte, 20
Atella, 240
Australia, 68, 68n
Azov, 247, 249

Baena, 41n, 99, 100n
Bagheria, 54, 63n
Barcelona, 111, 162, 162n, 163
Basel, 71
Belgium, 195

Benameji, 41n, 102, 103, 106
Benaocaz, 103
Benevento, 124
Bengal, 216n, 223
Berlin, 165
Bezdna, 160
Birmingham (England), 148n, 189n,
    192
Bisacquino, 133
Bologna, 151
Bolton, 192
Bordighera, 68n
Bornos, 103, 118
Boston (England), 258
Bova, 20, 22
Bradford, 190–1, 192
Bradshaw, 192
Brazil, xvi, xix, xx, xxiin, xxiii,
    xxiv–xxv, 83n
Brinkworth, 183
Britain (see also England; Scotland;
    Wales), xix, 10, 143, Chapter
    VIII passim, 204, 209, 211,
    212, 214
counties and districts:
  Berkshire, 182
  Cornwall, 181
  Cumberland, 184

Derbyshire, 184, 187
　Dorset, 181, 183, 184
　Durham, 6, 181, 183–4, 186,
　　187
　East Anglia, 30
　Essex, 175
　Kent, 179
　Lancashire, 181, 181*n*, 192
　Lincolnshire, 181, 233, 257–8
　Midlands, 182, 184, 186
　Norfolk, 181–2, 183, 184, 185*n*,
　　187, 196*n*
　North, 181, 183–7, 192, 193, 195
　Northumberland, 183, 186
　Shropshire, 183
　Staffordshire, 186
　Suffolk, 183
　Thames Valley, 182
　Tyneside, 4
　West, 25, 179, 181, 192
　Wiltshire, 183
　Yorkshire, 184–7
Brussels, 216
Buenos Aires, 111
Bujalance, 103*n*, 113
Bykhvostova, 36

Cadiz, xvi, 98, 100, 100*n*, 103–4,
　103*n*, 111
Cagliari, 235, 236
Canicatti, 131
Canolo, 67, 69
Carmona, 103*n*
Carpatho-Ukraine, 18
Carpathians, 19, 20, 25, 32, 33
Casas Viejas, 105, 106*n*, 111, 112,
　113, 114, 118
Castel del Piano, 88
Castro del Rio, 103*n*, 108, 113
Catania, 127, 155

Chernigov, 34*n*, 36*n*, 252–4
China, xxii, *148*
Cinigiano, 88
Cordoba, 24*n*, 41*n*, 98, 100, 101,
　103*n*, 104, 108
Corleone, 63*n*, 131
Cosenza, xvi, 96, 155, 155*n*

Delianova, 20
Denmark, 30
Dewsbury, 186
Dnieper, 247
Dobrianka, 253
Docking, 183
Don, 247
Dublin, 51, 159, 227

Eire, see Ireland
El Arahal, 103
El Bosque, 103
England (see also Britain), 17, 30, 112,
　168n, 180, 181, 189n, 195, 258

Farnworth, 192
Favara, 46*n*, 54
Fernan-Nuñez, 103*n*
Foggia, 95, 95*n*, 96, 240, 243
France (see also individual place-names),
　xix, 80, 91, 92, 158, 188, 194,
　195, 210, 213, 214, 224
　departments and regions:
　Corsica, 5, 6, 19, 23
　Nord, 164
　Normandy, 30
　Pas-de-Calais, 164
　Sarthe, 169
　Vendée, 163
Fuenteovejuna, 101, 102

Gallo, 124

Gaston County, 256

Gastonia, 174*n*, 176*n*, 179, 195

Geneva, 216

Gerace, 69

Germany, xix, 144, 158, 168, 170,
208–9, 211, 219, 224, 228, 247

  Central, 164

  Rhineland, 26, 31

  Silesia, 177

Gibraltar, 219

Gioia Tauro, 68

Gorodna, 252, 253

Grazalema, 97*n*, 103, 112

Greece, 20, 135, 139

Grimsby, 181

Grotte, 133

Guadalquivir, 98, 100

Gulai-Polye, 247, 249

Halifax, 192

Holland, 181

Hull, 191, 198

Hyde, 192

Iceland, 181

Ireland, 27, 51, 58, 159, 168, 173,
211, 216n, 217, 220, 220n, 223

Israel, 243, 244, 245

Istanbul, 152

Italy (see also individual place-names),
xv, xvi, xix, 1, 18, 24–32
passim, 26n, 55, 63–5, 84–96,
95n, 99, 106, 123–7, 126n,
135, 138n, 155–6, 222n,
241–3, 258–9, 261

  provinces, regions, and zones:

  Agrigento, 46*n*, 60*n*

  Apulia, xvi, 25, 27, 95, 221, 243,
    259

  Bari, 73

Basilicata (Lucania), 23, 23*n*,
  24*n*, 25

  Calabria, xvi, 6, 20–32 *passim*,
    20*n*, 41–2, 42*n*, 65-9, 68*n*,
    96, 155, 254–6

  Caltanissetta, 60, 60*n*

  Campania, 155

  Capitanata, 23, 25

  Caserta, 73

  Catania, 127, 155

  Cilento, 42

  Cosenza, xvi, 96, 155*n*

  Foggia, 95–6, 95*n*, 240, 243

  Latium, 26, 87, 155

  Liguria, 68

  Lombard, 42

  Lucania, *see* Basilicata

  Maremma, 24, 87

  Messina, 127, 155

  Monte Gargano, 95, 95*n*

  Naples, 38, 72–4, 136, 148–62
    passim

  Nuoro, 237

  Palermo, xxvi, 32*n*, Chapter
    III *passim*, 127, 134*n*, 135*n*,
    136, 137, 149–55, 162–5,
    245

  Piedmont, 42, 47, 49, 55, 89,
    241

  Reggio Calabria, 21, 42*n*, 66

  Romagna, 125*n*, 154

  Rome, xv, xvi, 18*n*, 58–63
    passim, 138, 149–55 *passim*,
    235, 241–4 *passim*

  Salerno, 42, 73

  Sardinia, 5, 21, 22*n*, 27, 32, 238

  Sicily, xvi, xxi, xxv, 4, 6, 8, 18,
    19, 22, 31, 35, Chapter III
    passim, 79, 81, 84, 85, 98,
    99, 106, 108, 121, Chapter

VI *passim*, 143, 149*n*, 159, 160, 236, 238, 245
Siena, 89
Sila (Calabrian), 31
South, xv, Chapter II *passim*, 55, 84, 94, 96, 99, 106, 125*n*, 127, 155, 243
Tavoliere, 96
Trapani, 60*n*, 63*n*, 141
Tuscany, xv, 8, 85–9, 92, 126*n*
Umbria, 87
Iznajar, 41, 102, 103*n*, 106

Jerez, 103, 103*n*, 105, 117
Jerusalem, 243

Kiev, 253
Kussiey, 253

La Linea, 103*n*
Lebrija, 118
Lecce, 233, 259
Leeds, 192
Leghorn, 111
Letino, 124
Liege, 195
Linares, 103*n*
Liverpool, 148*n*
Loja, 102
London, xv, 156, 163, 165, 170, 173, 174, 178*n*, 194, 216
Londonderry, 183
Loray, 256–7

Madrid, 111
Malaga, 100, 103*n*, 104, 109, 110
Manchester, xv, 189, 192
Marsala, 136
Medina Sidonia, 103, 103*n*
Messina, 127, 155

Milan, xvi, 151, 154, 164
Milazzo, 46
Minsterley, 183
Monreale, 46*n*, 49, 54, 54*n*, 59, 61, 63
Monte Amiata, 86–96 *passim*
Montelepre, 19, 22, 32
Montemaggiore, 22
Montilla, 41*n*
Morley, 192
Morón, 103*n*, 110*n*
Motcombe, 183

Naples, 38, 72–4, 136, 148–62 *passim*
Netherlands, *see Holland*
Newcastle-on-Tyne, 183
New Orleans, 56*n*, 62
Newport, 196
New York, 46*n*, 56*n*, 62, 111
Noca Inferiore, 73
Nola, 73
Norway, 181
Norwich, 194
Nuoro, 237

Orgosolo, 235, 236, 237, 238
Osuna, 103, 106

Palermo, xxvi, 31, 31*n*, Chapter III *passim*, 127, 134*n*, 135*n*, 136, 137, 149–55 *passim*, 162, 164, 165, 245
Paris, 147, 149, 153, 159, 162, 165, 165*n*, 69, 212, 215, 216, 219, 224
Parma, 154–5
Partinico-Monreale, 63*n*
Piana dei Greci, 56, 126, 131, 132, 135, 233, 245

Piana degli Albanesi, xvi, 121, 135
Plymouth, 191, 192
Poland, 17, 168
Poltava, 250–2
Porta della Ginestra, 35, 59, 139
Portugal, 101
Pozoblanco, 100, 102

Reggio Calabria, 21, 42*n*, 66
Rheims, 200
Rio Tinto, 100
Roccalbegna, 88
Rochdale, 195
Rockland, 183
Roichensky, 254
Rome, Rome, xv, xvi, 18*n*, 58–63
   passim, 138, 149–55 *passim*,
   235, 241–4 *passim*
Ronda, 100
*Russia (see also Ukraine; individual
   place-names)*, 37, 37*n*, 80, 104,
   114, 157, 160*n*, 216*n*, 219, 224,
   226, 247
Ryepki, 253–4

'sa verula', 235, 238
St Petersburg, 251
Salerno, 42, 73
San Fernando, 103*n*
San Giovanni in Fiore, xvi, 254–5
San Giuseppe Iato, 25, 141
San Nicandro, xvi, 95, 95*n*, 96,
   233, 243, 265
Santa Fiora, 88–9
Scafati, 73–4
Sciacca, 23
Scotland *(see also Britain)*, 188
Seville, 98, 100, 103, 103*n*, 156,
   162
Sheffield, 173, 182, 194

Shotley Bridge, 183
Sicily *(see also* Italy, *under* provinces,
   regions and zones), Kingdom
   of the Two Sicilies, 125
Sinopoli, 68*n*
Slovakia, 17
Spain (see also individual place-names),
   xvi, xix, xxii, 18, 79, Chapter
   V *passim*, 124–5, 135, 162
provinces and regions:
Andalusia, xvi, xxii, xxv, 6, 8,
   17, 23, 24, 41, 79, 82, 84,
   85, Chapter V *passim*, 123,
   125, 125*n*, 133, 134, 141,
   142, 143, 162*n*
Aragon, 102, 107, 163
Cadiz, xvi, 98, 100, 100*n*,
   103–4, 103*n*, 111, 111*n*
Castille, 99*n*, 100, 157
Catalonia, 101
Cordoba, 24*n*, 41*n*, 98, 100, 101,
   103*n*, 104, 108, 110
Granada, 100
Huelva, 98
Jaen, 98, 100, 103*n*
Malaga, 100, 103, 104, 109–10
Navarre, 107, 163
Seville, 98, 100, 103, 103*n*, 156,
   162
'Sicily of', 98
South, 18, 100, 124
Stoke-on-Trent, 165
Sturno, 241
Sydney, 68*n*

Thornley, 183
Tolpuddle, 184
Trapani, 60*n*, 63*n*, 141
Turin, 164
Turkey, 135

Ukraine, 18, 36, 37, 247, 250
United Kingdom (UK), *see Britain*
United States (US), see America

Vallata, 33*n*
Venice, 153
Versailles, 153
Vienna, 29*n*, 148, 149, 152, 153,
    162, 163, 165*n*
Villagrande, 235, 238
Villalba, 59, 59*n*

Villamartin, 103, 103*n*, 118
Volga, 160

Wales *(see also Britain)*, 164, 168*n*,
    172, 172*n*, 176, 182, 187, 188,
    196, 198
Wangford, 183

Yarmouth, 181

Zaporozhe, 249

Index of Names

Sources mentioned in the text or discussed are marked*. Where necessary, the persons indexed are briefly described.

Ackroyd, Seth, labour sectarian, 191, 191n, 198
Albert (revolutionary), 228n
Alexander II, of Russia, 160
*Alongi, G., 23n, 42n, 45n, 46n, 71, 71n, 72, 73, 130n
Angiolillo (bandit), 18, 19, 19n, 20, 27, 29, 38
Annicchiarico, Ciro (bandit), 39
Antonio the Counsellor (prophet), xxv, 83n
Apraxin, Gen., 160
Arch, Joseph, 184, 196n, 258

Bakunin, Michael, 36, 36n, 102, 103, 109, 114, 124, 219, 219n
Banks, W. (trade unionist), 258
Barbato (Sicilian family) 134, 135, 135n
Barbato, N. (socialist), 137–9
*Barzellotti, G., 86, 86n, 88n, 89n, 91n, 92n
Batey, J. (trade unionist), 186
Blake, William, 78, 78n

Blanqui, Auguste, 219n, 222, 223–4, 228–31, 228n
Blatchford, R., 170, 192
Bloor, T. (trade unionist), 186
Borjes, J. L. (soldier), 35
Bradlaugh, Charles, 170
Branca (policeman), 63, 149
*Brenan, G., 41n, 97, 97n, 99n, 100, 106, 106n, 107n, 109–10, 110n, 120, 163n
Broadhurst, Henry, 184
Brown, W. J. (politician), 187
Bunyan, John, 193, 194
Buonarroti, P. (revolutionary), 216, 218, 218n, 219, 219n, 230
Burt, T. (trade unionist), 184

Cabanas Silva, J. 113
Caffieri, G. (revolutionary), 259
Cafiero, Carlo, 124
*Cagnetta, F., 5, 235–9
Calabro, R. (*mafioso*), *68n*
Campesi (bandit), 21
Cape, Tom, 184

Capraro (bandit), 23
Cascioferro, Vito, 55
*Cassin, Elena, 95, 95n, 243
Castagna, Serafino, 66n
Castriot, George, *see* Skanderbeg
Cervantes, M., 71
Chalier, M. J. (revolutionary), 169
Championne, Gen., 160
Chapman, Joseph, 257–8
Cheremok, Pyotr, 36
*Cohn, Prof. Norman, xv, 14, 75–6
*Colajanni, N., 42n, 54n, 58, 127n, 128n, 130n
Coleman, Zachariah, 194, 196
Comte, Auguste, 169
Cook, A. J., 187
Copreaux (revolutionary), 261–2
Corrientes, Diego, 17, 101
Cowey, E. (trade unionist), 184
Crabtree, H. J. (preacher), 257
Crawford, William, 184
Croce, Benedetto, 19, 149n, 150, 150n, 151n, 160n
Cruz, Curro, 113
Cruz, Maria, 113
*Cutrera, A., 42n, 46, 49n, 50n, 56n

d'Agostino, Nicola, 67, 69
*Dakin, D., 219
Dallas, G., MP, 187
de Furia, Giuseppe, 25
de Serio, Vito, 259
*Diaz del Moral, J., 97n, 100, 109, 110, 112, 113, 115, 117, 119n, 265
Dick Turpin, 29, 30
Dimino, S. (heretic), 133
Dionigi, Mariano, 21

Di Pasquale (bandit), 22
Djilas, M., 80n, 81n
Donatello, Carmine ('Crocco'), 38
*Donini, Prof. Ambrogio, xv, 18n, 86n
*Douglas, Norman, 28
Dovbush, Oleksa, 19–20, 29, 29n, 33
Duca, A., *see* Angiolillo
Dugue, Saint Perrine, 169
Dunlop, John, 204

Edwards, Enoch, 184
Edwards, George, 184, 187, 196n
Engels, Friedrich, 225
Enko (landowner), 252

Fenwick, C. (trade unionist), 184, 186
Ferdinand II of Naples, 72
Finance, Isodore, 188n
Finney, Sam, 184
Fiore, Joachim of, 14
*Franchetti, L., 42, 43n, 50n, 126n
Francis I of Austria, 158
Francis II of Naples, 72, 241, 242
Francis, Saint, 133
Franco, Gen., 104, 108, 121

Garcia Lorca, F., 103
Gargaro, Pietro, 259
Garibaldi, G., 38, 49, 55, 58, 125, 136, 162–3
Giuliano, Salvatore, 19, 21, 22, 25, 26, 29, 31, 35, 53, 139, 235–6, 238
Goddi, G. (bandit), 21
Gooch, Edwin, 184
Gramsci, Antonio, 13

Harun-al-Raschid, 158
Hauptmann, Gerhart, 177
Heller, Justo, 113
Henderson, Arthur, 184, 186
Henry III of France, 159
Hepburn, T. (trade unionist), 184
Hill, Billy, 27
Hodde, de la (police spy), 221,
    222*n*, 226, 228, 228*n*
Holyoake, G. J., 170
Hood, Robin, *see* Robin Hood
Horner, Arthur, 187, 198
Hoxha, Enver, 139

Jacks, Samuel, 186
James, Jesse, 33
Janošik (legendary bandit), 17, 25
*Jennings, Hilda, 176, 176*n*
Johnson, John, 184
Joseph II of Austria, 158

*Kefauver, E., 44*n*, 62*n*
*Kendall, H. B., 179*n*, 181, 185*n*
Kenyon, Barnett, 184, 186–7
Kerensky, A., 250
Keufer, A. (trade unionist), 188*n*
Kropotkin, Peter, 111

*La Loggia, E., 128*n*, 130*n*, 136,
    136*n*
Lansbury, George, 170
Lazzaretti, Davide, xv, xviv, 8,
    75–96, 130, 132, 142–3, 244,
    265
Lee, Peter, 184, 186
Lenin, Vladimir, 94, 229, 230,
    250
Lepeletier (revolutionary), 169
Lerroux, Alejandro, 163
*Levi, Carlo, 28, 93

Libertaria, La, *see* Cruz, Maria
Li Causi, G. (communist), 59
*Linden, Franz, 170*n*, 187
Lo Cicero (bandit), 22
Loddo (policeman), 237–8
*Lombroso, C., 24*n*, 42*n*
Londonderry, Lord, 183
*Longnone, R., 20*n*, 22*n*, 66*n*, 67
Lopez, Giovanni, xvi,, 23, 254–6
Lorenzo, Fr (unorthodox priest),
    57*n*, 132*n*, 133, 138*n*
Loyacano (Sicilian family), 56, 135
Luther, Martin, 94

Macheath, Capt., 30
*Mack Smith, Denis, 127*n*, 163,
    264
Macri, Angelo, 20
Makhno, Nestor, 37, 247, 249
Malatesta, Errico, 109, 111, 124
Manduzio, D., prophet, 233, 243–5
Manzoni, Alessandro, 45
Marat, J. P., 169
Mariana, J. de, 102
Martina, Duke of, 20
Marx, Karl, 14, 109, 123–5, 170,
    171*n*, 195, 198, 219*n*, 220,
    224–5, 224*n*, 229, 230
Masaniello, 147*n*, 150–1, 151*n*
Matranga (Sicilian family), 56*n*,
    62, 135, 135*n*
*Maxwell, Gavin, 19, 19*n*
Mazzini, G., 38, 219, 227, 229
Meomartino, Gaetano, *see*
    Vardarelli, Gaetano
Messer, Fred, MP, 187
Miceli, Salvatore, 49, 59
Milton, John, 194
*Montalbane, G., 42*n*, 45*n*, 46*n*,
    48*n*, 49*n*, 54*n*, 55, 55*n*, 59*n*, 61

More, Thomas, 5
Murat, Joachim, 25
Musolino, Giuseppe, 31, 31n

Napoléon Bonaparte, 218
Nappi, Vittorio, 74
Nestroy, Johann, 162n
Nicholas II of Russia, 158

O'Casey, Sean, 159
*Olbracht, Ivan, 19n, 29n, 30n, 32, 33n, 34

Paine, Thomas, 170
Parrott, W. (trade unionist), 184, 186
Pastorelli (wealthy family), 93
Petrosino, Lieut (policeman), 56n
Pickard, Ben, 184
Pippin, King, 243–5
*Pitt-Rivers, J., 23n, 26n, 97n, 101n, 121
Pius IX, 38, 91, 92
Place, Francis, 170
*Pope, L., 174, 174n, 175–6, 175n, 176n, 178n, 186n, 256
Potapenko, V. (Cossack) 36
Prim, Gen., 162n
Provenzano (Camorrist family), 62

Reclus, E. (anarchist), 109
Reid, T. (trade unionist), 186
*Renda, F. (political organizer), 59–60, 59n, 61n, 62, 63n, 64, 64n, 129n, 137n
Ricciu (policeman), 238
Riego (Spanish Republican hero), 162n
Robin Hood, xx, 1, 5, 6, 17, 19, 25–30 *passim*, 234

Romano, Sergeant (bandit), 25, 33n
Romeo, Vicenzo, 20, 22
*Rossi, Adolfo, 128n, 131n, 132, 132n, 133n, 134n, 136, 136n, 137, 138n, 245
*Rudé, George, 146, 148n, 150n, 265
Russo, Genco, 51
Rutherford, Mark, 194
Ryedky, Fyodor, 254

St André, Jeanbon, 27
St Anne, 212
St Antonius, 160
St Crispin, 212
St Eligius, 212
St Francis, 133
St Januarius, 150, 160
St John the Baptist, 222
St Joseph, 212
St Paul, 197
St Peter, 212
Sta Rosalia, 150
St Simonian, 169
Salis, G. A. (landowner), 21
Sanchez Rosa, José, 112
Skanderbeg (Albanian nobleman), 139
Scelba, Mario, 236, 238, 239
Schiller, F. (poet), 36
Schinderhannes (bandit), 26, 29
Schirò (Sicilian family), 56n, 135, 135n
*Scotellaro, Rocco, 95, 95n, 155n
Sebastiano, Mereu, 238
Sen, Suriya (terrorist), 223n
Serra (policeman), 238
Shakespeare, William, 225–6
Shuhaj, Nikola (fictional bandit), 19–20, 19n, 25

Silverio (flamenco singer), 162n
Simons, C., MP, 187
Sinenko, V. (peasant), 253
Six Fingers, *see* Cruz, Curro
*Soboul, Albert, 169
Stalin, Joseph, 255
Stanley, Albert, 184
Stassi (Sicilian family), 135

Tanteddu, Pasquale, 27, 233,
    235–9
Tanteddu, Pietro, 237
Taras, Antonio, 235
*Thomas, Gwyn, 176
Thomas, J. H., 187
Tiburzi, Domenico, 25–6
Tillet, Ben, 191
Togliatti, Palmiro, 93, 255
Toyn, J. (trade unionist), 184
*Trevelyan, G. M., 136
Trevor, John, 189–91
Triana, Fernando el de, 162n
*Troeltsch, E., 178
Turpin, Dick, *see* Dick Turpin

Vallejo Chinchilla, M. (anarchist),
    113
Valvo (bandit), 22
Vardarelli, Gaetano, 2, 27, 38,
    233, 239–40
*Verga, G., 127
Verro, B. (socialist), 134
Victor Emmanuel I of Italy, 92,
    241
*Villari, L., 136
Vizzini, Calogero, 51
von Goethe, J. W., 150

*Wearmouth, R., 171n, 179n, 180n,
    182n, 185, 186n
Weitling, Wilhelm, 169
Wesley, John, 171n
Wicksteed Philip, 189
Williams, Zephaniah, 196
Wilson, John, 184, 187

Yeats, W. B., 81
Yevtushenko, Kirill, 253

Subject Index

abduction, marriage by, 20, 24, 68*n*
abolition:
—, commercial slavery, 190
—, feudalism, 50, 52, 125–6, 136
—, money, 108
—, taxes and excise, 130
abstinence, *see* Temperance
Adelfi, 218–19
Adventists, 94
Anabaptists (see also Baptism, adult), 85, 122
anarcho-syndicalism, 114, 120
anarchism, -ists *(see also* Bakuninists), xxii, xxv, 8, 36–7, 37*n*, 41*n*, 77–9, 82, 85, Chapter V *passim,* 123, 124, 125, 132, 133, 135, 143, 161, 165, 167, 247–9
anti-clericalism *(see also* Clergy), 96, Chapter V *passim,* 159, 163, 168, 194, 234
Armed Companies, 52
artisans *(see also* journeymen's societies; plebs), 47, 94, 95, 100–1, 129, 129*n*, 144, 148, 151, 156, 170, 173, 173*n*, 175, 194, 204, 209, 214, 221, 228

—, rural, 39, 67, 94
atheism, *see* freethinking

Babouvism, 219
Bakuninism, -ists *(see also* anarchism), 36, 102, 103, 109, 114, 124, 219*n*
banditry, xix, xx, xxvi, 1, 5–9, 12, Chapter II *passim,* Chapter III *passim,* 101, 101*n*, 103, 106–7, 121, 139, 143, 156–7, 233, 235–9
bandolero (see also banditry*) 18, 24, 32n, 107*
bands, peasant, 24–5, 30*n*, 35, 36, 47, 102, 235
baptism, adult *(see also* anabaptists; initiation), 113, 201, 208
baptists, 85, 94, 171, 181, 182, 186, 188, 189
barbers, 228
Bengali Terrorist Movement, 223
betrayal *(see also* informers; *omertà*), 19, 27, 35, 82, 109, 132, 148, 156, 226, 238, 243, 248
Bhawani Mandir, 223n, 226
Bible, 25, 176, 179, 190, 193, 197, 234, 244

Bible Christians, *25, 179*

Blanquism (*see also Society of the Seasons*), *219n*, 224, 228–31, *228n*

blood-brotherhood (*see also* brotherhoods; gilds; kinship, artificial), 46, 62

blood-feud, *see* vengeance, blood

boatmen, 151

Bolshevism (*see also* communism), *37n*, 80, 104, 110, 230, 247, 249

Bourbons, *20n*, 24–5, 28, 34–5, 38, 47, 49, 52, 55, 66, 72, 106, 125, 153, 157, 160, 162, 233, 241–3

Bourgeoisie (*see also* middle class), 27, 50, 51, 126, 155, 173, 193, 210, 228

—, petite, *see* shopkeepers

braceros, see landless labourers

brigands, *see* banditry

brotherhoods (*see also* blood-brotherhood, gilds; kinship, artificial), xxvii, 3, 11, 131, 159, 161, Chapter IX *passim*, 235, 260

Buddhism, 76

builders, 206

Bund der Geächteten, see League of Outlaws

Bund der Gerechten, see League of the Just

butchers, 151

cabinet-makers, *228n*

caciques, 18, 24, 107

Camere del Lavoro, 96

Camorra, 42n, 44, 46, 47, 62, 66n, 71–4, 71n, 162

campieri, 21, 51, 64, 65, 126, 137

cantonalism, 102

capitalism (*see also* liberalism, economic), xxii, xxiii, 2, 4, 11, 26, 30–2, 50, 55–7, 88, 105, 112, 118, 126, 128, 143, 144, 190, 191

carabinieri (see also police), 92, 93, 235–9, 255

Carbonari, 38–9, 66, 102, Chapter IX passim

cargo cults, 6, 86

Carlists, 107, 163

carters, 89–90, 151

Charbonnerie Democratique Universelle, 219

Chartism, 129, 172, 179, 195

Chiliasm, 76

Church of Christian Brothers, 94

Church of England, 171–2, 173

Church of God, 179, 257

Church, Pentecostal Holiness, 179

Church, Roman Catholic (*see also* Papacy), 10, 102, 135, 136, 168, 173, 212

'Church and King', 9, 37, 146, 148, 157, 159, 163, 234

Church-burning (*see also* Puritanism, revolutionary), 109

Circolo Savonarola, 133

cities (*see also individual towns*), xxvi, 4, 9, 47, 91, 127, 129, Chapter VII *passim*, 170, 174, 194, 195, 223, 234, 247–9

—, Capital, 146, 164–5

—, Patriotism, Chapter VII *passim*

—, planning, and riot, 165

civil servants, 4

Civil Service Clerical Association, 187
civil wars, 104, 121
Clarion, 192
clergy (*see also* anticlericalism;
    individual churches), 36n, 158,
    Chapter VIII *passim*
coachmakers, 204, 215
cobblers, xvi, 95, 111, 145, 150,
    162, 212, 228, 254–6
Cofradia del Monopodio, 71
Committee of Public Safety, 27
communism (*see also* Bolshevism),
    xxiv, 10, 27, 31, 56n, 95, 102,
    115, 118, 121, Chapter VI
    passim, 167, 181, 223, 255
Communist League, 266
Compagnonnages, see journeymen's
    societies
*Confederazione Generale Italiana del
    Lavoro (CGIL), 95*
Confraternity, 129n
Congregationalists, 182, 184, 198
contro-squadre, 52, 55
conversion, 70, 90, 139, 172–3,
    178, 179–80, 186–8, 243
co-operation, 38, 55, 138, 195–6,
    195n
coopers, 208
cosche 45, 53
cossacks, 36, 36n
cost of living, 147, 152
counter-revolution, 36, 151, 156
craftsmen (*see* artisans)
crime, 21, 24, 36, Chapter III
    passim, 103, 207, 235, 237,
    238, 242, 246–7

dealers and moneylenders, 26, 29,
    147, 148, 150
Decembrists, 219

Decisi, 39
deism, 159, 169, 171, 189
demonstrations, mass, 27, 58, 66,
    70, 98, 104, 105, 106, 121,
    123, 135, 150, 152, 160
depression, economic, 24, 70, 96,
    124, 129, 133, 137
destructiveness, 36, 234
dockers, 150, 199, 203n
drug-trafficking, 64

Easter Rising, Irish, 81, 227
elections, 60, 60n, 62, 68, 94n,
    100, 100n, 137–8, 154, 155,
    155n
élites, xxii, 4, 47n, 58, 62, 71, 81,
    82, 96, 144, 167, 174, 195,
    220, 227, 231
emigration, 32, 56n, 68n, 121, 128
Enclosures, *see* land, common
Enfants du Père Soubise, see
    journeymen's societies
Enfants de Salomon, see journeymen's
    societies
Enfants du Maître Jacques, see
    journeymen's societies
'Enlightenment, The' (*see also*
    deism; rationalism), 217
equality, 32, 81, 161, 234, 235,
    255
excommunication, 92, 33, 242,
    246
Fabian Society, 170, 220
Famine, 31, 104, 147, 157, 164
Farm Labourers, 105, 182, 185,
    185n, 187, 198
Fasci Siciliani, 56, Chapter VI passim,
    265
fascism, 59, 62–3, 63n, 94n, 96,
    120, 129n, 139, 155, 155n, 255

Fenians, *see Irish Republican Brotherhood*

feudalism, 6, 13, 42–4, 48, 50, 52, 55, 66, 105, 125–6, 136

fibbia, 65, 66n, 68n

fieldguards, *see campieri*

Filadelfi, 218–19, 221

First World War *see* World War I

fishermen, 47, 151, 181

fish-sellers, 150

folklore (see also literature, popular; Janošik; Robin Hood; Dick Turpin), 20, 158, 174

foreigners *(see also* nationality), 5, 9, 28, 29, 106, 149, 151

forest laws, 88, 89

Fratellanza, 46n, 54

fraternities, religious, *see* brotherhoods; gilds; kinship, artificial)

fraternity, 71, 73, 81, 212–15, 246

Fratuzzi, 54

Freemasons, 41, 66, 102, 202, 202n, 209, 210n, 216

freethinking, 85, 167, 168, 170, 188, 195, 196

friendly societies, 54, 204, 209n, 210, 212, 214, 260

Frontier, American, 180, 181

gabellotti (see also middle class, rural), 50, 57, 61, 126, 138

galantuomini, see gentry

Garibaldians, 38, 49, 55, 58, 125, 136, 162, 163

Gasworkers' Union, 192

General Italian Confederation of Labour, *95*

General Strike *(see also* strikes), 103, 105, 117

gentry *(see also* landlords; nobility), 26, 28, 35, 101, 117, 119, 124, 127, 247, 253

Gesellenverbaende, see journeymen's societies)

gilds and corporations, 33, 71, 144, 148, 151

gilders, 228n

gleaning, 27, 240

Gordon Riots, 148, 148n

Grand-Orient (see also Freemasons), 217

Great World *see* World War I

Guardia Civil, 106

guerillas, 7, 23, 24, 28, 34, 35, 55, 102, 121n

Heaven, mandate of, 57

herdsmen, 23, 38, 39, 52

Hinduism, 76, 223

homicide *(see also* vengeance, blood), 21, 66, 127n, 235, 238, 242

illiteracy, 3, 39, 42, 49, 58, 61, 88, 99, 113, 115, 195, 201, 213, 236

Illuminati, 217, 218n, 222

Immacolata, 129n

immigrants, *see* emigration

impossibilism, 79, 85

Independent Labour Party, 170, 189, 192

Industrial Revolution, 170, 171

Industrial Workers of the World (IWW), 33

industrialization, xxvi, 1, 8–10, 29, 90, 99, Chapter VIII *passim*, 209, 214

informers *(see also* betrayal;

individuals by name in Index of Names), xvi, 137, 235, 238

initiation (*see also* ritual), 46, 46n, 66, 201–11, 207n, 218–20, 224, 224n, 228

insurrection (*see also* Blanquism; peasantry risings; revolution), Chapter V *passim*, 127, 128 134, 150n, 159, 220

intellectuals, 39, 90, 109, 124, 129, 133, 167, 175, 179, 194, 226, 228n, 229

International, 102, 103, 105, 141, 219

  First, 195, 219n

  Second, 129

Irish Republican Army, 216n, 223

Irish Republican Brotherhood, 159, 220

Italian Unification, 31–2, 57, 127

Jacobinism, 2, 9, 10, 38–9, 80, 88, 145, 148–9, 162, 164, 170, 172, 173, 193, 194, 198

jacqueries, 36n, 106, 125, 127, 160

jails, 34, 37, 43, 46, 67, 72, 73, 156, 236–7, 253–4

Jehovah's Witnesses, 83, 94, 96

Jews (*see also* pogroms), 26, 62, 95, 96, 188, 201, 252–3, 265

Journalists, 12, 42, 65, 111, 131, 135n, 170, 228n, 236, 245

journeymen's societies (*see also* artisans; gilds; brotherhoods), 2, 10, 94, 200, 204–5, 208, 211, 212, 214

'just kings', 33, 234

king, *see* sovereign

kinship (*see also* vengeance, blood), xxiii, xxiv, 4–5, 85

—, artificial (*see also* brotherhoods), 46

kulaks, see middle class, rural

Labour Party (UK), 156, 170, 190n

labour sects, xxvi, 6, 9–10, Chapter VIII *passim*, 234

labourers, rising of (1830), 35n, 72, 182

labouring poor (*see* plebs; *individual occupations*)

land, church, 89, 105

—, collectivization of (*see also* co-operation), 138, 138n, 246

—, common, 88, 127

—, division of, 102

—, occupation of, 63–4, 84, 98, 124, 126, 127

— reform, 68

Landless Labourers, 36, 59, 88, 94, Chapter V *passim*, 126, 136

Landlords (*see also* gentry; nobility), 4, 5, 14, 17, 37, 99n, 100, 106, 118, 126, 137, 240, 248, 252

latifundia, 44, 45, 48, 89, 98, 112– 13, 130

law (*see also* crime; jails; police), 4, 5–7, 12, 14, 19, 19n, Chapter III *passim*, 88–9, 91, 105, 114–15, 126, 138, 161, 172, 182n, 201, 211, 213n, 234, 245, 253, 260

lawyers, 29, 45, 50–1, 61, 110

lay preachers, 180, 184, 186, 187

Lazzarettists, xv, xviv, 8, 75–96, 130, 132, 142–3, 244, 265

lazzari (*see also* plebs), 149, 150, 160, 162

League of the Communists, 225
League of the Just, 225, 228, 230
League of Outlaws, 224
legitimism, popular, 157–60
levellers, 194
Liberalism, economic, 5, 32, 42*n*,
    88, 89, 105, 107
Liberalism, 23*n*, 28, 38, 54, 55, 57,
    62, 63, 63*n*, 70, 72, 88–90,
    107, 125, 126*n*, 128, 156, 162,
    189, 190, 193
literature, popular (*see also* Bible;
    folklore), xix, xx, xxvii, 1, 28,
    42, 46, 59*n*, 71*n*, 80, 83, 99,
    109, 115, 128*n*, 130*n*, 135*n*,
    243, 264, 265
Luddism, 2, 158
lumpenproletariat (*see also* crime),
    72

*Mafia, xxi, xxii, 2, 6–8, 11, 12,
    18, 22, 23n, 35,* Chapter III
    passim, 264
magic and miracles, 19, 77, 134,
    157, 169, 176, 202, 234
magliari, 73, 74
Makhnovshchina, 37, 247
'mandate of Heaven', 57
Marxism, 14, 109, 123, 124, 125,
    170, 198, 219*n*, 224, 230
May Day, 35, 53, 139, 141
Mazzinians, 38, 219, 227, 229
menu peuple, see plebs
merchants, *see* shopkeepers
messianism, 76, 120
Methodists:
—, *Calvinistic, 172, 182*
—, *Kilhamite, 172*
—, *Primitive, 172n,* 179–89, 179*n*,
    196*n*, 257

—, *Wesleyan, 172n,* 179–84 *passim,*
    191
—, *Wesleyan Association, 172n*
—, *Wesleyan Reformers, 172n*
mezzadri, see share-croppers
middle class (*see also* petty
    bourgeoisie), xxi, xxii, 42, 50,
    50*n*, 65, 66, 129–33 *passim,*
    169, 171, 189, 193, 194, 197,
    228, 229
—, rural (*see also Gabellotti;*
    peasantry), 4, 28, 41, 52, 55,
    127
millenarian frenzy (*see also*
    revivalism), 121
millenarianism, xv, xx, xxvi, 1,
    2, 6, 8, 14, 15, 39, Chapter
    IV *passim,* Chapter V *passim,*
    Chapter VI *passim,* 158, 161,
    234
miners, 6, 48, 54, 54*n*, 59, 133,
    182–7, 195–8
mir, see village community
mob, city, 9, 37, Chapter VII
    passim
monarch, *see* sovereign
monarchists (*see also* sovereign), 31,
    63, 63*n*, 155, 155*n*
moneylenders and dealers, 26, 29,
    147, 148, 150

Narodniks, 216n, 224, 230
national minorities, 168
nationalism (*see also* foreigners),
    168
'ndranghita, 65, 66*n*
neofascists, 155, 155*n*
nobility (*see also* gentry; landlords),
    69, 82, 124, 131, 135, 135*n*,
    148

oaths (*see also* ritual), 83, 202–31
    passim, 235, 260–2
obreros conscientes, xxv, *111, 113, 114,*
    121
O'Brienites, 170
Oddfellows (*see* friendly societies)
omertà, 43, 47, *103n*
Onorata Società, 22, 66–70
outlaws, *see* banditry
Owenites, 170, 173, 195

'Pangs', *148*
Papacy, 90, 91, 153, 158, 241, 242
partisanship, 34, 81*n*, 151, 237
passwords (*see also* ritual), 45, 46,
    202, 213, 220, 224
peasantry (*see also* campieri;
    herdsmen; land; landless
    labourers; middle class, rural,
    share-croppers), xvi, xxi,
    xxv–xxvi, 1, 2, 5–8, 11, 13,
    Chapter II *passim*, Chapter
    III *passim*, Chapter IV *passim*,
    Chapter V *passim*, Chapter
    VI *passim*, 143, 153, 157,
    160–8 *passim*, 202, 227, 234,
    Appendices 1–8 *passim*
— leagues (*see also* Fasci Siciliani),
    31, 40, 59, 96, Chapter V
    passim, Chapter VI *passim*
— risings (jacqueries), 1, 2, 5, 6,
    31, 35, 56, Chapter IV *passim*,
    Chapter VI *passim*, 234, 245
Philhellenes 219
Picciotti 45, 55
plebs (*see also* individual occupations),
    Chapter VII *passim*, 228*n*
pogroms, 252–4
police, 4, 14, Chapter II *passim*,
    48–9, 51, 56*n*, 61, 65–8, 66*n*,

72, 93, 107, 118, 120–1, 137,
    151, 216, 221, 228*n*, 235, 237,
    238–9, 251, 252, 253
pomeshchiki (*see also* gentry), 247,
    248, 249
Popolino, Popolo Minuto (*see* plebs)
Popular Front, Spain, 100*n*
porters, 150, 151
positivism, 16, 42*n*, 169, 188, 188*n*
power, xx, xxi, 7–8, 9, 15, 23, 26,
    29–30, 29*n*, 33, 36*n*, 37, 43,
    47–62 *passim*, 67–9, 72, 81,
    81*n*, 93, 97*n*, 102, 104, 108,
    118–19, 128, 130, 138–9, 148,
    150, 161, 194, 197, 220, 237
precious-metal workers, 150
Presbyterians, 171, 188
printers, 188*n*, 208, 211, 228
property, 48, 51–5, 63, 64, 67, 70,
    73, 89, 98, 99*n*, 105, 108,
    126*n*, 131, 148, 150, 154
prophesies/prophets (*see also*
    individual prophets in Index of
    Names), xxv, 14, 77, 90, 91,
    93, 109, 122, 169, 177, 185,
    193, 245, 258
Protestantism (*see also individual*
    churches), 10, 25, 95–6,Chapter
    VIII *passim*, 208, 243
Proudhonists, 219
Purgatory, 129*n*, 222
puritanism, 113, 181*n*, 194

Quakers, 171, 188, 198
qualunquists, 155
queen, *see* sovereign

Radicalism, 2, 15, 55, 126, 156,
    164, 172, 180, 184, 189, 198
railwaymen, 187

Rational Society, 194

rationalism (*see also* freethinking),
3, 12, 16, 76, 78, 167, 171,
198, 200, 225

Reformism, -ists, xx, xxii*n*, xxiii,
7–10, 14–16, 64, 68, 70,
78–9, 83, 84, 88, 91, 99*n*,
111*n*, 114–15, 126, 129–30,
139, 154, 172, 172*n*, 180, 184,
188*n*, 198, 235

Republican Party (US), 58

Republicanism (*see also individual
Republicans by name in* Index of
Names; *organisations by name*),
23, 38, 104, 120, 159, 162*n*,
194, 195, 216*n*, 217, 220, 223,
259, 261

retainers, 6, 18, 24, 37, Chapter III
passim, 126, 127

revivalism (*see also* millenarian
frenzy), 173, 174–5, 174*n*,
194

revolutions, *passim* but especially,
xx, xxii–xxvi, xxvi*n*, 8–11,
70–4, Chapter IV *passim*,
Chapter V *passim*, Chapter
VI *passim*, Chapter IX *passim*

—, American, 167, 169

—, French, 1, 11, 77, 146, 147,
150*n*, 162, 164, 167, 169, 171,
215, 217

—, Neapolitan of 1647, 147, 150,
–1

—, of 1830, 218, 227–8

—, of 1848, 90, 125, 127, 128, 162,
162*n*

—, Russian, 37*n*, 80, 104, 114

—, Sicilian, 51–70 *passim*, 128, 141

riot, 90, Chapter VI *passim*,
Chapter VII *passim*, 236–9

ritual (*see also* brotherhoods; magic;
initiation; oaths; passwords;
symbolism), xxvii, 1, 3,
10–12, 46–7, 46*n*, 66, 66*n*,
71, 77, 145, 169, Chapter IX
passim, 235

ronde, 47

rope-makers 150

saddlers, 39

sailors 47

saints (*see individuals by name* in
Index of Names), 133, 150,
160, 197, 212, 222

Salvation Army, 175

Second World War *see* World War
II

secret societies, xxi–xxii, 1, 20*n*,
22*n*, Chapter III *passim*,
Chapter IX *passim*, 258–9,
261

secularism, *see* freethinking,
rationalism

separatists, Sicilian, 31, 35, 63

servants, domestic, 117, 150, 235

share-croppers (*see also* peasantry),
50, 89, 94, 95, 130

shoemakers, xvi, 95, 111, 145, 150,
162, 212, 228, 254–6

shopkeepers and dealers, 89, 148,
151, 156

silversmiths, 150

skhods, 247

smugglers, 18, 21, 41*n*, 101

Social Democratic Federation (SDF)
170

socialism (*see also individuals by name
in* Index of Names), xxvi*n*,
10, 31, 56*n*, 79–80, 85, 100,
Chapter VI *passim*

—, Christian, 133, Chapter VIII
      passim
—, Italian, 155
—, Utopian, 2, 8, 169
Societé des Nouvelles Saisons, 228n
Society of the Families, 229
Society of the Seasons, 222, 223–4,
      228n, 229, 262
soldiers as rebels, 17, 34–5, 221,
      228n
sovereign (*see also* 'just kings';
      legitimism, popular;
      monarchists; 'unjust kings'),
      9, 20n, 27, 29, 36, 37, 38, 43,
      91, 107, 130, 136, 146, 148–9,
      157, 158–63, 200, 234, 242,
      243, 245, 250–2
Spenceans, 170
squadre, 49, 52, 53–5, 59
State, the, 4, 6, 17, 20–2, 26,
      36n, 43, 48, 67, 72, 93, 103,
      106–8, 146, 148, 156, 160,
      161, 191, 194
Stoppaglieri, 46n, 49, 54, 56n
strikes (*see also* General Strike),
      79, 103–4, 105, 110, 110n,
      117–18, 124, 128, 130, 140–1,
      155, 179, 184, 256–7
Sublime Perfect Masters, 219
symbolism (*see also* ritual), 44,
      202–3, 203n, 213, 214n, 217,
      220

tailors, 150, 228, 228n
tanners, 150, 151
tax collectors, 4, 107
taxation, 48, 87–90, 98, 130, 147,
      150n, 250
temperance, 184–5, 204
terrorism (*see also* Bengali Terrorist
      Movement; Narodniks; Irish
      Republican Army; Irish
      Republican Brotherhood),
      59, 216n, 220, 223, 223n, 226,
      238
textile workers, 214
trade unions (*see also individual trade*
      unions), 2, 4, 10, 95, 114, 120,
      144–5, 145n, 154, 178, 179,
      183–7, 195, 199, 203–4, 203n,
      214–15
traders, *see* shopkeepers
tranquillity, 119, 158
tsar, *see* sovereign
Tugendbund, 218, 219

unemployment, 60, 147, 150, 164,
      182, 226, 239
Unitarians, 171, 184, 188, 189,
      198
United Irishmen, 217
'unjust kings', 158
urbanization, *see* cities
usury, 5, 133, 246
utopianism, 2, 8, 16, 78, 79–80,
      84, 107, 119, 169

Valdensians, 94
vengeance, xx, 7, 17, 26, 29, 33–4,
      36n, 54, 127, 127n, 176, 177,
      234
—, blood, 5–6, 67, 68, 156
village community, 36, Chapter V
      passim, 247, 249
—, industrial, xxvi, 1, 143–4,
      152–3, 171–5, 175n

Walworth Jumpers, 178
women (*see also* abduction; sexual
      relations), xvi, 31, 37, 81n, 82,

92, 99, 108, 118, 131, 137, 141–2, 152, 163, 174, 175, 180, 201
woodworkers, 150
working class, 8–10, 100, 146, 164, Chapter VIII *passim*, 214, 228

World War I, 6, 31, 32, 59, 61, 128, 138
World War II, 51

Zion, 83
—, Communist 15

Viva la Revolución

Hobsbawm on Latin America

Edited by Leslie Bethell

In his autobiography *Interesting Times: A Twentieth Century Life,* published in 2002 when he was eighty-five years old, Eric Hobsbawm wrote that Latin America was the only region of the world outside Europe where he felt entirely at home.

After the triumph of Fidel Castro in Cuba in January 1959, and even more after the defeat of the American attempt to overthrow him at the Bay of Pigs in April 1961, 'there was not an intellectual in Europe or the USA', he wrote, 'who was not under the spell of Latin America, a continent apparently bubbling with the lava of social revolutions'. The Third World 'brought the hope of revolution back to the First in the 1960s'. The two great international inspirations were Cuba and Vietnam, 'triumphs not only of revolution, but of Davids against Goliaths, of the weak against the all-powerful'.

Viva la Revolución is Hobsbawm's magisterial work on Latin America, the fruit of forty years' writing about the continent.

To buy any of our books and to find out
more about Abacus and Little, Brown, our authors
and titles, as well as events and book clubs,
visit our website

www.littlebrown.co.uk

and follow us on Twitter

@AbacusBooks
@LittleBrownUK

To order any Abacus titles p & p free in the UK,
please contact our mail order supplier on:

+ 44 (0)1832 737525

Customers not based in the UK should contact
the same number for appropriate postage
and packing costs.